NF

D0891777

A Publication of the Egon-Sohmen-Foundation

Springer
Berlin
Heidelberg
New York
Barcelona
Budapest
Hong Kong
London
Milan
Paris
Santa Clara
Singapore
Tokyo

Publications of the Egon-Sohmen-Foundation

Herbert Giersch (Ed.)
Towards a Market Economy in Central and Eastern Europe
1991, IX, 169 pp.
3-540-53922-0
Out of print

Herbert Giersch (Ed.)
Money, Trade, and Competition
1992, X, 305 pp.
3-540-55125-5

Herbert Giersch (Ed.)
Economic Progress and Environmental Concerns
1993, X, 302 pp.
3-540-56466-7
Out of print

Herbert Giersch (Ed.)
Economic Aspects of International Migration
1994, X, 275 pp.
3-540-57606-1
Out of print

Herbert Giersch (Ed.)
Urban Agglomeration and Economic Growth
1995, VIII, 278 pp.
3-540-58690-3

Herbert Giersch (Ed.)

for the Egon-Sohmen-Foundation

Fighting Europe´s Unemployment in the 1990s

**With 19 Figures
and 23 Tables**

 Springer

Prof. Herbert Giersch
Past President
Kiel Institute of World Economics
P.O. Box 4309
D-24100 Kiel

---

*This book was produced with financial support
of the Egon-Sohmen-Foundation*

ISBN 3-540-60833-8 Springer-Verlag Berlin Heidelberg New York

Library of Congress Cataloging-in-Publication Data
Fighting Europe's unemployment in the 1990s / Herbert Giersch (ed.)
for the Egon-Sohmen-Fundation.
p. cm. -- (A Publication of the Egon-Sohmen-Foundation)
Includes bibliographical references.
ISBN 3-540-60833-8 (hardcover)
1. Full employment policies--Europe--Congresses. 2. Unemployment-
-Europe--Congresses. I. Giersch, Herbert, II. Egon-Sohmen
-Foundation. III. Series: Publications of the Egon-Sohmen
-Foundation.
HD5764.A6F543 1996
331.13'794--dc20

© Springer-Verlag Berlin • Heidelberg 1996
Printed in Germany

SPIN 10517326   42/2202-5 4 3 2 1 0 - Printed on acid-free paper

Preface

Following the five books listed above on an earlier page, the Egon-Sohmen-Foundation herewith submits its sixth volume. Once again, it is a collection of academic papers that were discussed at a symposium sponsored by the Foundation and subsequently revised.

Readers not familiar with the Foundation may be interested to know that it was established in 1987 by Helmut Sohmen of Hong Kong in memory of his late brother, Egon Sohmen (1930–1977). Egon Sohmen was an international economist highly respected in North America and in Europe, notably for his work on flexible exchange rates and on the economics of allocation and competition.

Born in Linz (Austria) and educated as an economist in Vienna, Tübingen, and Cambridge, Mass., Egon Sohmen held teaching posts in several places (M.I.T., Yale, Frankfurt, Saarbrücken, Minnesota, and Heidelberg). As an active participant in numerous international conferences and workshops, he truly belonged to the international research community of his time and age cohort. His lasting reputation greatly helped me to convene the active participants of this symposium.

While at previous occasions it was easy to identify the person who suggested the topic for the symposium, I must report this time that the subject of unemployment in Europe had been on the list for years. It came up again as a spontaneous suggestion from various quarters for the Foundation's 1994 conference. At that time, we considered the neglect of the unemployment problem in the public policy debate to be so alarming that we contemplated issuing a manifesto.

The Symposium took place on August 27–28, 1994, in the festival town of Salzburg. Apart from reviewing the papers, we had general discussions about a possible consensus for the manifesto along the lines of a draft that Sir Samuel Brittan had prepared on the basis of various suggestions submitted to him earlier in writing. We broadly agreed on the text reproduced below, though none of the participants would like to feel committed to every word. The reason for the reservation is essentially that circumstances naturally differ from country to country and, in addition, may change over time. However, all would be glad if the self-correcting forces would soon work in such a way as to make the manifesto obsolete. Those who were skeptical in this respect quickly suggested the topic for the 1995 symposium: "Reforming the Welfare State." That is where the problem may have its roots. We shall see.

It remains for me to thank Thomas Tack for effective support in organizing the meeting, Uwe Siegmund for help in editing this volume, and, last but not least, Regine Sohmen for preparing the German version of the manifesto.

Herbert Giersch
August 1995

Contents

Fighting Europe's Unemployment in the 1990s
— Salzburg Manifesto —

Samuel Brittan, et al.   Europe
E24
J68

This manifesto has been issued by a group of economists brought together by the Egon-Sohmen-Foundation in Salzburg in late August 1994. The meeting was chaired by Professor Herbert Giersch, a former head of the Kiel Institute of World Economics and Founding Member of the German Council of Economic Advisers (1964–1970). The economists taking part covered a wide range of the political spectrum and came from a variety of personal and professional backgrounds. The manifesto has been drawn up on the initiative of Professor Giersch. Most of those present accepted it, but are not committed to every detail.

September 1994

Fighting unemployment is imperative for economic as well as human-itarian reasons. Europe could offer gainful work opportunities to mil-lions of people now on the dole and produce more valuable goods and services. Discouraged job seekers, notably among older and young people, would find a new perspective on life, instead of seeing them-selves separated from society. Once labour is again in high demand, people will welcome rather than discriminate against new entrants to the labour force whether from inside the country concerned or abroad. With the unemployed back at work, Europe could enlarge its tax base and thus make progress on its fiscal problems. Higher employment would thus contribute to European prosperity as well as social cohe-sion and co-operation among the EU countries as well as with other states.

All markets work with some stock or reserves. Present unemploy-ment rates in Europe are however abnormally high, whether judged by comparison with other periods or other parts of the industrialised world, such as the US or Japan. There is no need for such high rates.

Labour, like other resources, is fundamentally scarce in view of vast potential demands for its use. There is still a mass of unsatisfied human wants, even in the industrial West. Environmental requirements make extra claims on resources and provide an additional reason for available human labour to be fully and efficiently used. Yet a substantial part of the labour force is not engaged in meeting this demand (outside the black economy).

The choice between take home pay and leisure is one for workers and employers to make on a voluntary basis in the light of preferences and opportunities. Make-work measures such as compulsory reductions in working hours, job-sharing or enforced early retirement tend to impoverish the whole economy and merely tinker with unemployment statistics.

Present unemployment has three proximate roots: pay and associated labour costs which price workers out of jobs; intermittent periods of low demand growth; and capacity shortages which emerge in many countries during each economic recovery while unemployment is still high. These elements are interrelated. If labour is too expensive to employ it will not pay businesses to make capital-widening investments. Insufficient capacity itself results in inflationary bottlenecks when employment is still unsatisfactory. Demand squeezes—whether in response to inflation, exogenous shocks or simple policy errors—lead to longer spells of unemployment and, thus, to workers becoming less easily re-employable (the so-called hysteresis effect). The most fundamental obstacles are, however, in the labour market; other remedies will not work unless pay costs move nearer market-clearing levels.

The amount of different kinds of labour that it pays to employ depends on their prices, which include both wages and additional non-wage costs. The problem is that pay is not only a price for the employer. It also provides most people with their main source of livelihood.

There have been forces, such as globalisation and technical change, which have depressed the market value of many kinds of labour, especially unskilled workers. In the USA they have led to severe pressure on the living standards of the lowest paid workers. In Europe they have shown themselves in obstinately high rates of long-duration unemployment. Neither outcome is satisfactory.

Under present European conditions the public interest largely coincides with the interest of unemployed persons who are being priced out of work. If market-clearing pay for some workers is below a tolerable minimum, their fellow citizens should use the tax and transfer system to top up their income by direct payments. This is a way of tackling the problems of the least well paid, far superior to restrictive devices which prevent pay from reaching market clearing levels, or to restrictions to keep out imports from poor countries. In contrast to prevailing protectionist sentiments, we want to express a strong commitment to an open trading system which enhances the welfare of both the rich and the poor countries.

A 9-Point Agenda

1. Appropriate macroeconomic policy can provide a helpful background for stable growth. Inflationary dashes for growth should be strictly avoided. Once inflation is at low levels monetary authorities have as much responsibility for avoiding nominal demand deficiency as inflationary excess. In practice the responsibility for achieving this must be largely that of central banks. Thus we recommend that the European Monetary Institute should monitor the development of nominal GDP at an EU level. This is entirely consistent with its anti-inflationary responsibilities and will be worth pursuing irrespective of whether a European currency is established.

2. The key to more jobs lies in following the signals given by rapid changes in relative prices and sales conditions which reflect underlying changes in relative scarcity and opportunities both for workers and for products. Collective bargaining still prices workers out of jobs in many parts of Europe. In the years to come, the level of contractual minimum wages should not rise in real terms so that productivity growth can be translated into an expansion of employment. A growing proportion of the pay packet should be determined by local labour market conditions and differentiated according to skill, region, district and place of operation. The practice of uniform pay increases, or legislation which generalises collective bargaining settlements to employers and workers who wish to remain outside, should be re-examined.

3. The power of workers already employed (insiders) to preserve customary pay scales will not disappear overnight. Under present conditions the principle of "equal pay for equal work" stands in the

way of full employment in an economy with fast growth and structural change. It is desirable to pay newly-hired persons less—or occasionally more—than those already in employment, depending upon whether their skills are ample or in tight supply in the places and regions where they are needed.

4. The wage dispersion required for high employment in an advanced economy must be sufficiently wide to encompass the full range of skills and of relative scarcities. With the move towards an integrated world economy where unskilled workers are abundant, the market incomes of such workers in the West will tend to move nearer those in developing countries. This is not a cause for panic. First of all, pay scales in developing countries are already rising and will rise further. Secondly, the real national income in advanced countries will benefit from the gains from trade which should provide a surplus to channel towards those most hard hit by economic change.

5. Ultimately, the best way of reversing the present widening of market wage disparities is investment in human capital. The formation of human capital by education and training should bring its own rewards. But we should avoid the trap of "credentialism," that is of inventing more and more paper qualifications which may have little relevance to future skill requirements. We are doubtful whether education or training bureaucrats have a better sense of future labour market requirements than young people themselves. Intervention in the training market could take the form of credit vouchers (to be used for training on the job or in institutions chosen by the applicant) preferably repayable on concessionary terms along the lines of student loans. Such credits should also be available later in adult life, obviously on a strictly monitored basis.

6. The restoration of high employment will require physical investment as well. We do not recommend generalised fiscal subsidies which have frequently encouraged the wrong kind of investment, notably capital intensive projects. Public policies should be directed towards removing any existing barriers to capital formation and the establishment of new firms. The best contribution that governments could make to encourage capital formation would be to reduce their own structural budget deficits, especially by curbing expenditure. No individual European government can decisively affect world real

interest rates, but the collectivity of European governments is large enough to have an impact. We would note that the Japanese current account surplus—provided it is not achieved at the expense of a depressed economy—is a contribution to world savings.

7. Support for poorer workers in wealthy countries, provided for reasons of equity or social cohesion, should be given to them as citizens rather than as employees. There should be a shift in the emphasis of the welfare state from dole payments for non-workers to top-up payments for low-income households. (This of course implies means tests.) As incomes rise, these top-up payments should decrease, but by less than income increases. Recipients who cannot work should receive a larger transfer than those who are able to work. (The UK Family Credit scheme is of this type and worth investigating.) Another useful safety net would be a fiscal rule providing temporary tax relief for people returning from spells of unemployment.

8. To the extent that long-term unemployment support is not based on insurance principles but is financed by general taxes, the link between unemployment benefit and previous earnings is an undesirable feature of dubious equity, which increases the minimum reservation wage below which people will not take jobs. It should be abolished, as it was in the UK in the 1980s without any political outcry.

9. Legitimate social concerns motivated the Social Chapter of the Maastricht Treaty, but there are risks that the measures adopted will limit employment and should be watched carefully in that respect. Some of the proposed rules, e.g., limiting working hours, are derived from controversial pre-Maastricht decisions; so the issue goes well beyond the Treaty itself.

Conclusion

We put forward these suggestions in the knowledge that it can take a long time for measures on the supply-side of the economy to work in reducing unemployment. We therefore urge their prompt adoption along with supportive non-inflationary demand policies. If such a balanced approach is soon adopted there will be a reasonable chance of reducing unemployment in Europe.

SAMUEL BRITTAN, UK
MICHAEL C. BURDA, Germany
RICHARD N. COOPER, USA
BARRY EICHENGREEN, USA
HERBERT GIERSCH, Germany
PATRICK MINFORD, UK
KARL-HEINZ PAQUÉ, Germany
WOLFGANG RIEKE, Germany
ROLAND VAUBEL, Germany
CHARLES WYPLOSZ, France

Part I
The Historical Record

Unemployment and the Structure of Labor Markets: The Long View

USA
UK
N30
J64

Barry Eichengreen

Understanding the causes of high unemployment requires first under-standing the structure of labor markets. The latter is necessarily a his-torical agenda, since it is only over time that one observes significant variation in the socioeconomic institutions structuring labor market outcomes. While some investigators have fruitfully adopted interna-tional comparisons as a way of gaining purchase on institutional varia-tion, contemporary labor markets share many common features, ren-dering the relevant variation fairly modest.

This paper therefore adopts a long view on the operation of labor markets in order to provide a context for discussions of sources and solutions to the current problem of unemployment. It attempts to char-acterize the operation of labor markets following the advent of indus-trialization—essentially the second half of the 19th century. It pursues some comparisons with market structure and performance in the inter-war years and concludes with some implications for today.

Any survey of such a vast topic must be partial and limited in scope. Here I confine myself to Anglo-American labor markets, not because these are exceptionally interesting and important or because they are representative of labor market structures elsewhere in the industrial world. But the majority of historical research has focused on the U.S. and British labor markets. And historical statistics documenting the operation of these two markets are relatively well developed.

Rather than focusing exclusively on the level and incidence of unemployment, I embed my discussion of these issues in a broader analysis of labor market dynamics. Following recent research by his-torical scholars, I relate the incidence and duration of unemployment

I thank Karl-Heinz Paqué for helpful comments.

to the incidence and duration of employment and connect those variables, along with the dispersion and flexibility of wages, to the institutional structure of the labor markets in which these outcomes were generated.

I Labor Market Structure and the Incidence of Unemployment

Four distinctive features of 19th-century industry—what is called the factory system—were centralized power, the concentration of different activities under one roof, the foreman or overseer, and the "drive system" with which he was associated. In early textile mills, the first modern factories of any consequence (aside, perhaps, from "state enterprises" like armories and mints), the overseer rather than the enterprise owner-manager selected the workers, assigned them tasks, and monitored their activities. The overseer operated as an independent contractor, arranging with the proprietor to deliver the product within a specified time at a specified cost. He hired skilled workers directly; those skilled workers in turn hired their unskilled counterparts and worked in self-contained teams. By the 1880s, the self-contained teams had disappeared but many of the other arrangements remained. The overseer had evolved into the foreman, who had free rein in hiring, paying, and supervising those employed in a particular division of the firm. When hiring, he might favor relatives, friends, or fellow countrymen, or he might toss apples into the crowd assembled at the factory gate as a way of picking job candidates. He could set wages and offer jobs for as little as part of a day. A worker might be fired by one foreman in the morning and hired by another in a separate division of the same company in the afternoon.

Associated with these practices was the "drive system." Workers were driven to move faster and work harder by close supervision, abuse, profanity, and threats. They risked immediate dismissal if they did not perform as demanded.

This characterization, admittedly stylized, of labor market arrangements in 19th-century Anglo-American industry suggests two questions. First, what features of 19th-century technology and socioeconomic structure encouraged the development of this form of labor organization? To put the question another way, what developments in 20th-century industrial organization have caused employment relations to assume a very different form? And second, what were the implications of the drive system and its concomitants for the incidence and character of unemployment?

A   Sources of Labor Market Structure

To understand the prevalence of subcontracting within the factory, it is useful to recall the activities that manufacturing firms subcontract today. An example is janitorial services that are provided at night. These are low-marginal-productivity activities that, because they occur during off-hours when regular supervisors are absent, have high monitoring costs for the employer. Since these tasks do not need to be coordinated with those of other workers, they can be subcontracted to an independent janitorial firm. This example suggests that much manual labor in 19th-century industry was undertaken by unskilled workers whose low productivity rendered costly their monitoring by upper-level management. Although much early factory production may have made use of a centralized power source, often it did little more than bring under one roof artisans or putting-out workers who continued to labor in a self-contained way. Only with the emergence of the multidivisional enterprise in the final decades of the 19th century, which adapted hierarchical management techniques from the army and the railways, and the development of the continuous-process, mass-production techniques pioneered in slaughter houses and foundries, was this early shop-floor labor organization systematically reorganized.[1] It follows that these same large, multidivisional enterprises served, after World War I, as the hotbed for personnel departments and other modern labor market practices.[2]

The way in which workers were hired and fired points to a lower prevalence of firm-specific skills than is typical of 20th-century industry. Employers would not have been inclined to take on workers with-

---

[1] Alfred Chandler is the exponent of this view. See Chandler (1990) for his latest statement.

[2] Sundstrom (1988a) provides evidence on the precocious development of internal labor markets before the 1920s.

out screening them or to dismiss them when the volume of work declined even temporarily had productivity depended significantly on formal training or on-the-job experience. Arbitrary hiring and firing were not characteristics of all 19th-century jobs, as we will see when considering evidence on labor turnover and unemployment duration; education, training, and experience were by no means irrelevant in all 19th-century occupations, in other words. The point is that in the 19th-century world of more primitive and standardized technologies, firm-specific skills were less important than today.

Further evidence of this point is the emphasis placed by contemporaries, especially in Britain, on the problem of casual labor.[3] The Fabian Socialists and other social reformers lamented the instability of employment—the fact that many workers drifted from job to job, with periods of gainful employment separated by repeated spells of idleness. That idleness was regarded as a source of inefficiency for society and of demoralization for the worker who experienced it. Major employers of casual labor included the dockyards and the construction trades, in which workers might be taken on for a part of a day and in which an individual might average no more than two or three days of work a week. But casual workers could also be found in numerous other occupations such as land transport, personal services, and various declining manufacturing and outwork trades. Industries whose demands for labor fluctuated widely across seasons and over the cycle relied on a substantial fringe of casual workers to perform less-skilled tasks. Stedman Jones (1976) estimated that 10 percent of the labor force of London in 1891 was made up of casuals. Rowntree (1911) calculated that half of the unemployed in York in 1910 were casuals. The prevalence of short spells of employment and repeated spells of unemployment in the construction trades today suggests that some workers preferred the freedom that casual labor conferred and that the practice was not always inefficient. Still, the emphasis placed by late-19th-century social reformers on the problem of casual labor suggests that short employment durations and repeated unemployment spells characterized the situation of workers in a wider segment of the economy in the 19th century than today.

The prevalence of the drive system reinforces this presumption of the lesser importance of firm-specific skills. Insofar as productivity

---

[3] See Phillips and Whiteside (1985) for references.

depended on brute force and physical effort rather than attention to detail, it was possible to reduce unit labor costs simply by driving labor to work harder. That the drive system utilized the threat of dismissal to elicit effort points out the fact that firing costs—whether in the form of experience-rated unemployment insurance contributions, inverse-seniority layoff rules, or union protection against arbitrary employer treatment—were weaker than today and sometimes nonexistent.

Again, such characterizations are likely to mislead if we apply them to an entire economy or generalize them across countries. Substantial portions of British industry operated in the presence of strong trade unions that allowed workers considerable shop-floor autonomy. In the final decades of the 19th century, British firms "opted for collective accommodation with unions of skilled and strategically positioned workers" rather than risking industrial conflict in order to restructure the organization of work (Elbaum and Lazonick, 1986, p. 4). British trade unions staged successful strikes, gained local autonomy in bargaining, and exerted control of shop-floor organization. The power of these well-entrenched, craft-based unions and the failure of management to provide an effective counterweight slowed the adoption of the kind of modern multidivisional, continuous-process mass-production methods increasingly prevalent in the United States. At the same time, unions protected their members against arbitrary dismissal and enhanced their senior members' job security.

Late-19th-century labor markets, this suggests, were divided into segments with different characteristics: a high-turnover segment comprised of some less-skilled blue-collar laborers, and a low-turnover segment comprised of skilled blue-collar workers and their white-collar counterparts. The distinctiveness of these segments varied across countries: in the United States, for example, where trade unionism was slower to develop than in Britain, differences in the condition of skilled and unskilled blue-collar workers may have been less pronounced.

Segmented labor market theorists would observe that there is nothing distinctive about these characteristics of 19th-century labor markets; they would diagnose the operation of modern labor markets in similar fashion. But there is reason to think that the secondary segment characterized by high turnover and repeated spells of unemployment was larger, as a share of the labor force, than it is in most advanced economies today.

B   Evidence on Labor Market Dynamics

Empirical work on the history of labor market dynamics is in its
infancy. The research that exists is consistent with the picture of a
market characterized by high turnover, frequent short spells of unemployment, and pronounced differences in the experience of blue- and
white-collar workers.

Thomas (1990) studies labor market dynamics using the records of
Britain's newly established Unemployment Insurance Scheme in 1911–
1913, a time when the unemployment rate was 3.7 percent. He confirms
the picture of rapid turnover and short unemployment spells. Estimated
weekly rates of inflow and outflow from the pool of the unemployed, at
9 and 25 percent, were much higher than those for post–World War II
Britain. The expected duration of a spell of unemployment, calculated
as the inverse of the outflow rate, was only four weeks (compared to
more than 30 weeks in the 1980s).[4]

Thomas's evidence also suggests that unemployment was spread
relatively evenly across sectors and workers. The differential in the unemployment rate between the high-unemployment construction trades
and the low-unemployment mechanical engineering industry was only
2.8 percentage points, for example. Fewer than 1 percent of all claims
in 1913 were filed by individuals who remained unemployed for the
entire year. Before leaping to the conclusion that long-term unemployment was rare, however, it is important to bear in mind that a claim is
not the same as an individual, since workers were entitled to file separate claims for successive spells. Thomas calculates that the average
claimant experienced three spells of unemployment a year. Given an
average spell duration of three to four weeks, this is still consistent with
a relatively low level of long-term unemployment. Additional evidence
from trade union returns for engineers indicates that in 1904 the average unemployed worker spent 67 days out of work. Only 11 percent of
the unemployed spent more than 12 weeks out of work.

Jacoby (1983) confirms the picture of high turnover rates in the
United States. He concludes that monthly separation rates in excess
of 10 percent were common in the 1900s and 1910s (compared to 2–4

---

[4] The duration of actual spells recorded in the 1911–1913 insurance statistics
(which differs from the inverse of the outflow rate because the unemployment rate
was not in a steady state) was shorter still.

percent in the 1960s). Case studies bear this out; a survey of 14 industrial firms in Detroit in 1913–1914, for example, indicated an average monthly separation rate of 15.3 percent.

Margo (1990a) uses data drawn from the public use sample of the 1910 U.S. Census of Population to characterize the labor market experience of non-self-employed American males between the ages of 18 and 64 in nonfarm occupations. It is useful to follow his procedure of comparing labor market dynamics in 1909 with those in 1977–1979, as analyzed by Murphy and Topel (1987). Murphy and Topel analyzed U.S. labor market dynamics for an identically defined sample of nonfarm males drawn from the Current Population Survey, in which questions on unemployment that parallel those of the 1910 Census were asked. An additional convenience is that measured unemployment rates in the two periods were remarkably similar (4.9 percent in 1910 and 4.7 percent in 1977–1979).

Margo confirms the existence of striking differences in the speed of flow through the pool of unemployed. Compared with 1977–1979, workers in 1909 had a 38 percent higher monthly entry hazard from employment to unemployment and a 32 percent higher monthly exit hazard. As Keyssar (1986) has emphasized, the chances of becoming unemployed were higher in the early 20th century, but unemployed workers were reemployed more quickly than today.

In 1909, 18.5 percent of men reported experiencing some unemployment. This is higher than the comparable figure for 1977–1979—14.9 percent—again suggesting that the same level of unemployment was spread more evenly across the labor force at the beginning of the century. Unemployment was also more evenly spread among socioeconomic and demographic groups.[5] The mean duration of an unemployment spell was less than four months in 1909, compared to more than five months in 1977–1979.

Shift-share analysis adjusting the 1910 data to correspond to 1977–1979 industry shares does not alter the picture, but adjusting for 1977–1979 occupational shares reduces the percentage of men experiencing some unemployment from 18.5 to 14.9 percent, identical to that for 1977–1979. Thus, the more even incidence of unemployment toward

---

[5] As Margo (1992) puts it, "The probability of becoming unemployed was less a function of personal characteristics, such as age, work experience, education, marital status, than in the post-World War Two period."

the beginning of the century appears to have been associated not with changes in the relative importance of mining and construction, non-durable goods manufacturing and durable goods manufacturing, or with the shift in employment from manufacturing to government and services, but to the relative importance of white- and blue-collar labor in a wide range of sectors. This is confirmed by the fact that 26 percent of unskilled blue-collar workers, 20 percent of semiskilled blue-collar workers, and 24 percent of skilled blue-collar workers experienced some unemployment in 1909, two or three times the incidence reported among white-collar workers. Thus, there is no evidence here that the cleavage in unemployment experiences in 1909 was between skilled and unskilled factory laborers; rather, the gulf was between blue-collar workers on the shop floor and accountants, clerks, middle managers, and others in the front office.

Shifts in occupation can explain most of the long-term decline in the entry hazard but only a portion of the decline in the exit hazard. Margo interprets this as suggesting that factors such as unemployment benefit and unionization were more important than changes in occupational mix for the long-term increase in the duration of unemployment spells.

It is tempting to infer from the even incidence of idleness and the prevalence of repeated short spells of unemployment that job attachment was looser in the 19th century. This would be consistent with the emphasis in the literature on the lesser importance of firm-specific skills. Yet just as Hall (1982) found for the 1970s that, despite the brevity of the typical job, most employment was concentrated in near-lifetime jobs, it could be that at the beginning of the century turnover among newly hired workers was high but that the job of the average worker was lengthy. Slichter's (1919) suggestion for the United States that most labor turnover was due to a few workers changing jobs rapidly is consistent with this hypothesis, although the relatively even incidence of unemployment is more difficult to reconcile with this view.

Akerlof and Main (1981) calculated that the average male in the modern U.S. economy could be expected to stay with his employer for 18 years. The simplest way of constructing comparable historical estimates is to assume that the economy was in a steady state and to therefore double the length of the average employment spell in progress (since observation is equally likely to occur at any point in a job). Carter and Savoca (1980) report data on various types of late-19th century workers: these suggest that males employed in the Michigan fire clay industry surveyed in the late 1880s stayed with an employer for an average of 9.2 years, gypsum industry workers for 7.3 years, grindstone industry workers for 7.8 years, furniture workers for 6 years.[6] Males in San Francisco in the early 1890s stayed with their employer for 7.8 years, males in New Hampshire for 7.4 years. The consistency of these averages suggests that job tenure was shorter in the late 19th century than today, but that the picture of extremely short tenure and high turnover can be overdrawn.

More sophisticated analysis involves estimating a model of job duration. Carter and Savoca do so using data from a survey of workers conducted by the California Bureau of Labor Statistics in San Francisco in 1892. They estimate an average completed job duration of about 9 years. This may be an underestimate insofar as the San Francisco survey undersampled married, homeowning workers. Adjusting their estimates for marital status, home ownership, and number of dependents implies an average job length of 13 years.

Estimating a proportional hazards model using a sample containing information on a range of personal characteristics permits Carter and Savoca to address further claims about the causes of unemployment. Some historians argue that the persistence of nonindustrial work cultures led workers to quit unexpectedly, while the absence of union work rules and the power of the foreman allowed workers to be dismissed arbitrarily. The implication is that personal and professional characteristics that explain the incidence of terminations and quits today should have little explanatory power a century ago. Carter and Savoca in fact find remarkably little difference between the 1890s and today in the role in quits and layoffs played by personal and economic characteristics. Thus, married workers with children and mortgages were significantly less likely to quit, for example. The presence of capital-intensive production processes was associated with lower separation rates.

Carter and Savoca's results, subversive as they are to characterizations of the prewar labor force as a floating pool of casual workers, have not gone unchallenged. Jacoby and Sharma (1992) point out that San Francisco was disproportionately unionized, and that unionism, by protecting workers against arbitrary dismissal, increased job duration.

---

[6] All of these data are from surveys conducted by the Michigan Bureau of Labor Statistics.

In 1892, a recession year in San Francisco, poor job prospects should have led workers to hesitate before quitting. And Chinese workers, who accounted for 20 percent of the local labor force and who were concentrated in short-duration jobs, were not surveyed by the California State Bureau of Labor Statistics. For all these reasons, Jacoby and Sharma reject Carter and Savoca's challenge to the high-turnover model.

The obvious way of reconciling these views is by invoking the segmented labor market model. A majority of blue-collar workers may have experienced relative unstable employment, while a minority held lengthy, stable jobs. The difference from the U.S. economy in the 1970s and 1980s lies in the relative importance of the two segments. Abraham and Farber (1987) estimate that 49 percent of blue-collar workers had completed job durations of ten years or more in 1968–1981, while Carter and Savoca's figure for San Francisco in 1892 is only 27 percent. Near-permanent jobs existed in medium to large firms in industries such as meat packing, print, and rail transportation, where workers were protected against arbitrary dismissal by unionism and craft control. But this sector was small relative to the post–World War II period, condemning more workers to lives of unstable employment.

What were the implications of this structure of labor markets for the responsiveness of wages to unemployment? Before considering explanations, it is important to acknowledge disagreement over the facts. Allen (1988) argues, upon constructing a consistent time series on U.S. wages from the 1890s, that wages a century ago were no more sensitive to the business cycle than they are today, and that they may have been less sensitive. Hanes (1993), on the other hand, finds that there was a decline in the flexibility of nominal wages in American manufacturing, but that this was missed by previous investigators because it occurred before their sample period began. American manufacturing firms had been inclined to cut money wages in response to declining demand for 20 years after the Civil War. Following the labor unrest of 1886, however, there was a shift in behavior. Time-series evidence to this effect, plus the cross-section finding that wage cuts were less prevalent in industries with a greater incidence of strikes, leads Hanes to conclude that the increased bargaining power of workers and threat of labor unrest led to the decline in wage flexibility.[7]

---

[7] Sundstrom (1992) also emphasizes the association between nominal wage rigidity and the strike threat in the 1890s.

Since the U.S. economy featured low levels of unionization before the turn of the century, the credibility of the strike threat must have resided elsewhere. Hanes notes that large firms were notorious hotbeds of strikes. One interpretation is that as firms grew more capital-intensive, they adopted high-speed-throughput, mass-production techniques that rendered them vulnerable to temporary shutdowns. The growing sophistication of the prevailing technology placed a greater premium on firm-specific skills, making it increasingly difficult to replace striking workers on short notice.[8] Workers used this leverage to limit wage cuts. Following the eight-hour-day movement and Haymarket riot of 1886, firms adapted their behavior accordingly. In the short run, they hesitated to cut nominal wages in recessions.[9] In the long run, they developed administered wage scales and centralized the personnel management function in an effort to control the labor market.

II Interwar Comparisons

World War I was a watershed in the organization of Anglo-American labor markets. The British and U.S. governments sought to collaborate with organized labor to secure labor peace and insure that industrial disputes did not disrupt the war effort. "Military victory required a radical redirection of economic resources and the maintenance of social solidarity," as one set of coauthors (Phillips and Whiteside, 1985, p. 112) put it. Labor's position strengthened as unionization scaled new heights. Labor markets tightened, encouraging industrial disputes despite government's best efforts to suppress them. Employers

---

[8] Sundstrom (1992), using data for a cross-section of Cincinnati manufacturing firms in the recession of 1893, finds that the prevalence of wage cuts was less in relatively capital-intensive sectors where few workers were paid by the piece. Raff's (1988) explanation of Henry Ford's five-dollar day in terms of the threat of labor action is also consistent with this interpretation.

[9] Ozanne (1967, p. 239) describes the change in practice at McCormick and International Harvester. "The depression of 1893, coming close on the heels of the terrible labor troubles of 1885 and 1886, brought a dramatic change in the company's wage-cutting tactics even though at that time there were no unions in the plant. Instead of an across-the-board cut as in 1884, the company maintained its common labor rate through three years of depression, cutting it only at the end of 1896" (as quoted in Sundstrom, 1992, pp. 449–450).

responded by improving working conditions and bidding for the allegiance of a core group of workers by rewarding them with employment security. While not all of these changes proved permanent (unionization rates, for example, fell back following the conclusion of hostilities), the war still represented a break with prewar modes of labor market organization.

The wartime shock also lent impetus to the development of personnel management practices.[10] Government intervention in the industrial relations of sectors regarded as essential to the war effort encouraged firms to innovate so as to preempt official incursions. As the labor market tightened, effort norms and shop-floor discipline were eroded. The spread of unionism and the availability of alternative job opportunities undermined the effectiveness of the drive system: as absenteeism and tardiness rose, productivity declined. In response, firms established compensation schedules that rewarded employees for tenure and encouraged internal promotion.[11] They created personnel departments designed to screen workers for reliability. The proportion of firms with more than 250 workers that had personnel departments rose from perhaps 5 percent in 1915 to 25 percent in 1920. Increasingly, managers assumed responsibilities that had traditionally been delegated to foremen.[12] They issued rules and regulations regarding the compensation and promotion of workers, superseding the drive system of previous years.

---

[10] Importantly, this bureaucratization of labor relations appears to have been a distinctively American phenomenon. In Britain, where the emergence of the large multidivisional corporation lagged behind, this development was less common. I return to this point below.

[11] Sundstrom (1988b) dissents from the view that the establishment of centralized, job-based wage determination was a response to the threat of unionization and the tightening of the labor market, arguing instead that the increasing size and complexity of the firm aggravated the principal-agent problems between owners and lower-level managers that inevitably arose when the latter were delegated responsibility for wage determination. As Sundstrom notes, however, the two explanations are not really incompatible: the difficulty of monitoring the wage-setting decisions of lower-level managers became especially severe "in the extraordinarily tight labor market conditions of World War I" (p. 202).

[12] At the same time, Jacoby (1985, p. 237) notes that as late as 1935, half of all U.S. firms still allowed the foreman to be the sole arbiter of dismissal. See also Nelson (1975).

Once the war ended and soldiers were demobilized, labor markets loosened and many of these wartime developments were reversed. Some, however, proved permanent, especially when reinforced by public policy. In the United States, the most significant policy initiative may have been the end of large-scale immigration. As the supply of immigrants was curtailed, firms found it necessary to restructure the organization of work. Skilled natives had to be substituted for unskilled immigrants. Machinery came to be used in more complex ways. This increased the cost of turnover, reinforcing the bureaucratization of the labor market and the spread of personnel management techniques.[13]

In addition, in the 1930s the National Industrial Recovery Act (NIRA) sanctioned the right of workers to organize and bargain collectively. It encouraged trade associations to submit to the National Recovery Administration labor codes detailing standards and conditions of work. The development of internal labor markets was given another boost as firms further bureaucratized their employment practices under NIRA pressure and sought to preempt unionization. In response to these pressures, practices like inverse-seniority layoff rules finally became widespread.[14]

In Britain, meanwhile, the government attempted to "decasualize" the labor force. Ministry of Labour and Board of Trade officials sought to encourage the development of more stable employment relationships on the docks and wherever casual labor prevailed. They encouraged port employers to offer a guaranteed minimum income and job tenure to dockers. These initiatives were not entirely successful, but they reinforced other trends, such as the increasingly capital-intensive and skilled nature of dock work and similar forms of labor, leading to more stable employment relationships.

British labor market dynamics were further transformed by unemployment insurance. Public insurance had first been provided in selected sectors in 1911. But the scheme's coverage was limited. Starting in 1920, it was extended to virtually all workers outside the agricultural and personal service sectors. Because of the particular form of the

---

[13] See Slichter (1929) and Scott (1941) for details.

[14] Jacoby (1985) notes that at the beginning of the 1920s only a small minority of industrial firms had definite procedures governing layoffs. Hence, foremen continued to exercise extensive control of the discharge process.

Unemployment Insurance Scheme, it is not clear whether it was conducive to repeated short spells of unemployment or to an increasing prevalence of long spells. Rules limiting the length of time for which benefits could be drawn should have limited the incentive to remain unemployed for extended periods. But these regulations were relaxed when high unemployment became a pressing problem in the 1930s. Workers entitled to draw half or more of their regular earnings for an unlimited period and relieved of commuting costs and other professional expenses may have been encouraged to shun short-term jobs. On the other hand, the short waiting period prior to qualifying for benefit may have encouraged job sharing and short spells of unemployment. The scheme treated any three days of unemployment occurring in a period of six as continuous with previous days unemployed; it thus required no further waiting period prior to drawing benefits. This gave rise to the "OXO system," named for the arrangement of days of work (O) and leisure (X). Individuals could work for three days each week and be idle for three, permitting two workers to share a single job and, courtesy of unemployment insurance, sacrifice little income. Even before the Great Depression struck, systematic short time was used as a means of job sharing; nearly one in five cotton industry workers was on short time in the second half of the 1920s. "Work pools" were common in the shoe and hat trade and the coal industry as well (Gibson, 1931). One can imagine how this encouraged repeated short spells of unemployment, but not of the irregular and unorganized nature of prewar casual work.

In the United States, the advent of federal unemployment insurance did not occur until later.[15] Meanwhile, a surprising number of private

---

[15] The first compulsory state unemployment insurance law was that of Wisconsin, adopted in 1932. The fact that work sharing increased in the United States as well as the United Kingdom after 1929 undermines the notion that the OXO system was wholly responsible for British short time. Thus, in the United States the number of establishments that had part-time employment rose from 15 percent in September 1929 to 42 percent in January 1931 (Jacoby, 1985, p. 212). The practice was promoted by the Hoover Administration, through the President's Emergency Committee on Employment and its successor, the President's Organization on Unemployment Relief. Bernanke (1986) models the simultaneous determination of wages, hours, and workers in the 1930s, emphasizing that more adjustment occurred on the hours margin than has been typical of post-World War II recessions.

firms provided relief programs for their employees.[16] Some unemployed workers also had the option of public works employment. Margo (1993) reports that persons on work relief had longer incomplete spells of unemployment than other unemployed persons. Compared with unemployed persons not on work relief, twice as many of those on relief in 1940 had been without a nonrelief job for a year or longer. It is hard to know whether the provision of public works employment encouraged workers to shun regular jobs, or whether those least able to obtain regular employment had preferential access to public works employment. But this pattern is at least consistent with the view that the increased provision of public employment increased the length of time for which many of those who became unemployed in the 1930s remained out of work (Kesselman, 1978).

While these developments hardly transformed labor markets into their late 20th-century form, they do appear to have slowed the rate of turnover and lengthened the average duration of unemployment spells. Trends are unfortunately obscured by the fact that not just institutional arrangements but also macroeconomic conditions had changed. That a larger share of unemployed workers in the 1930s now experienced long spells of idleness may say more about the depressed state of the macroeconomy than about changes in labor market structure. Thomas (1988) reports rates of inflow into unemployment in 1931 that were essentially the same as those of 1911–1913. This may indicate that turnover rates were little different than 20 years before, or more plausibly that turnover had declined somewhat but that current circumstances were atypical, with inflow rates temporarily boosted by the onset of the Great Depression. By how much is difficult to say. The difference on the outflow side was more dramatic: the average outflow rate was 11.6 in 1926–1938, compared to 24.9 percent in 1911–1913. The fall relative to 20 years before presumably reflected both some secular decline in the average rate of flow through the labor market as well as the depressed employment prospects of the 1930s. It is worth noting that at 11.6 percent the outflow rate, even in these adverse conditions, was still more than double that for Britain in the 1970s.[17]

---

[16] One in three large enterprises did so in 1930–1933 according to the National Industrial Conference Board (1934).

[17] Baily (1983) provides comparisons for the United States that point in the same direction.

These inflow rates (and the steady-state assumption) imply that the expected duration of a spell of unemployment rose from 4 weeks in 1913 to 23 weeks in 1931 (compared to 32 weeks in 1984) (Thomas, 1988, pp. 103, 127).[18] The steady-state assumption is problematic, however. Outflow data suggest shorter average expected durations (on the order of eight weeks, but these are still double the average for 1911–1913). They suggest that only half as many of the unemployed suffered from prolonged spells in 1934 as in 1984 (20 versus 40 percent).

Interwar data also suggest that the burden of unemployment was shared less evenly across socioeconomic groups than before 1913. In Britain, male unemployment rates in 1931 ranged from 1.8 percent for highly trained professionals to 5.6 percent for clerks, 12 percent for skilled and semiskilled manual workers, and 22.5 percent for the unskilled. Average expected unemployment durations for males ranged from 4 weeks for 18–20-year-olds to 10 weeks for 35–44-year-olds and more than 22 weeks for 60–64-year-olds. In Michigan, male unemployment rates as of 1935 were less than 10 percent for white-collar workers but more than 20 percent for blue-collar workers (Jensen, 1989, p. 569). They ranged from 10 percent for clerical workers, to 16–17 percent for skilled and semiskilled manual laborers, to 29 percent for the unskilled. If the spread of firm-specific skills gave firms additional incentive to hoard workers during downturns, this was clearly more the case for the skilled than the unskilled.

Thus, the picture is one of an interwar labor market in which rates of turnover had slowed and the incidence of unemployment had grown more uneven, though neither change was as pronounced as it was to become in the 1970s and 1980s.[19]

Again, it is worth inquiring into the implications of these changes for wage flexibility. Gordon's (1982) time-series analysis reveals a decline after World War I in the responsiveness of wages to fluctuations in GNP for the United States but not for Britain. Hatton's (1988)

---

[18] The same rate of inflow implies a longer average duration because the unemployment rate had risen.

[19] As Thomas puts it, "although the total insured population in 1933 was only half that of fifty years later, the volume of inflows on to the register was almost three times as large. The rapid rate of turnover is reflected in a considerably lower mean duration of completed spells, despite a higher unemployment rate" (1988, p. 127).

prewar and interwar comparisons for Britain similarly do not indicate a decline in wage flexibility. Nor does Thomas's (1992) analysis of the interwar United Kingdom.

The key differences between the two countries may have been the rise of internal labor markets and bureaucratized wage setting in the United States but not in the United Kingdom, plus the policies of the American government. As Sundstrom (1988b) shows, the bureaucratization of wage setting in the United States made it increasingly difficult after World War I for employers to adjust wages in response to demand fluctuations. The growing inertia of American wages was reinforced by the policies of the Hoover Administration, which, in a misguided effort to sustain the level of demand, jawboned major employers to refrain from initiating wage reductions. While the provision of unemployment benefits for virtually unlimited periods could not have encouraged job search by British workers and enhanced the flexibility of sterling-denominated wages, there is little evidence that its effects were as profound as those of bureaucratized labor relations and industrial policy in the United States.

III   Implications for Today

Any analysis of the historical evolution of industrial labor markets is necessarily a tale of continuity and change. There is continuity in the differing degrees of job stability enjoyed by white- and blue-collar workers and in the imperfect wage flexibility that appears to characterize all labor markets. There is change in the secular decline in the speed of job turnover and the more uneven incidence of unemployment.

While industrial labor markets never resembled the perfectly flexible spot markets of textbooks, from a long-term perspective it is possible to discern a decline in the degree of nominal wage flexibility and an increase in the incidence of long-term unemployment. Commentators considering the problem of unemployment from the viewpoint of Europe in the 1990s are tempted to attribute these phenomena to the market power of unions and the adverse incentives created by unemployment insurance and other forms of government intervention. While nothing in this paper leads one to dismiss factors such as these, the present analysis points also to technological and institutional factors working in the same direction. Over the last century, the growing capital intensity of production, the greater complexity of technology, the heightened interrelatedness of tasks, and the rising importance of firm-specific skills have all enhanced the ability of insiders to resist wage cuts and the incentive for management to adopt alternative strategies for coping with demand fluctuations. The internal labor markets and personnel management practices developed in response reinforced the trend toward greater nominal inertia.

Reforms of public programs and limits on monopoly power in the labor market are all to the good, but they alone will not restore the wage flexibility, high turnover, even incidence of unemployment, and limited prevalence of long-term joblessness that were characteristic of earlier eras.

Bibliography

Abraham, K., and H. Farber. 1987. "Job Duration, Seniority, and Earnings." *American Economic Review* 77:278–297.

Akerlof, G., and B. Main. 1981. "An Experience-Weighted Measure of Employment and Unemployment Durations." *American Economic Review* 71:1003–1011.

Allen, S.G. 1992. "Changes in the Cyclical Sensitivity of Wages in the United States, 1891–1987." *American Economic Review* 82:122–140.

Baily, M.N. 1983. "The Labor Market in the 1930s." In: J. Tobin (ed.), *Macroeconomics, Prices and Quantities*, pp. 21–61. Washington, D.C.: The Brookings Institution.

Bernanke, B.S. 1986. "Employment, Hours and Earnings in the Depression." *American Economic Review* 76:82–109.

Carter, S., and E. Savoca. 1990. "Labor Mobility and Lengthy Jobs in Nineteenth-Century America." *Journal of Economic History* 50:1–17.

Chandler, A. 1990. *Scale and Scope: The Dynamics of Industrial Capitalism.* Cambridge: Harvard University Press.

Elbaum, B., and W. Lazonick. 1986. *The Decline of the British Economy.* Oxford: Clarendon Press.

Gibson, M.B. 1931. *Unemployment Insurance in Great Britain.* New York: Industrial Relations Councilors.

Gordon, R.J. 1982. "Why U.S. Wage and Employment Behavior Differs From That in Britain and Japan." *Economic Journal* 92:13–44.

Hall, R. 1982. "The Importance of Lifetime Jobs in the U.S. Economy." *American Economic Review* 72:716–724.

Hanes, C. 1993. "The Development of Nominal Wage Rigidity in the Late 19th Century." *American Economic Review* 83:732–756.

Hatton, T.J. 1988. "Institutional Change and Wage Rigidity in the U.K., 1880–1985." *Oxford Review of Economic Policy* 4:74–86.

Jacoby, S. 1985. *Employing Bureaucracy: Managers, Unions and the Transformation of Work in American Industry 1900–1945.* New York: Columbia University Press.

Jacoby, S., and S. Sharma. 1992. "Employment Duration and Industrial Labor Mobility in the United States, 1880–1980." *Journal of Economic History* 52:161–180.

Jensen, R.J. 1989. "The Causes and Cures of Unemployment in the Great Depression." *Journal of Interdisciplinary History* 19:553–585.

Kesselman, J.R. 1978. "Work Relief Programs in the Great Depression." In: J. L. Palmer (ed.), *Creating Jobs*. Washington, D.C.: The Brookings Institution.

Keyssar, A. 1986. *Out of Work: The First Century of Unemployment in Massachusetts*. Cambridge: Harvard University Press.

Margo, R.A. 1990a. "Unemployment in 1910: Some Preliminary Findings." In: E. Aerts and B. Eichengreen (ed.), *Unemployment and Underemployment in Historical Perspective*, pp. 51–60. Leuven: University of Leuven Press.

Margo, R.A. 1990b. "The Microeconomics of Depression Unemployment." NBER Working Paper No. 18. Cambridge, Mass.: NBER.

Margo, R.A. 1992. "The Labor Force in the 19th Century." NBER, Working Paper Series on Historical Factors in Long Run Growth, No. 40. Cambridge, Mass.: NBER.

Margo, R.A. 1993. "Employment and Unemployment in the 1930s." *Journal of Economic Perspectives* 7:41–59.

Murphy, K., and R. Topel. 1987. "The Evolution of Unemployment in the United States: 1968–1985." *NBER Macroeconomics Annual*, pp. 11–58.

National Industrial Conference Board. 1934. *Effect of the Depression on Industrial Relations Programs*. New York: NICB.

Nelson, D. 1975. *Managers and Workers: Origins of the New Factory System in the United States*. Madison: University of Wisconsin Press.

Ozanne, R. 1967. *A Century of Labor-Management Relations at McCormick and International Harvester*. Madison: University of Wisconsin Press.

Phillips, G., and N. Whiteside. 1985. *Casual Labor*. Oxford: Oxford University Press.

Raff, D. 1988. "Wage Determination Theory and the Five Dollar Day at Ford." *Journal of Economic History* 48:387–400.

Rowntree, B.S., and E. Lasker. 1911. *Unemployment: A Social Study*. London: Macmillan.

Scott, W.D. et al. 1941. *Personnel Management*. Third edition. New York: McGraw Hill.

Slichter, S. 1919. *The Turnover of Factory Labor*. New York: Appelton.

Slichter, S. 1929. "The Current Labor Policies of American Industries." *Quarterly Journal of Economics* 43:393–435.

Stedman Jones, G. 1976. *Outcast London*. London: Penguin.

Sundstrom, W.A. 1988a. "Internal Labor Markets Before World War I: On-the-Job Training and Employee Promotion." *Explorations in Economic History* 25:424–445.

Sundstrom, W.A. 1988b. "Organizational Failures and Wage Determination: A Historical Case Study." *Journal of Economic Behavior and Organization* 10: 201–224.

Sundstrom, W.A. 1992. "Rigid Wages or Small Equilibrium Adjustments: Evidence from the Contraction of 1893." *Explorations in Economic History* 29:430–454.

Thomas, M. 1988. "Labor Market Structure and the Nature of Unemployment in Interwar Britain." In: B. Eichengreen and T.J. Hatton (eds.), *Interwar Unemployment in International Perspective*, pp. 97–148. Dordrecht: Martinus Nijhoff.

Thomas, M. 1990. "Unemployment in Edwardian Britain: A New Perspective." In: E. Aerts and B. Eichengreen (ed), *Unemployment and Underemployment in Historical Perspective*, pp. 36–50. Leuven: University of Leuven Press.

Thomas, M. Forthcoming. "How Flexible Were Wages in Interwar Britain?" In: G. Grantham and M. MacKinnon (eds.), *The Evolution of Labor Markets*.

Doing It Right? The U.S. Labor Market Response to the 1980s–1990s

Richard B. Freeman

USA
J31
J21
J64

Many European analysts and policymakers view the U.S. labor market as a paradise of neoclassical flexibility. Wages respond rapidly to changes in supply and demand in local labor markets with little institutional intervention. Jobs are readily created for those who seek them. Firms hire and fire at will, with little government or union restrictions. Spells of unemployment are short in duration, and unemployment benefits modest. As a result, the story goes, the United States has avoided the long extensive joblessness that has characterized Europe since the early 1980s.

These observations about the American job market are factually correct. There is much about the American response to the economic shocks of the 1980s–1990s that merits approbation.

Many American analysts and policymakers, however, view the U.S. job market differently. Wage inequality grew in the 1980s. The real earnings of the less-skilled plummeted, to the point where workers in the lower parts of the earnings distribution have living standards below those of comparably situated workers in Europe (Freeman, 1994a, Chapter 1). Many young men found crime more attractive than work. Child poverty rose, and the country developed a seemingly permanent underclass of the homeless and beggars.

These observations are also factually correct. There is much about the American job market that merits disapprobation. Americans did not vote George Bush out of office merely because he had never seen a supermarket checkout counter.

Parts of this paper are taken from my work for Chapter 1 of the *Fact Finding Report* of the United States Commission on the Future of Worker-Management Relations, issued in May 1994.

In this paper I examine both the positive and negative aspects of the U.S. labor market response to the economic world of the 1980s–1990s. I review the economic developments that created difficulties in the United States and other advanced economies post the first oil shock, consider how a decentralized labor market might be expected to respond to them, and summarize the American response. I conclude by assessing the social welfare consequences of the American response relative to that of Europe.

I The Developments

From the early 1970s (roughly post the first oil shock) through the mid-1990s Western economies had slower economic growth than in the 1950s and 1960s (Figure 1). This made it more difficult to provide rising wages or employment for those seeking jobs than in the previous twenty years or so. The extent to which the post-oil-shock slowdown fundamentally breaks with the past is open to debate. Growth rates of real earnings and per capita income vary over extended periods. Since the Industrial Revolution the United States and Europe have suffered depressions and periods where living standards deteriorated for many citizens. Perhaps the 1970s–1990s is one of these long cyclic slowdowns. The successful recovery from world war and depression of the

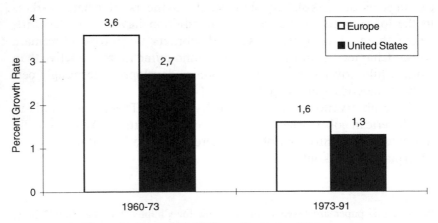

Figure 1. Growth of GDP per Capita per Year.
Source: OECD, Historical Statistics (various editions).

1950s and 1960s may have given us an exalted view of the economic opportunities capitalism normally provides workers. Alternatively, however, the economic performance of advanced countries in this period may represent a particularly unsuccessful adjustment to specific developments.

Many things changed in the 1970s and 1980s from earlier decades, besides the slowdown in growth. The composition of the work force, the structure of industrial output, the level of foreign trade, the technology of production—all changed. Analysts disagree about the extent to which these changes contributed to the economic ills of the period, but most would concur that along with slow growth the following were important:

Technological change. Although the period was *not* one of rapid productivity growth in the United States or other advanced countries,[1] nor of an *accelerating* shift in employment against unskilled labor,[2] there was a clear change in the type of work performed at most workplaces, with evidence that the expanded use of computers shifted labor demand toward more educated workers (Krueger, 1993). Most analysts believe that technological changes contributed to the reduction in the relative earnings of unskilled Americans (U.S. Council of Economic Advisors, 1994).

The growth of trade. World trade grew from the 1970s through 1980s, as it had from the 1950s through the 1970s, though with no ac-

---

[1] In the United States from 1973 to 1992 the rate of growth of GDP per employee was 0.5 percent a year, compared to 2.5 percent per year from 1950 to 1973. In manufacturing the growth of productivity fell in the 1970s but recovered in the late 1980s and 1990s to its historic level of approximately 2.5 percent per year. Measured by GDP per employee or manufacturing output per hour, the United States had slower growth of productivity than other advanced countries.

[2] Employment shifted toward the skilled within industries no faster than in earlier decades. In manufacturing, the ratio of nonproduction to production workers rose from .264 in 1973 to .318 in 1993, but the ratio had risen proportionately faster in the preceding two decades from .199 in 1953. The Economic Policy Institute estimates that occupational upgrading raised compensation by 0.18 percent per year from 1972 to 1979, and by 0.19 percent per year from 1979 to 1993, implying no change in the rate of acceleration of skill upgrading.

celeration of the trend.[3] Beginning in the 1980s, a growing proportion of manufacturing imports to the West came from low-wage developing countries, such as China. By 1992, in fact, mainland China and Taiwan were together the third largest importer into the United States. Some analysts, notably Adrian Wood, argue that the growth of manufacturing imports from third world countries is the main reason for the problems facing less-skilled workers in the United States and Europe. Others (Borjas, Freeman, and Katz, 1992; Sachs and Shatz, 1994) place a smaller weight on trade, in large part because the vast bulk of less-skilled workers are employed outside the traded goods sector; while still others have argued that the trade effects are negligible (Bhagwati, 1994; Lawrence and Slaughter, 1993).

Increased immigration. Most Western countries experienced an increased flow of immigrants from developing countries. The proportion of the population who are foreign-born in the United States rose from 4.7 percent in 1970 to 7.9 percent in 1990. Since the Census fails to count perhaps one-third of illegal immigrants, most of whom work, the proportion who are foreign-born in the work force may be as high as nine percent. Following the Immigration Act of 1964, the bulk of immigrants were from developing countries, often with little schooling and few skills. In 1990, one in five American workers with less than a high school education was foreign-born, and one in seven American men in the bottom quintile of the income distribution was foreign-born.[4]

Increased supply of women. The proportion of the labor force that is female increased;[5] and many families have come to rely on two earners or on single female heads. The proportion of "traditional couples" in the United States—man works, wife stays home—fell from 44 percent of the total to 23 percent between 1975 and 1993. The increased role of women as both breadwinners and homemakers challenges traditional work arrangements and raises demands for flexible

---

[3] In the United States the most commonly used measure of the magnitude of trade in the economy, the ratio of exports and imports to GDP, rose by 3.3 percent per year from 1959 to 1973 and increased thereafter by 2.9 percent per year.

[4] This is based on tabulations from the 1990 Census public use data set.

[5] In 1953, 34.4 percent of women of working age were in the labor force. In 1973, 44.7 percent were in the labor force. In 1993, 57.9 percent were in the labor force.

working hours, job sharing arrangements, child care benefits, and parental leave.

Still, it is important to recognize that the growth of the female share of employment did not accelerate in the 1980s or 1970s. The proportion of females in the work force increased by 30 percent from 1953 and 1973 and from 1973 and 1993, though the absolute change in the proportion in the work force was bigger in the latter period.

Changed supply of educated workers.   The years of schooling attained by the work force increased greatly. In the United States in 1970, 12 percent of the labor force 25–64 years old had more than 12 years of schooling. In 1992, 52 percent had more than 12 years. In the 1970s, with the baby-boomers entering the job market, the flood of college graduates reduced the pay of college graduates relative to less-educated workers (Freeman, 1976). Other advanced countries had a similar experience: increased numbers of graduates reduced educational differentials. In the 1980s, by contrast, the rate of growth in the relative supply of college graduates lessened in the United States (it actually fell for 25–29-year-old men), contributing to the rise in educational differentials.

Turbulence in other markets.   Developments in other markets also "shocked" the U.S. labor market. The United States moved from creditor to debtor nation. The U.S. dollar rose in value in the mid-1980s, devastating employment in many export sectors. The government deregulated air transportation and trucking and broke up AT&T, putting downward pressure on wages in those sectors. There was a savings and loan banking crisis, a third world debt crisis, and so on. Following the Reagan tax cuts, the federal budget deficit skyrocketed. Whatever the reason, saving rates were exceptionally low in the United States, making investment funds depend on foreign investors, particularly the Japanese. Market reforms, currency fluctuations, and flows of capital also greatly affected labor markets in other advanced countries.

Institutional changes.   The major institutional change in the United States was the fall in union representation of workers. In part, this reflected the demographic and market developments given above, but to a large extent, it was an independent change, resulting from the U.S. process of determining union representation in an adversarial election where management greatly affects outcomes, in some cases by committing illegal "unfair labor practices." The fall in union density to 11.4 percent in the private sector by 1993 meant that most workers had to find means other than union representation to give them a voice in company affairs.

Did the economic developments of the 1980s–1990s demand greater structural adjustment in the American job market than was required in earlier decades? The *1994 Economic Report of the President* noted that one indicator of turbulence in the job market—the sum of the absolute value of changes in the proportion of the work force in different industries—shows no trend since 1945. Abraham and Katz (1986) examined changes in the composition of the labor force across industries and found no evidence of greater turbulence over time. Consistent with this, Steve Allen and I have calculated the amount of shifting among industries since the 1920s and found that the 1980–1992 period is not extraordinary in its degree of change (Allen and Freeman, 1994). The most turbulent decade was the 1940s, followed by the 1920s and 1930s. Similarly, we examined the amount of shifting of employment across occupations and found that compared to earlier decades the 1980s-early 1990s were a relatively quiet period in terms of changes in the occupational structure.

In sum, most of the changes in the economy during the 1980s–1990s were not sharp breaks with the past, nor marked accelerations of previous trends, but continuations of longer-run developments; and the overall "flux" in the market was not more marked than in earlier decades. What differentiated the troubled times of the 1980s–1990s (or 1970s–1990s) from earlier periods was the direction/bias of changes that put extraordinary pressure on low-skill workers and the interaction of the developments outlined above with slow growth.

II   Responses of a Decentralized Labor Market

How might a decentralized labor market respond to weakened demand for labor relative to the supply of labor? In the basic supply-demand model, the wages of workers facing reduced demand for labor should fall, and their employment should drop, but most of those who lose work should find employment quickly elsewhere in the job market.

There ought to be no increase in joblessness, beyond some temporary or frictional level.

Consider first the wage side of the story.

A   Flexible Wage Adjustments

1. The real hourly compensation of American workers stagnated from 1973 to 1993 and fell for full-time males—a development unprecedented in the past 75 years in the country.   Table 1 documents the stagnation or fall in real earnings for Americans over this period. The compensation series in the table differ in various ways—the sample covered, inclusion or exclusion of fringe benefit, the particular years covered—but they tell the same story: that from 1973 or thereabouts to 1993, real pay did not increase at anything like its historic growth rate of 2 or so percent per year.

The real pay in Table 1 deflates earnings by the consumer price index. This is appropriate for comparing living standards but is not the right price index for analyses of labor demand, where a producer price index is superior. The bottom lines of the table record rates of change in the consumer price index, and two measures of output prices, the producer price index (PPI) and the GDP deflator. Output prices increased less rapidly than the consumer price index (CPI), implying that the decline or stagnation in consumption wages overstates the change in product wages that affect labor demand. OECD data on hourly earnings and producer prices in manufacturing show that from 1979 to 1989 real product earnings grew by 0.7 percent per year in the United States compared to 1.6 percent in EEC countries. From this perspective, falling or stagnant real earnings in the United States contributed less to the growth of employment than is suggested by the CPI-deflated figures, though it still contributed to the better U.S. employment experience.

2. The gap in wages between more/less-educated and skilled workers rose greatly in the 1980s after falling in the 1970s.   The increased gap in pay between high-skill and low-skill workers is the most widely noted change in the U.S. job market—documented extensively in Current Population Survey (CPS) files. The following data show the changes in real earnings from 1972 to 1990 in the CPS by sex and education (Commission on the Future of Worker-Management Relations, 1994):

Table 1. Compound Annual Growth of Real Earnings and Prices in the United States, 1973–1993

	Compound Growth Rate Per Year
Establishment Survey Data	
Average hourly earnings, private nonagriculture production and nonsupervisory workers	−0.8
Hourly compensation, business sector	0.4
Total compensation, employment cost index (1979–1993)	0.1
National Income and Products Account, 1975–1993	
Wages and salaries of full-time equivalent workers	−0.1
Compensation of full-time equivalent workers	0.2
Household Survey Data	
Median Weekly Earnings, Full-Time Workers, 1979–1993	
All	−0.2
Male	−0.8
Female	0.5
Median Annual Income, Full-Time Workers, 1973–1992	
Male	−0.5
Female	0.7
Price Indices, 1973–1993	
Consumer price index	5.9
Producer price index	5.0
GDP deflator	5.5

Source: Updated and adapted from Commission on the Future of Worker-Management Relations, Fact Finding Report, May 1994.
Note: Figures for median weekly earning differ slightly from those in the Commission report because different government documents report different medians for 1979. Wages and salaries or earnings figures differ from compensation figures, because compensation includes employer contributions to "fringe benefits," such as health insurance, pensions, and government-mandated costs such as payroll taxes.

	Men	Women
Less than High School	−23%	−5%
4 Years of High School	−19%	1%
1–3 Years of College	−14%	8%
4 Years of College	−8%	9%

Real earnings fell most for male workers with less than high school education, but they also fell for female workers with less than high

Table 2. Estimates of the Effect of Education on Ln Hourly Earnings of American Men Aged 18–64, 1970–1990

Education	1969	1979	1989
8 years or less	−0.44	−0.48	−0.41
Some high school (9–11 years)	−0.20	−0.25	−0.24
High school (12 years)	−	−	−
Some college (13–15 years)	0.11	0.10	0.17
College (16 years)	0.43	0.34	0.49
College plus (>16 years)	0.65	0.41	0.63
Other Controls			
9 experience dummies	×	×	×
2 race/ethnic dummies	×	×	×
Number of Observations	335,423	373,139	406,931
R^2	0.168	0.180	0.227

Source: Tabulated from U.S. Census of Population public use data files, 1970, 1980, 1990.

Note: Because of the large sample sizes all of the standard errors on the coefficients are less than .01 except for the following:

(1) 1969: College Plus (>16 years) = .18
(2) 1989: 8 years or less   = .01

school education and for all other groups of men. A group (not shown in these data) that fared particularly poorly in terms of earnings growth was younger men, who also are less likely to have pensions and other fringe benefits than similarly aged men years ago.

Table 2 gives regression coefficients and standard errors for the effect of different levels of education in 1970, 1980, and 1990 from the Census of Population. The estimated coefficients are based on multivariate regressions with hundreds of thousands of observations, so that with rare exception all of the coefficients have standard errors below 0.01. The estimates show a fall in educational differentials in the 1970s followed by a rise in those differentials in the 1980s. This pattern corroborates findings based on CPS data. The changes in educational premium are strong evidence of the flexibility of relative wages by education to shifts in the demand and supply of labor with different levels of schooling in the United States.

3. The earnings distribution widened greatly from the early 1970s to the 1990s, producing an extraordinarily unequal income distribution. When

Bluestone and Harrison (1986) first reported the "great U-turn" in the American earnings distribution from modest declines (or stability) in inequality to increased inequality, many analysts were suspicious of their claims. Perhaps the results reflected the particular series and measures chosen and the 1980s recession—the worst since the Great Depression—rather than a secular change. A decade and a host of studies later, it is common wisdom that the American earnings distribution has undergone an extraordinary widening. The Bureau of the Census reports that in 1992, 18 percent of the nation's year-round full-time workers were low-wage workers (earning less than $13,091)—a 50 percent increase over the 12 percent of the work force in the low-wage category in 1979.

Measures of the pay gap between workers in the highest decile of earnings and those in the lowest decile show that the United States' earnings distribution is the most unequal among developed countries (OECD, 1993). Male workers in the bottom decile earn 38 percent of median earnings in the United States, whereas in Western Europe male workers in the bottom decile earn 68 percent of median earnings (Freeman, 1994a). In the upper rungs of the distribution, top-decile men in the United States earn 2.14 times median earnings whereas top-decile men in most European countries earn 1.4 to 1.7 times the median. As a result, the ratio of earnings in the top decile to the lowest decile in the United States is 5.63—by far the widest among OECD countries. The rise in inequality exceeds, moreover, the rise that would be expected simply given the rising educational or occupational differentials: it has occurred within groups of seemingly similarly skilled workers.

The positive side of the earnings story for the United States is that relative and absolute earnings are quite responsive to economic conditions. The negative side is that market conditions demanded falls in real earnings for low-paid workers and increases in inequality to levels that trouble even a country with considerable tolerance for inequality.

B   Job Creation and Mobility

4. The United States was more successful in generating work for those who seek it in the 1980s and 1990s than European countries. Measured by either employment-population rates or unemployment rates, the

U.S. labor market has done a better job than European labor markets in "creating jobs." In 1974 the ratio of employment to the population aged 15–64 was *the same* in the United States and in OECD-Europe: 64.8 percent. In 1992 the employment to population rate was 71.1 percent in the United States and 60.1 percent in OECD-Europe. Prior to the 1980s, the rate of unemployment in the United States exceeded the rates in Europe (a fact which led one of my European colleagues to say he could never take seriously the standard neoclassical model of the labor market). After 1983 the rate of unemployment has been considerably higher in Europe. For over a decade the United States has produced an unemployment rate roughly 3 percentage points below that in Europe. This change is not, however, the result of the United States reducing its unemployment rate. To the contrary, the U.S. unemployment rate has drifted upward decade by decade, as the following decadal average rates of unemployment show: 1950s–4.5, 1960s–4.8, 1970s–6.2, 1980s–7.3. In addition, many Americans are involuntarily employed part-time. In 1991 the proportion of the U.S. labor force that was involuntarily employed part-time was 4.0 percent compared to 1.5 percent for the OECD-Europe countries for which data are available (OECD, 1993, Table 1.5).

Data on hours worked show that the American employment growth was not fueled by reduction in hours and work-sharing of the type widely discussed in Europe. Americans put in more hours of work than Europeans, and have increased their worktime—possibly in response to slow growth/decline of earnings. U.S. workers currently work about 200 hours more during a year than workers in Europe. In 1993 the OECD reports that Americans put in 1,743 hours compared to 1,534 hours for Germans, 1,542 hours for the French (1992), and 1,409 hours by the Dutch. A major reason for this difference in working time is the smaller vacations of Americans, who at most take about 2 weeks a year compared to the 4–5 weeks common in Europe. The length of vacation and holiday time in the United States has actually declined in the past 20 years. In addition, many Americans hold more than one job. In 1991 over 6 percent of Americans held a second job. Over 18 percent of workers reported that they did job-related work at home. With a higher fraction of the work force employed and putting in more hours than Europeans, one might expect that Americans would be eager for time off. Surveys of preferences for work show the opposite: Americans want to work more than Europeans and report themselves working harder and being more devoted to work than Europeans (Bell and Freeman, 1994). The American response to the economic problems of the 1980s was to work more, not to seek to share the available work.

5. Duration of unemployment in the United States is shorter than in Europe, so that unemployment is more widely shared among the population. Unemployment in the United States affects many workers. In 1992, 16 percent of the work force experienced some joblessness—nearly three times the proportion unemployed at any time in the year. Spells of unemployment are much shorter in the United States than in Europe: 11 percent of American workers who were unemployed in 1992 were unemployed for more than one year compared to 30–50 percent in most OECD-European countries (OECD, 1994, Table P). The movement into and out of joblessness in the United States is nearly 10 times as fast as the rate of movement into and out of joblessness in Europe, according to OECD figures. In 1986, 46 percent of Americans unemployed in one month left that state by the next month; the comparable flow out of unemployment for Europeans was 5 percent. But, the flip side of this was that 2 percent of Americans became unemployed in a month compared to 0.4 percent of Europeans (OECD, 1990, Table 1.2). In one sense, the flexible U.S. market produces substantial work-sharing over time: workers hold a job for a certain period and are jobless for a certain period in contrast to the insider-outsider distinction between the employed and unemployed in Europe.

Still, this does not mean that the unemployed American does not have a problem. The median spell of reported joblessness in the United States of approximately 12 weeks understates the length of completed spells. The amount of time these people will be unemployed is likely to be twice as long—nearly half a year. This can be quite painful given the low level of U.S. unemployment benefits, potential loss of health insurance between employment spells, and low levels of personal savings. Over time, moreover, the proportion of unemployment that is long-run has increased in the United States: Topel and Murphy (1987) estimate that 62 percent of the secular increase in unemployment from 1968–1970 to 1980–1985 was due to the increase in spells that lasted over six months. Finally, empirical studies of unemployment show that workers displaced from a job into unemployment take large wage cuts when they return to work—on the order of 23 percent (Topel, 1994).

6. *Groups whose earnings fell in the 1980s had the worst problems in joblessness.* Ideally, substantial wage reductions for workers facing reduced labor demands will maintain their employment levels. This has not occurred in the United States to any noticeable degree. In 1993, the unemployment rate for those with less than a high school education was 12.6 percent; for those with only a high school education, 7.2 percent; for those with some college, 5.7 percent; while for those with a bachelor's degree, it was 3.5 percent. In the 1980s, unemployment for men aged 25 to 64 steadily increased for high school dropouts and high school graduates relative to those with some college or college graduates; and despite concerns about rising joblessness among white-collar workers and an upward trend in the ratio of white-collar to blue-collar unemployment rates in the 1980s, a blue-collar worker still had roughly 3 times the chance of being unemployed as a white-collar worker in the early 1990s. Among the young, whose wages have fallen relative to older workers, unemployment rates are also high–2–3 times those in Germany, for instance, though less than those in France or Italy. Employment-population rates for out of school 20–24 year olds were lower in the United States than in most advanced OECD-European countries–a trifle above the rates in France despite much lower relative pay in the United States (OECD, 1994, Table 1.20). For young blacks, many who are not involved in the work force at all, joblessness is huge even by European standards. In 1993 just 51 percent of 16–24 year old blacks not enrolled in school were employed compared to 73 percent of 16–24 year old whites not enrolled in school. For those in the labor force and not in school, the rate of unemployment was 27 percent for young blacks; 11 percent for young whites, and 16 percent for young Hispanics.

Topel (1984) has used the CPS to examine the work activity of adult men according to their position in the wage distribution (which limits the sample to persons who work at least one week in the year). He finds that those with low wages work less than those higher in the income distribution and that joblessness grew more concentrated among the low-paid over time, despite their falling wage. For instance, between 1967–1968 and 1987–1989 weeks of joblessness increased by 8.5 weeks among men in the lowest decile of the wage distribution but did not change for those in the upper 4 deciles (Topel, 1994, Table 1). My analyses of the annual hours of workers in Census of Population given in Figure 2 Panel (a) reveals a rising inequality in hours worked among

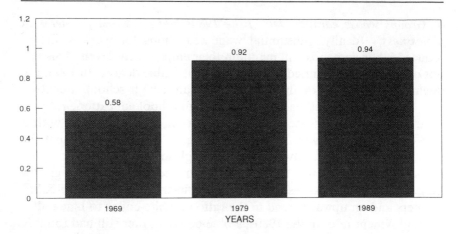

Panel a. Ninth Decile minus First Decile in Ln Hours Worked.

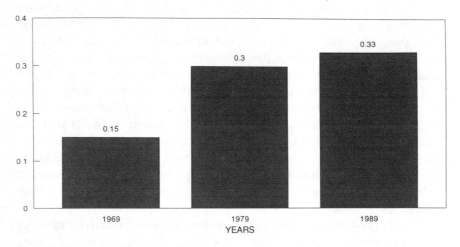

Panel b. Variance of Ln Annual Hours

Figure 2. Rise in Inequality in Hours Worked in Year (Men Aged 18–64).
Source: Tabulated from U.S. Census of Population public use data files, 1970, 1980, 1990.

Table 3. Mean Annual Hours Worked, by Wage Decile, Male Workers, 1970–1990	Wage Decile	1970	1980	1990	Percentage Change, 1970–90
	0–10	2,108	1,758	1,719	−18
	10–20	2,239	1,919	1,924	−16
	20–30	2,256	2,010	2,064	−9
	30–40	2,162	2,041	2,107	−3
	40–50	2,192	2,104	2,108	−4
	50–60	2,142	2,081	2,115	−1
	60–70	2,090	2,091	2,129	2
	70–80	2,075	2,055	2,106	1
	80–90	1,993	2,028	2,092	5
	90–100	1,766	1,721	1,953	11

Source: Tabulated from U.S. Census of Population public use data files, 1970, 1980, and 1990.

Americans: in 1969 the top decile of American men worked .58 ln points more, in terms of annual hours, than the bottom decile, whereas in 1989 the top decile worked .94 ln points more than the bottom decile. The rise in hours inequality, however, occurred largely in the 1970s, rather than in the 1980s, when hourly pay inequality grew. Similarly, the variance in the log of annual hours worked doubled from 1969 to 1979, then rose modestly through 1989 (Panel b). Table 3 shows that the rise in inequality in hours worked was associated with level of pay: in the 1980s, hours worked declined most among those with low wages. The covariance between hours worked and wages increased from the 1970 Census to the 1990 Census, implying that the increased inequality in work time contributed to the rise in annual earnings inequality.

A market-clearing interpretation of these results (which does not take measured unemployment seriously) is that falling real wages reduced the work time of the low-paid or less-skilled along a labor supply curve. The low wages that "solved" the problem of inadequate demand created a supply side incentive problem. A disequilibrium interpretation of these results (which views measured unemployment as real) is that even huge real wage cuts were insufficient to create adequate demand for less-skilled young labor. Regardless of which interpretation one prefers, it is clear that massive wage cuts were no panacea for the less-skilled.

C   Problems

7. The rate of poverty and "extreme poverty" has increased to levels beyond that in other advanced countries. Every visitor to the United States sees some of the downsides of the U.S. economic system: crime-ridden slums in which a large proportion of American children are brought up in poverty, and homeless men and the beggars reminiscent of the worst of Dickens' England. These are not social aberrations in an otherwise neoclassical nirvana, but the tail end of a widening income distribution. With only a modest safety net for citizens who fail in the job market, increased inequality in earnings and time worked translates into increased inequality in family incomes and poverty. The U.S. Council of Economic Advisors (1994) reports that mean family income in the lowest quintile declined by 14 percent from 1973 to 1992. The child poverty rate rose in the 1980s and shows little sign of falling with economic recovery. For children with single parents, the level of AFDC benefits declined from the mid-1970s through the early 1990s. As a result, despite higher income per head, the rate of child poverty in the United States exceeded that in most other advanced countries, even with poverty measured on the same "purchasing power" absolute income scale.

The homeless—an estimated 500,000 at the outset of the 1990s—are also partly the result of the widening income inequality. Increased inequality has given the wealthy a greater edge over the poor in competing for land and dwellings, while the hollowing out of the middle class has reduced the number of old dwellings that are available to the poor as middle-income earners leave for newer residences (O'Flaherty, 1994). With diminished financial resources, poor families find it difficult to take care of troubled family members, and let them seek respite in shelters or on the street. Social spending for the homeless has been meager. Finally, as the wages of the less-skilled have fallen, begging has become more attractive, even for those with normal residences.

Some Europeans might wonder if the problem of increased poverty and incumbent social ills is peculiarly American, because of America's minority populations or immigrants, rather than part-and-parcel of a response to the American reliance on market forces to determine incomes. While Americans differ in some ways from Europeans, I would not downplay the effect of labor market and economic institutions on behavior. In joint work with Anders Bjorklund (Bjorklund and Freeman, forthcoming), I examined the income distribution of Americans of Swedish descent and found that this distribution was as unequal as that of other Americans, producing U.S.-style poverty among Swedish-Americans leagues greater than that of their Swedish brethren in Sweden, despite a sizable American advantage in GDP per head. The European country whose labor market most resembles the American, the United Kingdom, has seen rising inequality, increased homelessness and crime.

8. A large number of American men, particularly less educated young minority men, have been involved in crimes that have led to incarceration.   Most visitors to the United States are aware of another downside of American society—the high level of crime. Few realize that the high crime rate has occurred despite the nation's incarcerating extraordinary numbers. In 1993 roughly 2 percent of the American male work force was in jail or prison. The 2 percent does not refer to minority men or to young men, but to *all men.* An additional 5 percent of men were on probation or parole, so that approximately 7 percent of American men were under supervision of the criminal justice system. Most of these men have relatively little schooling and limited work skills. Among subgroups 3 percent of men aged 18–34 were incarcerated; 9 percent of all black men were incarcerated; and 13 percent of black men aged 18–34 were incarcerated (Freeman, 1994b). These extraordinary levels are the result of an 8.5 percent growth in the prison and jail population in the 1980s that shows no sign of leveling off.

The United States has avoided the heavy expense of a welfare state and dole for the long-term jobless, but has developed something comparable through its jails and prisons. The 2 percent incarcerated are in for long periods of time at an average annual cost of $25,000 or so. While no one can say for certain what proportion of the crime problem results from income inequality, a growing body of studies find that inequality and low wages are important economic factors in maintaining the rate of crime, despite massive incarceration (Freeman, 1994b). At the minimum, arrest and prison records show that the criminal population has the same characteristics as the population doing poorly in the job market. Many inner city youths report that they can earn more from crime than from legitimate employment and have substantial opportunities for illegal earnings.

9. Government regulations of the labor market, and individual court suits over worker rights, have increased greatly. The image of the U.S. labor market as the least regulated among major Western countries is true in four respects: collective bargaining is limited to 11 percent of the private sector; most collective agreements are between local unions and establishments; national regulation of wages, fringe benefits, or hiring and firing is minimal; and there are few barriers to exit and entry of firms. But talk to an American businessperson about labor market regulations and you will hear bitter complaints about government policies and court actions. The reason for these complaints is that the United States gives individuals many rights at workplaces that can be enforced through court actions. The number of federal statutes covering the workplace increased since the 1970s under the administrations of both political parties. The enactment of laws regarding occupational health and safety, pension plans, employment of immigrants, family and medical leaves, and various amendments to the equal opportunity statutes, including acts giving the disabled the right to sue if they believe an employer has discriminated against them by not adjusting the job they are seeking to take account of their disability, are illustrative of major regulatory developments.

While American workers are more protected at their workplace with statutory rights than in the past and firms more restricted in what they can do to workers, appropriations for organization and staff to enforce legal rights have not increased. Given limited regulatory staff, and absent works councils or other local groups of employees to work with management to monitor local work conditions, American workers have flooded agencies and courts with suits on employment issues (Commission on the Future of Worker-Management Relations, 1994). Between 1971 and 1991 the number of court cases filed in federal district courts on individual employment issues increased by 430 percent. In 1971, employment law cases were 6 percent of all cases in these courts. In 1991, they were 16 percent of all cases. Equal Employment Opportunity Commission complaints rose by 56 percent between 1981 and 1993, and the number of discrimination suits before state agencies also skyrocketed. The American Civil Liberties Union, which is hardly a union grievance committee, receives hundreds of calls per day asking for legal assistance on workplace issues, as do a variety of other civil-rights-type organizations.

This court-based system of workplace justice adds to the inequality in the American labor market, since only those with enough gumption and/or income are likely to take an employer to court over violations of workplace rights. Ms. Jones may sue her employer for alleged sexual harassment or discrimination, while Ms. Smith does not do so because she cannot afford a lawyer. Ms. Jones may convince a jury to give her hundreds of thousands of dollars in settlement, while Mr. Smith may fail to do so. A company that sells consumer products may settle a workers' complaint out of court to avoid bad publicity, while one that sells producer products may decide to go to court with the same case. And so on. Most labor relations experts regard the system as a costly inequitable "lottery."

III   Evaluating the American Response

To judge the response of the American labor market to the developments of the past several decades requires two things: a welfare function to assess the level and the distribution of economic outcomes, and a counterfactual measuring rod for comparison. I am not so bold as to write down either "the" social welfare function or "the" counterfactual, and so will limit my concluding comments to some observations about the positive and negative aspects of the U.S. response; and the possible lessons of this experience for Europe.

By any plausible metric, the United States has done well in the level of unemployment and in its distribution among workers compared to Europe. Given two ways of producing a 10 percent unemployment rate—having 10 percent of the work force unemployed for a year and 90 percent employed versus having all workers unemployed 10 percent of the time and employed 90 percent of the time—the latter, which comes closer to the United States than to Europe, would get higher marks. If Europe could import U.S. unemployment patterns and maintain (most of) its wage distribution, it would benefit. At the same time, the United States has done poorly in the level of income for those in the bottom rungs of the distribution, compared to Europe. Analysts can weigh increased inequality differently when the "rising tide raises all boats," but few would give high grades to an income distribution where increased inequality means falling real incomes for the low-paid. If the United States could import a European earnings distribution without (much) cost in jobs or changes in the distribution of joblessness, most welfare functions would rate this a gain.

These considerations do not, however, take us very far, for if lower unemployment requires lower wages for the less-skilled, and higher wages for the less-skilled requires greater unemployment for them, we are left with a Hobson's choice between two undesirable outcomes—joblessness or poverty wages for the less-skilled. Many Europeans—seeing first hand the unemployment problem—believe that a better level and distribution of unemployment is more important; while many Americans—seeing first hand the social and economic effects of a worsened income distribution—cast wishful eyes at the European welfare state. And both may be right, given their starting points. The United States could arguably benefit from a bit more redistribution of income and a stronger social safety net (vide the Clinton Administration effort to enact national health insurance). And Europe could arguably benefit from a bit less redistribution and lower social safety net (vide the efforts of most European governments).

But there is more that we can say about the U.S. and European responses to the economic problems of the past two decades. A key issue in assessing these responses is their viability or lack thereof over the long run. The European response of maintaining a reasonably constant earnings distribution in the face of market trends toward inequality faces problems of fiscal feasibility at high levels of unemployment. Regardless of how highly one values the preservation of real incomes in the bottom rungs of the distribution, it is difficult to see how a welfare state developed in a world of 2–3 percent joblessness can prosper over the long run in a world of 6–10 percent unemployment and slow economic growth.

But the U.S. response also has problems of viability. The American job market serves well the best firms and the skilled workers, and generates self-correcting forces, in the form of increased investment by young persons in education and training in response to educational differentials. But it does a poor job in preparing less-skilled Americans for the modern world of work and has shortchanged the children brought up in poverty and surrounded by crime. The economic and social conditions that produce crime burden the United States with a huge criminal justice system.

Recent economic theorizing about growth suggests, moreover, that a large population of poorly skilled persons can detract from the productivity of the highly skilled through spillovers. Even if one does not accept this argument and believes, as I am inclined to do, that an economy can succeed with a highly unequal distribution of income—a dual economy of the sort usually associated with third world countries—few would laud such an outcome. In its May 1994 Fact-Finding Report, the Commission on the Future of Worker-Management Relations wrote: "A healthy society cannot long continue along the path the United States is moving, with rising bifurcation of the labor market." This assessment was widely cited and accepted in public discussion of the Report.

There are thus dangers in the American response to the economic developments of the 1980s–1990s that Europeans and others who look admiringly at the U.S. experience should bear in mind. If OECD-Europe were to copy the United States whole hog, it would find itself facing many of the same problems that bedevil the United States today; just as the United States would likely face European problems if it expanded its welfare state and adopted European modes of labor market operations. But such stark transformations are not realistic. Labor markets in Europe differ in so many ways from the U.S. labor market that even with substantial changes, I would not expect the European labor situation or problems to mirror those in the United States in the foreseeable future.

The real question is less far-reaching but also more difficult to answer given our current state of knowledge. This is determining which, if any, U.S. practices could be crafted or designed to "fit" with the other parts of European economic systems, to create better outcomes and, conversely, which, if any, European practices could be designed to fit with the U.S. labor relations system, in ways that would avoid simply trading one set of ills for another. If we knew the answer to this dual question—to how to combine the best of American flexibility and reliance on market forces with the best of European social protections—we would turn discussions of labor market reforms, flexibility, and the like from alchemy and ideology to science. It is, in my opinion, finding the right combination that is the economic challenge of the 1990s.

Bibliography

Abraham, K., and L.F. Katz. 1986. "Cyclical Unemployment: Sectoral Shifts or Aggregate Disturbances?" *Journal of Political Economy* 94:507–522.

Allen, S., and R.B. Freeman. 1994. "Quantitative Flexibility in the U.S. Job Market." Conference on Labor Market Flexibility, October 5, Guadalajara, Mexico.

Bhagwati, J. 1994. "Trade and Wages of the Unskilled: Is Marx Striking Again?" In: J. Bhagwati and M. Kosters (eds.), *Trade and Wages*. American Enterprise Institute.

Bell, L., and R.B. Freeman. 1994. "Why Do Americans and Germans Work Different Hours?" NBER Working Paper No. 4804. Cambridge, Mass.: NBER.

Bjorklund, A. and R.B. Freeman. Forthcoming. "Generating Equality and Eliminating Poverty—The Swedish Way." In: R.B. Freeman, B. Swedenborg, and R. Topel (eds.), *Reforming the Welfare State*. Cambridge, Mass.: NBER.

Bluestone, B., and B. Harrison. 1986. *The Great U-Turn*. New York: Basic Books.

Borjas, G., R.B. Freeman, and L.F. Katz. 1992. "On the Labor Market Effects of Immigration and Trade." In: G. Borjas and R.B. Freeman (eds.), *Immigration and the Work Force: Economic Consequences for the United States and Source Areas*. University of Chicago Press for NBER.

Commission on the Future of Worker-Management Relations. 1994. *Fact Finding Report, May 1994*. Washington, D.C.: U.S. Department of Labor and U.S. Department of Commerce.

Freeman, R.B. (ed.). 1994a. *Working Under Different Rules*. NBER Research Volume. New York: Russell Sage Foundation Press.

Freeman, R.B. 1994b. "Crime and the Labor Market." In: J.Q. Wilson and J. Petersilia (eds.), *Crime*, pp. 171–191. San Francisco: ICS Press.

Freeman, R.B. 1976. *The Overeducated American*. New York: Academic Press.

Juhn, C., K.M. Murphy, and R. Topel. 1991. "Why Has the Natural Rate of Unemployment Increased Over Time?" *Brookings Papers on Economic Activity* 2:75–142.

Krueger, A. 1993. "How Computers Have Changed the Wage Structure: Evidence from Microdata, 1984–89." *Quarterly Journal of Economics* 108:33–60.

Lawrence, R.E. and M.J. Slaughter. 1993. "Trade and U.S. Wages: Giant Sucking Sound or Small Hiccup?" *Brookings Papers on Economic Activity, Microeconomics* 2:161–210.

OECD. Various editions. *Employment Outlook*.

O'Flaherty, B. 1994. "Homelessness." Manuscript, Columbia University.

Sachs, J., and H. Schatz. 1994. "Trade and Jobs in U.S. Manufacturing." *Brookings Papers on Economic Activity* Spring: 1–83.

Topel, R. 1994. "What Have We Learned from Empirical Studies of Unemployment?" *American Economic Association, Papers and Proceedings*, May: 110–116.

Topel, R., and K. Murphy. 1987. "The Evolution of Unemployment in the United States?" *NBER Macroeconomics Annual* 2:7–58.

U.S. Council of Economic Advisors. 1994. *Annual Report 1994*.

Wood, A. 1994. *North-South Trade, Employment and Inequality: Changing Fortunes in a Skill-Driven World*. Oxford: Clarendon Press.

Unemployment in the OECD and Its Remedies

Patrick Minford

OECD
E24
F16

There is evidence today of dramatic changes in the labor market as a result of competition between low-wage "emerging-market" economies and the rich OECD countries. In previous work I and others (for example, Bean, Layard, and Nickell, 1986; Davis and Minford, 1986; Layard and Nickell, 1985; Minford, 1983; and see Layard, Nickell, and Jackman, 1991, for other relevant work) have explored how far one can account for changing unemployment in the OECD through general equilibrium models of the open economy. These models have used conventional "elasticities" equations for the current account, assuming that the prevailing competition facing OECD countries was imperfect competition in manufactures from other OECD countries.

Such models have given fairly plausible results to date. The story they have told has also been qualitatively persuasive. In summary, it has identified the basic cause of high unemployment as long-duration unemployment benefits or equivalent social support. Given such a source of "real wage rigidity" all sorts of developments whose effect would under flexible wages be to lower real wages have the effect of causing unemployment. It is possible to estimate the "natural rate" of unemployment within such models, as the equilibrium once macro-economic shocks to demand have died away. Theories of "efficiency wages" are really, for all the claims one finds for them as a "general" theory of unemployment (e.g., Phelps, 1993), merely one special development of the sort just described: if the "outsiders" do not exhibit real wage rigidity, then the fall in outsider real wages would displace downwards the comparator for insiders and the whole wage structure would be flexible. Thus unions, insiders, or other sources of employee wage premia all can contribute to the explanation of unemployment within this framework of real wage rigidity created by social support.

This model remains adequate as a representation of the supply of labor. But if the nature of competition in the goods market is changing because of low-wage countries then some adaptation of the model is in order. In this paper I sketch out a theoretical framework for this adaptation, review some evidence bearing on it, speculate on the implications this work may have for the natural rate estimates we have made to date, and consider the implications also for social policy. The empirical research agenda opened up is formidable and like Vasco da Gama the sight of it fills me with awe, but like him, too, the conquest of it is another matter.

I   Trade, Development, and Global Competition

As we have watched the rapid, and sometimes explosive, growth first of Japan, then of the "Little Dragons," and now most recently of the other "emerging markets" (of Asia, Latin America, and Eastern Europe), we must all have wondered whether there was not some secret formula that could suddenly turn previously torpid or declining economies into growth miracles. There is some evidence by now that there is indeed such an elixir and that it works for a country regardless of history, culture, ethnicity, and religion. The most recent example is Dollar (1992), and in the theory of growth Parente and Prescott (1993a, 1993b) have developed a formal framework in which what they call "business capital," their name for the formula, is the key input into the growth process. The elixir could also be called "open economy capitalism": the adoption of secure property rights, not merely for home nationals but also for foreigners. The latter is a vital component because of the role played by foreign investment and technology transmission in the traded sector (perhaps also, but to a far more modest extent, the nontraded sector). The purpose of this paper is to link the processes of growth, convergence, and trade into a single theory, no component of which should prove unfamiliar but whose linkage has not hitherto to my knowledge been made. I hope also to offer a little bit of new evidence on the combined process; but inevitably the canvas is so huge that I will rely on previous evidence mainly and hope to lay the groundwork for more and perhaps better-focused empirical work in the future.

The large and rapidly expanding literature of endogenous growth and convergence (for example, Romer, 1986; Lucas, 1988; Barro, 1991; Rebelo, 1991) has paid little attention to the role of trade and comparative advantage; the same was true of an earlier postwar literature (Solow, 1956; Dennison, 1967, 1974). Yet it is in the traded sector of developing countries that growth tends to manifest itself first—it is also through this sector that technology is mostly transferred and one of the major forces of convergence is exerted, namely, that of wage equalization. It therefore seems worthwhile to examine how far trade theory can add to the insights already achieved in this area.

This paper is an attempt to do so, in a fairly specific way: it sets out a particular model of two linked open economies, "North" and "South," and examines the nature of ultimate convergence and what the key elements determining its pace are. The theory on which it is based is that of Heckscher, Ohlin, and Samuelson (HOS; Heckscher, 1919; Ohlin, 1933; Samuelson, 1948), with some suitable modifications to be discussed. There are many other trade theories: for example, industrial oligopoly, intraindustry, product cycle, as well as the Ricardian (production-function-less) theory. However, the relative attraction of HOS in the context of growth is that it is focused on the production function and its factor inputs. The dynamics by which factor and product properties evolve need to be captured by other theories; but these can be, as it were, bolted on to HOS.

The key assumption in HOS of constant returns to scale needs to be defended, especially as it is rejected in the industrial oligopoly approach. Again, the latter may perhaps be thought of as a theory of first-mover advantage, giving insight into the dynamics of industrial competition. Yet ultimately constant returns to scale must prevail because increasing returns must be exploited by expanding firm size (if necessary at the international level) while decreasing returns are eliminated through competitive entry by new firms. In such a world where constant returns have been produced, first-mover advantage ceases to be relevant if it can be challenged by new entrants. Thus the United States may have been the first successfully to establish a huge firm in aircraft production but that cannot prevent a firm in other countries challenging it and perhaps ultimately displacing it on cost grounds. HOS theory examines such industrial patterns purely on a cost basis without considerations of corporate history. It seems hard to argue with such a position from a long-term perspective: once a worldwide industry has exploited its increasing returns, then if its firms, however new, are cheaper in country X they will surely displace those of country Y, however long established.

The other key assumption of HOS, that factors of production can be distinguished by broad type, is self-evident. But as has long been recognized by HOS theorists (Jones, 1967), if less in application, it is important to distinguish mobile from immobile factors of production; only the latter play the usual HOS role of determining comparative advantage. Mobile factors accommodate to that pattern. Thus, for example, if capital is mobile at a price set internationally, its quantity will not help to determine comparative advantage (most empirical studies have dubiously proceeded as if capital were immobile: see Minford, 1989; Wood, 1994).

The model in this paper builds onto these two basic HOS assumptions three main elements:

1. A division of factors of production into mobile and immobile, mainly based on the degree of international market integration.
2. A nontraded goods sector, familiar from open-economy macro-economics.
3. A number of hypotheses about the supply of factors and the transfer of technology; these provide the dynamics of the model. Some of them are quite rudimentary (and "ad hoc"), based on ideas from other areas of study; all invite much further research.

The rest of this paper sets out the model and its broad implications—briefly, as a fuller account is contained in Minford, Riley, and Nowell (1995); it then reviews some simulations from a calibrated version of the model. Finally, it discusses the implications for policy.

II The Model

We distinguish five factors of production: capital, raw materials, land, unskilled ("raw") labor, and skill or human capital (embodied in labor).

Land is of course immobile. Labor we also treat as immobile, for two main reasons: politics and preferences. Politics applies to unskilled labor. This would like to migrate from low- to high-wage countries ("wages" will always refer to the pay of unskilled labor). But high-wage countries limit entry for such labor: a well-known political fact, to be accounted for partly by preferences of citizens (they wish to keep their country to "their own type"), partly by the economics of public goods (the immigrants, having low taxable capacity, will contribute less for the public goods than they will consume—but the extra numbers will imply more public goods to avoid congestion). Hence unskilled labor is prevented from migrating.

As for skilled labor with human capital, they are generally welcome migrants because they can "buy their way in" to other countries. But they have limited mobility (that is to say, only a limited number will become expatriates in response to differential rewards) because of their own preferences: since they have large incomes anyway, the marginal utility of location (relatives and friends close by, access to favorite leisure pursuits, whether going to London plays, playing golf in Scotland, or enjoying their dacha near Moscow) increases relative to the marginal utility of general consumption goods. Hence, though there is some migratory supply curve of skilled labor, it is steep and for simplicity, we treat human capital, too, as immobile.

Capital and raw materials are quickly dealt with. The latter are traded routinely. It is true that because transport costs per cash load fall sharply with refinement, which raises value and usually reduces bulk, the processing of bulky raw materials tends to be located close to their source of supply. But even this immobility of bulky materials is progressively being eliminated by modern bulk transport. Again, we simplify by assuming complete mobility of all raw materials.

Capital consists of produced capital goods combined with finance. The latter is obtainable through the international capital market and though on occasions extreme "country risk" may put a premium on its cost we shall neglect this on the grounds that diversification and market efficiency drive this "nonsystematic risk" close to zero. The former, capital goods themselves, are to a high degree traded, being either plant and machinery or inventory; the exception is factory building which if built locally is nontraded. However, even here the importance of prefabricated factories dilutes the point. We shall assume therefore that capital goods are traded. Thus, in sum, capital is assumed to be completely mobile.

Of our five factors, therefore, three only are immobile: labor, human capital, and land. These, then, become the key determinants of comparative advantage and development.

We now turn to the nature of the industries which may use them. There has been much mathematical ink spilt on the relative numbers of factors and industries and the problems for the HOS theory of different sets. The fact is that, if using this theory, one logically divides industries into groups corresponding to the factor divisions. For example, if the two factors determining comparative advantage among traded goods were just labor and human capital, we would want to divide traded industries into those intensive in labor and those intensive in human capital; nothing is gained by further subdivision.

It turns out in our analysis here that something like this applies. There is a complication, however: nontraded goods. This is a category resolutely ignored by HOS; but it is impossible to ignore in development, since it is typically such a huge component of most economies (60 percent or more in most developed economies and in the least developed much higher still, how high depending on the valuation of subsistence industry and agriculture). It is perhaps no more surprising that the development literature on endogenous growth has shied away from considering trade and concentrated on total GDP: for it trade is as great a complication as nontraded goods are for HOS.

If one considers the industries that make up nontraded goods and services, one quickly realizes that here is the land-intensive industry par excellence. The biggest nontraded industries are housing and leisure, recreation, and sport; the land needs of these industries are rapacious indeed. Add in subsistence agriculture and other industries (crafts and ancillary services) for developing countries and the picture is complete. Countries absorb enormous amounts of land in providing for needs that are not satisfied by trade. As one progresses down the list of the less land-intensive nontraded industries—education, health care, hotels, distribution, transport, construction, government services such as defense, law and order, and administration—again, their needs for land are clearly far from negligible. One might query construction: but then think of how much land is tied up in building sites.

By contrast, traded industries—most of them manufacturing or financial services—are light users of land.

Nonsubsistence or "cash" agriculture is the exception. This is, in principle, a third traded industry, one that is intensive in land; and in less-developed countries (LDCs), clearly it is simply that—the third traded industry. However, through most of the developed world, cash agriculture is heavily protected, both directly through subsidy and indirectly through planning consent to the nonagricultural use of land (which artificially holds down agricultural land prices). Our theory predicts that, if it were not, it would contract massively because the high demand for land in nontraded use would preempt its use by farmers forced to compete in world markets. Hence, in developed countries we could treat agriculture as a special sector of exogenous size, this being determined by political decision: the country would then achieve this size by whatever protection is required. However, it turns out that such protection ultimately causes wages in LDCs actually to overtake, not merely to become equal with, wages in developed countries; this of course reflects the inefficiency of such protection, which for this reason appears unsustainable in the long run. Hence we will ignore agricultural protection in what follows.

With three immobile factors and three traded goods, our 3 × 3 system determines the absolute level of wages, returns to human capital and land rents given world prices of traded goods: these relative factor prices then fix factor shares in the three traded industries, whose size in turn depends on the amounts of the three factors available to the traded sector.

To determine these amounts, we note that domestic goods prices are fixed by the costs of the three factors, given constant returns of scale and competition here as elsewhere. Hence prices of domestic goods relative to traded goods are given by world prices and technology; by implication any exogenous rise in demand for domestic goods is satisfied by a supply shift into domestic goods at constant prices: infinite supply elasticity. We therefore determine the amounts of the immobile factors available to traded goods industries simply by subtracting from their total supplies the requirements of domestic industry demand.

It follows that total supply is strictly limited by immobile factor supplies, while its composition depends partly on the size of the demand for domestic goods and partly on the relative supplies of immobile factors left over after the satisfaction of this demand. We may now ask how total demand is determined.

Total supply and its composition will create a demand for capital goods: investment demand. The flow of real income from supply over time will create a dynamic problem of intertemporal utility maximization for consumers. Government demands and tax rates, treated here as exogenous, modify this problem: but the government's intertemporal budget ensures that the present value of taxes equals that of government spending. Consumers' transversality condition ensures that their present value of consumption equals that of their net income (i.e., that of total income less government spending): they then set an optimal rate of consumption that, if we treat households as infinitely lived, will obey the permanent income hypothesis. It follows that a "young" LDC will, both in anticipation of rising income and in response to the high investment needs of growth, have demand typically well in excess of supply: the counterpart will be capital inflows on the balance of payments, its net demand on the international capital market.

The model of the developed country is under the assumption of no agricultural protection no different in specification: only its technology is superior.

Having sketched in the demand and productive conditions in both North and South, we now turn to the supply of immobile factors, hitherto held fixed, and to the transfer of technology.

Land supply is assumed to respond to its rent relative to wages, taken as a measure of its opportunity cost in noncommercial use (for example, as common land). Hence there is a "supply curve" of land to the traded sector, unlike the usual HOS setup.

Human capital is plainly the result of investment in education and training (in its widest sense). We assume that this investment is affected by the country's structure of marginal tax rates: the incentive to upgrade human capital depends on its returns, and the steeper the marginal tax rates schedule, the less the posttax pay differentials, and the less, therefore, the return to this investment.

Further, the supply of hours of high-grade labor, for a given stock of human capital, is assumed to be affected by the absolute level of the higher marginal tax rates. We assume that there are zero income effects on labor supply of government spending: the extra utility provided by public goods is assumed to be equal to that of the private goods removed by taxation. This is more a simplification than an empirically accurate assessment: the utility of parks may be more or less than that of Mars bars but there seems little to be gained here by allowing for any difference.

Thus the supply of human capital both in the long and the short term is related here to marginal tax rates.

The supply of raw labor is assumed to depend on the marginal tax rate on participation and the supply of hours by low-paid workers: this rate is overwhelmingly determined by the social security system, its benefits and conditionality. We summarize this for participation by using the ratio of unemployment benefit to (unskilled) wages and the severity of "worktesting" conditions (checking on the genuineness of search), and for the supply of hours by the net benefit withdrawal rate (the rate of "negative income tax") for in-work benefits and the degree of monitoring of need for these (i.e., monitoring not related purely to actual means, but rather evaluating potential means).

We abstract in this study from the rate of population growth itself by expressing the theory entirely in per capita terms. Our concern is with living standards not with the size of nations: this is a massive challenge (to the dynamic theory of dynastic household formation, to be contrasted with the Malthusian theory that population grows until wages fall to subsistence level) that must be deferred or left to others.

Finally, we consider technology, which we represent for simplicity as a factor-neutral multiplicative term in our constant-returns production functions. Under HOS theory, if these terms were identical across nations, there would be immediate factor-price equalization.

We do not observe such rapid convergence. Accordingly, we assume here that we do not have the same technology across nations: again, this does not violate our perceptions of the real world—for whatever reason, the schools, hospitals, factories, and financial intermediaries (to take a few examples at random) of Bangladesh do not use the same advanced technologies as their equivalents in New England.

The basic reason for this, we suggest, is that technology is invented in one place (usually in a developed country [DC]) and then must be transferred, mainly through inward investment, though also by licensing and technical assistance to local investors. Either way, it requires investment (either physical or equivalent investment in the license contract) by foreign companies with the prospect of returns through outward transfer of profits. Our assumption is that these returns depend on a framework of property rights that provide foreign investors with some guarantees against expropriation. The speed of technology transfer, we assume, thus depends on the strength of property rights (for foreigners in particular), besides the technology of transfer itself (as set by computer power and transport costs). Hence the level of an LDC's technology term depends on the integral over time of these rights.

This idea has similarity to that of Parente and Prescott's concept of "business capital." They enter this term directly as a factor input in the production function and proxy it by the level of the aggregate tax rate, this being the stimulus to entrepreneurship and business formation. In effect, we have divided their notion into two parts: the effect of marginal tax rates on the supplies of labor and human capital and the effect of property rights guaranteeing the appropriation of contracted returns. (We do not concern ourselves with taxes on capital because their incidence does not fall on capital owners in conditions of complete capital mobility: the issue is one of time-inconsistency, whether they can be sure to get their returns at all.)

There is also a relation here to work on "self-enforcing" contracts between investors and (unreliable) LDCs—see Worrall (1990) and Thomas and Worrall (1994). Plainly, there must be some such contract for any country with a given degree of unreliability. Our point could be put in those terms by relating the inefficiency of the contract (as compared with one written without concern for self-enforcement) to the poorness of property rights.

III   Empirical Investigations and the Model's Broad Implications

This line of reasoning has some fairly striking empirical implications.

A   Comparative Advantage

The implication here is that it is endowments of immobile factors that determine trade patterns. In respect of manufactures that use little land, it is essentially endowments of raw labor and human capital. This hypothesis—which suggests that LDCs should export raw-labor-intensive products and DCs export skilled-labor-intensive ones—has by now been widely supported empirically: see Minford (1989) and Wood (1994) who both comprehensively survey the available work and provide much new evidence of their own. It turns out that much of the early "testing" of HOS failed to notice the mobility of capital: hence the huge Leontief Paradox literature, which agonizes over the (physical-)capital-intensiveness of some less-developed countries' exports is flawed, since the physical capital "endowment" is endogenous.

B   The Measurement of GDP

There are implications for the measurement and comparison of GDP across countries, rather in the manner already much investigated by

Summers and Heston (1988, and most recently, 1991; and see the references in these for their huge amount of earlier work). The model here suggests an alternative ("supply-side") correction to their demand-side approach. This is discussed in Minford et al. (1994) and suggests even larger corrections than they have used.

C   The Sources of Convergence

The third set of implications is about how and why convergence occurs. The model implies there are three sources: The main one is the convergence of local factor prices as a result of convergence of productivity in traded goods and services. The second is convergence of labor participation rates (i.e., labor supply per capita) and mix of labor endowments towards higher skill. The third, which affects GNP but not GDP, is the accumulation of savings and so income from owned capital (as opposed to employed capital).

It is also possible for a country with lower per capita income than another to innovate independently and so generate what we might call primary growth in productivity, which creates the possibility of catch-up in the richer country. This will enhance observed convergence. But in this model we ignore such primary technology creation and focus on convergence proper where catching-up is occurring. This is our first source of convergence. Furthermore, the second and third sources are, within the model, largely dependent on the first. As local factor prices converge, so do the incentives to participate and to gain skill; so also, as GDP per capita increases because of increased productivity, does savings income grow. The basic source of convergence is therefore that of productivity.

The model stresses that this comes about through catching-up or technology transfer. Data on productivity across countries is scarce. But our model implies that they will be reflected in differential labor costs, on which there is a huge quantity of data, both current and historical.

I suggested earlier a number of ideas about how technology transfer might be determined. These included the firmness of property rights in the transferee country (perhaps proxied by the number of lawyers, and by the absence of such controls as exchange controls) and the progress of the technology of communication itself (the information and computer "revolution" obviously affecting the ease of transfer). I suggested, therefore, that we should have some index of a country's "openness" or "capitalist values", as well as some index internationally of the level of communications technology (perhaps the speed with which a piece of information could be sent a given distance).

These ideas have been investigated empirically by Dollar (1992) and Parente and Prescott (1993, a and b). Dollar finds an index of external price distortion (adapted from Summers and Heston, 1988), Parente and Prescott the aggregate tax rate; each being an index of "open economy capitalism," these are important contributors to an explanation of cross-country growth differences since the 1960s. Parente and Prescott also find that the rate of growth convergence, for countries which "take off," has speeded up steadily over the past three centuries: this confirms that the technology of transfer itself has become steadily more powerful.

However, Dollar controls for investment that is endogenous according to our model; while the aggregate tax rate may not capture the wider aspects of capitalist systems—many poor and unsuccessful countries have low tax rates because they have not developed their infrastructure, for example, and yet adequate infrastructure goes with the recognition of property rights as part of a wider capitalist program. I repeated Dollar's tests, using his price distortion variable, on the growth of dollar wage costs (total including taxes and social security) relative to the United States, this being the measure of (wage) factor price inequality. The only control I investigated is the initial level of this inequality, since the less this is, the less the scope for catch-up, and hence, if this process is asymptotic (or S-shaped), the slower the rate of catch-up would be.

The results confirm the importance of the price distortion index. A regression for 37 countries yields (standard errors parenthesized):

$$\% \; WG \; (\$) = 10.5 - 0.059 \; PDI - 0.00115 \; GP \; (\%)$$
$$\qquad\qquad (4.2) \; (0.028) \qquad (0.0008)$$

$$\text{adjusted } R^2 = 0.08$$
$$\text{standard error } (\%) = 6.06,$$

where WG is wage growth, PDI is the price distortion index, and GP the 1980 gap between own and U.S. per capita GDP. Clearly, much else is unexplained, as one would expect in a cross-section across such a huge variety of countries. But the significance of the distortion index is clear. The initial gap is marginally insignificant, suggesting that "convergence" per se exists but is weak.

IV   Simulation of the North–South Model

To explore the nature of the future developments that may face the OECD, it is helpful to simulate the model described above. The general nature of these results will be no surprise given the model's parentage. But it is impossible to work out the detailed implications of such a complex general equilibrium system even qualitatively, let alone quantitatively, without simulation; remembering the huge nonlinearities in it, we can see that the sort of shocks of interest that displace the model hugely away from its base trajectory cannot be assessed even by comparative statics of a linearized model (even this would be a computer task for such a large model).

The shock that is of primary interest is that of progressive technology transfer to the manufacturing sector of the South. Choose a growth rate of productivity in this Southern sector of 2.3 percent a year: this generates about 4 percent per year wage growth (relative to world manufacturing prices) for their unskilled workers. This seems a reasonably realistic order of magnitude to use as a benchmark for these countries as a group: the wage growth (deflated by dollar prices) among manufacturing workers of 9 newly industrializing countries reviewed by the U.S. Bureau of Labor Statistics (Mexico, Hong Kong, Korea, Singapore, Taiwan, Pakistan, India, Sri Lanka, Israel) was about 5 percent p.a., unweighted, from 1975 to 1992 (or the nearest available year).

The mechanism underlying the simulation can be quickly summarized in familiar HOS terms (for full details of it and the model, see Minford, Riley, and Nowell, 1995). The rise in Southern productivity in manufacturing raises the relative reward to the (immobile) factor in which manufacturing is intensive, namely, unskilled labor. The supply of this factor rises in the South, and, via the Rybcynski theorem, the expansion of manufacturing is accompanied by a contraction in the Southern supply of traded services and agriculture. The additional income in the South is spent broadly across all traded goods as against the additional Southern supply of manufacturing and contraction in that of services and agriculture. This raises world prices of services and agriculture, improving the terms of trade of the North and so its welfare. This fall in manufacturing's relative price, however, causes, via the Stolper-Samuelson theorem, a fall in the real wages of the factor, unskilled labor, in which manufacturing is intensive, and a rise in the rewards of the factors, skill and land, in which it is not intensive. Overall both the North and South gain from the rise in the South's productivity by more than the crude addition to world disposable income that this represents—in other words there are gains from trade. But there is a strong distributional effect in the North against unskilled labor.

It is worth pointing out, though it is obvious enough, that there may well be many other supply shocks hitting the world economy. These would overlay the effect here. I mention this because a recent Brookings study (Lawrence and Slaughter, 1993) concluded that such forces as shown in this simulation could not have been of any significance in the United States because the precise pattern of trends depicted here cannot be found in the U.S. data. In the absence of a fairly complete analysis of other shocks, however, this conclusion is unsound. There is no space here to discuss this and other skeptical recent U.S. studies (I have done so elsewhere [Minford et al., 1994]); however, Figure 1, which shows the terms of trade between the manufactured exports of the LDCs on the one hand and on the other the sophisticated manufactures (machinery and transport equipment) and the service exports of the DCs, reveals a steady and marked decline in the relative prices of the "manufactures" of our model, exactly as predicted in this simulation.

The simulation's orders of magnitude are of some interest and do not seem wholly implausible. Within the OECD the rewards to skill and land grow respectively by 2.6 and 2.8 percent p.a. and unskilled workers' wages fall by 1 percent p.a. relative to the numeraire, manufacturing prices. In real terms (i.e., relative to the consumer price deflator, which rises by 1 percent p.a.) figures are all reduced by 1 percent p.a.: hence real wages fall by 2 percent p.a., a pretty serious development. As a result there is a contraction of unskilled labor supply by 0.5 percent p.a., 11 percent overall in the 23 years. In that period both human capital and land in use rise by 50 percent. Real disposable income rises by 1.9 percent p.a.

In the South, unskilled workers' wages relative to manufacturing prices rise by 4 percent p.a., and relative to a general basket by 2.5

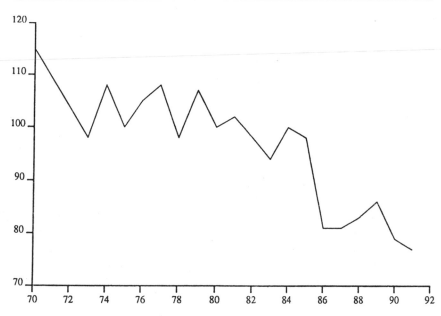

Figure 1. Ratio of Developing Countries' Manufacturing Export Prices to Developed Countries' Export Prices of Machinery and Transport Equipment and of Services (in dollars).
Source: UN International Trade Statistics Yearbook, Various Issues. For services the source is UK Pink Book, export of services price index converted into dollars. The weights are based on shares of non-oil exports and exports of services in UK trade of these, respectively 0.73 and 0.27.

percent p.a. (the overall deflator rises by 1.5 percent p.a.). There are also rises in the rewards of skill and land, by about one-third of this rate. The supply of unskilled labor rises, by 56 percent over the 23 years (2 percent p.a.) and there are contractions in the supplies of both skill and land in use by 1.1 percent p.a., or 20 percent over the 23 year period—remember this is before other shocks and policy changes in these countries. Real disposable income rises by 2.8 percent p.a., or 90 percent over the whole period.

The weighted average growth in real disposable income across the world economy is 2 percent p.a. against the direct effect of the productivity shock at 0.35 percent p.a. The reason for this huge trade gain multiplier is that additional supplies of factors are released as well as the gains from exchange and specialization.

V General Implications

The integrated approach set out here has 4 main implications:

1. Comparative advantage depends on endowments of immobile factors. These are (raw) labor, skill (human capital), and land.
2. Differences in relative income per capita are determined basically by differences in the relative technology of a country's traded sector: the rest arises from the resulting accumulation of savings and skills.
3. Because the nontraded sector's technology differs little internationally, a "purchasing power parity" correction can be achieved by revaluing this sector's output at common factor prices: this suggests that the pioneering work of Heston and Summers still understates the necessary correction.
4. The speed of foreign investment and technology transmission in exploiting differences is determined by the property rights environment as well as the sheer physical power of communications and transport technologies themselves.

We have found that there is by now a substantial and growing body of evidence supporting these ideas about trade, growth, and convergence. It is satisfying to notice that these ideas have a long intellectual pedigree, and that the experiments in social and economic engineering undertaken over the years, so bravely sometimes, so foolishly often, have served to confirm a long-standing precept of the classical economists—namely, that economic success depends on an ordered environment of incentives, the elixir of growth, at least for those who wish to catch up on the leaders.

VI Implications for the OECD Natural Rate of Unemployment

The HOS model set out here has strong implications for income distribution in OECD countries. Given that social support in these countries stresses the importance of an income "safety net," the form that this safety net takes will greatly affect unemployment rates among low-wage workers according to the theory of labor supply with which we began and which is preserved in this HOS framework. Let us remind ourselves of the "unemployment trap" model, which underpins the labor supply curve with real wage rigidity. Figure 2 Panel (a) shows

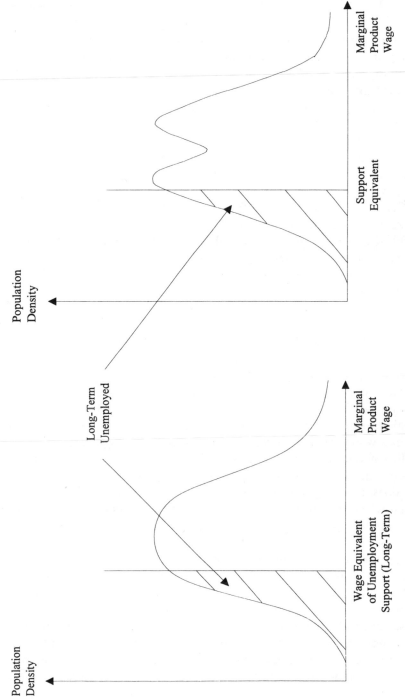

Figure 2. Panel a. The Usual Distribution. **Panel b.** Distribution after Low-Wage Competition.

how for a given population distribution over marginal value product a certain minimum support level may work to affect labor supply and unemployment.

Low-wage competition has the effect of concentrating large numbers of people at low levels of marginal value product. The distribution could tend to a bimodal one, as illustrated in Panel (b). The effects of unconditional income support on low-wage work could be quite literally to destroy it, creating a huge fiscal burden and massive (even 100 percent) low-wage-worker unemployment. The seriousness of this can be seen from the fact that in the United Kingdom, a fairly typical OECD economy, no less than 50 percent of the work force are manual workers, half of whom have "skills" of questionable value in today's world. If one goes on to question the value of the skills of many non-manual workers, the percentage of workers at risk escalates.

This creates most serious and obvious problems for social policy to which I now turn.

VII   The Social Problem of Low-Wage Competition

Three main approaches are put forward for income support.

One is negative income tax (NIT). This is pretty much what we do now in the United Kingdom (since Sir Norman Fowler's reforms of social security in 1987). In this system, help is given to many poor families whose breadwinners may be the wife working part-time with the husband in casual work, or both working part-time, or one working full-time at low wages. Judging from our experience to date, this system does a fairly good job in keeping the social peace. The problem with it is that to prevent it from becoming hugely expensive, it has to be means-tested rigorously and benefits have to be withdrawn gradually as incomes rise. This withdrawal rate runs at 70 percent or more (100 percent for part-timers) under our present system, and it is of course an equivalent marginal tax rate for these families.

A second approach is the basic income guarantee (BIG), whereby the marginal tax rate is brought down to the normal rate by giving a "basic income" that is not means-tested or withdrawn. Any income other than this state transfer is taxed in a normal way. The difficulty with BIG is that the huge expense of giving this universal flat rate benefit raises the average tax rate. Hence, while the marginal tax rate

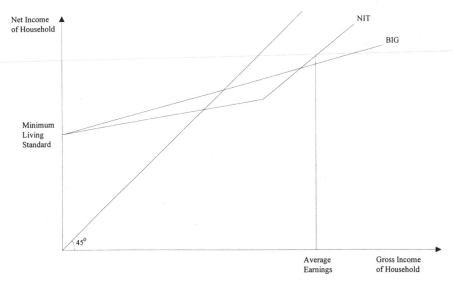

Figure 3. Basic Income Guarantee (BIG) and Negative Income Tax (NIT).

for the poor family is lowered as compared with NIT, that for the average family is raised. Since the latter is both far more numerous and more productive, this is a poor result overall from the viewpoint of incentives and efficiency. The comparison is illustrated in Figure 3.

Hence, to this point, we appear to be stuck with NIT, at some optimal withdrawal rate, as the least bad approach. The optimal rate is the best point on the implicit tradeoff just described between lowering the withdrawal rate for the poor and raising the marginal tax rate for the rest as you do so (because more receive benefit and so face the poverty withdrawal rate and also the cost goes up, raising the average tax rate). Optimality can be judged by overall efficiency. I made a rough effort at this calculation for the United Kingdom in Minford (1990) and concluded that the post-Fowler rates were then about right: some quarter of a million households in work faced high withdrawal rates (the "poverty trap") but this could be expected to fall as real wages grew provided real benefits were kept constant. I have seen no attempt to update that sort of calculation, and it may well still be about right for households in work.

We should, however, note that unemployment benefits can also create a dependency trap. Clearly, an assumption of the NIT system is that there is tight monitoring of job search with benefit withdrawal as the sanction for refusal to take available jobs. The idea, then, is to push people into the job market and support them there through in-work NIT.

A third approach is low-wage job subsidies. These might seem to be analytically the same as in-work NIT. It is of course irrelevant to their incidence whether they are paid to employer or employee. But the difference is that job subsidies are attached to particular jobs rather than to people with low household incomes. This means that from the viewpoint of income distribution—by which I mean the support of people in poverty they are less well targeted, because many with low-wage jobs (such as second earners and juveniles) are not in poor households. This creates the problem that they do not achieve their social objective. At the same time, precisely because they are not related to household income, they may diminish labor supply disincentives less. They create a distortion between types of job: jobs just outside the subsidy net will lose supply because given the fixed gross wage cost they will pay less (net) to workers than jobs just inside. Though this distortion could be minimized by tapering the job subsidy as the wage rate rises, it still creates a disincentive to take a better job. It does not, however, discourage working longer hours, as the NIT does. (In this model neither NIT nor job subsidies affect the gross wage cost to employers: all the incidence is on the net income of the employee and the effect on jobs comes then through employees' labor supply.) It also has, like the NIT, a good effect on unskilled labor supply and so unemployment. However, it damages training incentives and reduces human capital: it does so more than NIT because NIT is less correlated with low wages.

More recently, there has been a revival of interest in a fourth approach: income support systems modeled on charity, like that of the Victorians. In these, welfare assistance is put on a selective basis, decentralized in the hands of local agencies whose job is to use judgment about need: this is related not so much to actual income as potential income and unavoidable commitments or circumstances. Incentives can then be maintained, help targeted on those in need, and costs kept down. This approach in effect extends monitoring from job search—the "worktesting" that underlies NIT as a way of getting people back to work without forcing down their income—to efforts to improve in-work circumstances. This is a harder task than checking on search but some progress in it should be feasible.

We will undoubtedly (in the United Kingdom) be investigating how far we can move away from a general NIT system towards more such selectivity ("targeted NIT"), given the cost even of the benefit system we have and the prospect that the low-wage competition we are facing will increase the scope of the problem.

VIII   Judging Policies to Deal with the Low-Wage Dilemma

If we leave BIG on one side, then we could categorize the welfare effects of the three main policies low—wage subsidies, NIT, and targeted NIT—as follows. NIT is distributed according to household income at a point in time. As argued above, this is not particularly well correlated with low wages at a point in time, because of second earners and juveniles. Hence NIT should not have such a pronounced effect on the relative (lifetime) earnings of skilled workers relative to low-wage workers and, accordingly, should not affect the incentive to train so badly. At the same time, it is better targeted on income distribution. Since it is related well to household income, it improves the incentive for those with high unemployment benefits to leave unemployment and take a job: low-wage subsidies do this less well because they are less well related to household income.

The drawback of NIT is that it creates a poverty trap for those on low household incomes in work, damaging their incentive to supply more effort either by working more hours or by taking a better-paid job. This drawback is still present under wage subsidies that reduce the relative rewards of better-paid jobs, but to a lesser extent as it does not apply to hours.

It is this drawback that could be improved by targeted NIT where the additional monitoring of *potential* income could improve these incentives.

There is a further dimension that is important once one recognizes political pressures: the (political) "shock-proofness" of the system, by which I mean its capacity to become more supportive if the environment turns out more hostile (with large drops in the lowest real wages) or to wither away if there is little problem (if trickle-down turned into a downpour). The dilemma is related to an ongoing process, not a one-off shock, and we do not know whether it will intensify, be offset by other developments, or much else. In this dimension, low-wage subsidies that require a large political effort to install appear quite inflexible. NIT, whether targeted or not, is related to changes in low incomes by construction and therefore has shockproofness built in.

IX   Conclusions

The growing threat of low-wage competition to the living standards of unskilled workers in rich countries is likely to put a strain on those countries' commitment to free trade. It is important for their overall welfare as well as that of the developing countries that this commitment be maintained: both global and rich-country welfare is maximized by free trade in our model.

How then to relieve the strain under free trade? We have seen that a system of income supplementation for those in work (negative income tax) offers a way forward, and that incentive problems created by it (the "poverty trap") could be minimized by a targeted system administered locally with discretion—the Victorian model. Britain is increasingly experimenting with such systems in different benefit areas (e.g., the social fund and sickness benefit) and the same principle is used in monitoring unemployment benefits.

In moving forward, much will depend on how fast these low-wage trends develop. British experience suggests that people will tolerate a system that does not drive household incomes below some basic subsistence level, much as defined in the price-indexed official income support levels. It may well be that while low wages in Britain do not grow much in real terms (as has happened in the last two decades), they do not fall either. In that case we could manage without any significant increase in the cost of social benefits. But the situation on mainland Europe with its higher wage costs may well be much more difficult.

Bibliography

Barro, R.J. 1991. "Economic Growth in a Cross Section of Countries." *Quarterly Journal of Economics* 106:407–444.

Bean, C., R. Layard, and S. Nickell. 1986. "The Rise in Unemployment: A Multi-country Study." *Economica* 53:S1–22.

Benjamin, D., and L. Kochin. 1979. "Searching for an Explanation of Unemployment in Inter-War Britain." *Journal of Political Economy* 87:441–470.

Davis, J., and P. Minford. 1986. "Germany and the European Disease." *Recherches Economiques de Louvain* 52:373–398.

Denison, E.F. 1967. *Why Growth Rates Differ: Postwar Experience in Nine Western Countries*. Washington, D.C.: Brookings Institution.

Denison, E.F. 1974. *Accounting for United States Economic Growth, 1929–1969*. Washington, D.C.: Brookings Institution.

Dollar, D. 1992. "Outward-Oriented Developing Countries Really Do Grow More Rapidly: Evidence from 95 LDCs, 1976–85." *Economic Development and Cultural Change*, pp. 523–544.

Friedman, M. 1968. "The Role of Monetary Policy." *American Economic Review* 58:1–17.

Hayek, F.A. 1945. "The Use of Knowledge in Society." American Economic Review 35:519–530. Reprinted in *Individualism and Economic Order*. Chicago: University of Chicago, 1948.

Heckscher, E. 1919. "The Effect of Foreign Trade on the Distribution of Income." *Economisk Tidskrift*, pp. 497–512. Reprinted as Chapter 13 in *AEA Readings in the Theory of International Trade*. Philadelphia: Blakiston, 1949, pp. 272–300.

International Monetary Fund. 1993. *World Economic Outlook May:* 197.

Jones, R.W. 1967. "International Capital Movements and the Theory of Tariffs and Trade." *Quarterly Journal of Economics* 81:1–38.

Lawrence, R.Z., and M.J. Slaughter. 1993. "International Trade and American Wages in the 1980s: Giant Sucking Sound or Small Hiccup?" *Brookings Papers, Microeconomics* 2:161–226.

Layard, R., and S. Nickell. 1985. "The Causes of British Unemployment." *National Institute Economic Review* 111:62–85.

Layard, R., S. Nickell, and R. Jackman. 1991. *Unemployment—Macroeconomic Performance and the Labour Market*. Oxford: Oxford University Press.

Lucas, R.E., Jr. 1988. "On the Mechanics of Economic Development." *Journal of Monetary Economics* 22:3–42.

Minford, P. 1983. "Labour Market Equilibrium in an Open Economy." *Oxford Economic Papers* 35:S207–244.

Minford, P. 1989. "A Labour-Based Theory of International Trade." In: J. Black and A.I. MacBean (eds.), *Causes and Changes in the Structure of International Trade 1960–85*, pp. 196–240. London: Macmillan.

Minford, P. 1990. "The Poverty Trap after the Fowler Reforms." In: A. Bowen and K. Mayhew (eds.), *Improving the Incentives for the Low-Paid*. Macmillan for the National Economic Development Office.

Minford, P. 1994. "The OECD Unemployment Problem and the Role of Welfare." Conference paper forthcoming in D. Snower (ed.), *Policies To Deal with High Unemployment*, CUP for CEPR, proceedings of CEPR conference of the same name in Vigo, N. Spain, September.

Minford, P., J. Riley, and E. Nowell. 1995. "The Elixir of Growth: Trade, Non-Traded Goods and Development." CEPR Working Paper No. 2. London: CEPR.

Ohlin, B. 1933. *Interregional and International Trade*. Cambridge, Mass.: Harvard University Press.

Parente, S.L., and E.C. Prescott. 1993a. "Technology Adoption and Growth." *Research Department Staff Report* 136, revised September 1993, Federal Reserve Bank of Minneapolis. Forthcoming in *Journal of Political Economy*.

Parente, S.L., and E.C. Prescott. 1993b. "Changes in the Wealth of Nations." *Federal Reserve Bank of Minneapolis Quarterly Review* Spring: 3–16.

Rebelo, S. 1991. "Long-Run Policy Analysis and Long-Run Growth." *Journal of Political Economy* 99:500–521.

Romer, P.M. 1986. "Increasing Returns and Long-Run Growth." *Journal of Political Economy* 94:1002–1037.

Rybczynski, T.M. 1955. "Factor Endowments and Relative Commodity Prices." *Economica* 22:336–341.

Samuelson, P.A. 1948. "International Trade and the Equalisation of Factor Prices." *Economic Journal* 58:163–184.

Solow, R.M. 1956. "A Contribution to the Theory of Economic Growth." *Quarterly Journal of Economics* 70:65–94.

Stolper, W., and P.A. Samuelson. 1941. "Protection and Real Wages." *Review of Economic Studies*, pp. 58–73.

Summers, R., and A. Heston. 1988. "A New Set of International Comparisons of Real Product and Price Levels Estimates from 130 Countries, 1950–1985." *The Review of Income and Wealth* 34:1–25.

Summers, R., and A. Heston. 1991. "The Penn World Tables (Mark 5): An Expanded Set of International Comparisons, 1950–88." *Quarterly Journal of Economics* 106:327–368.

Thomas, J., and T. Worrall. 1994. "Foreign Direct Investment and the Risk of Expropriation." *Review of Economic Studies* 61:81–108.

Wood, A. 1994. *North–South Trade, Employment and Inequality—Changing Fortunes in a Skill-Driven World*. Oxford: Clarendon.

Worrall, T. 1990. "Debt with Potential Repudiation." *European Economic Review*.

Part II
Europe's Present Unemployment Crisis

Immigration and the European Labor Markets

Charles Wyplosz

Europe
J61
J64
F22

I Immigration and Jobs

The public debate on the economic effects of migration is ancient. It is back again in Europe, as always charged with social emotions and political undertones. Widely held fears that immigrants displace national workers through underbidding of wages and working conditions appear to be backed by casual observation. Quite regularly, the media reveal cases of illegal immigrants working long hours at extremely low wages, powerfully suggesting that both immigrants and native workers suffer from migration. Yet, in striking contrast, the economic literature fails to theoretically predict and empirically document unambiguously adverse effects from migration. In fact, in the long run when prices and wages are flexible, immigration is more likely to raise welfare in both origin and recipient countries. Freeman (1993) observing that few economists actually go on to support free migration suggests that the economic theory of migration must be modified to account for economically motivated resistance to immigration.

This paper does not attempt to extend the economics of migration (for recent references, see OECD [1993] and the collection of papers in Giersch [1994]). Rather, its objective is to draw from this literature, both theoretical and empirical, what is needed to evaluate the links between unemployment in Europe and the immigration experience and outlook. It surveys arguments and facts concerning the effects of migration on labor markets in recipient countries. The paper also examines the labor market determinants of migration.

I thank the conference participants, in particular Barry Eichengreen, and Maurice Schiff, for useful comments. The opinions expressed in the paper remain my own.

One important conclusion is that migrants face very large fixed costs, so that migration is little responsive to moderate changes in labor market conditions. Large migration flows typically occur under two conditions: when nationals have just established in the recipient country a "bridgehead" (connections to find jobs, housing and social support) which lowers the cost of migration, or when political upheavals disturb the existing balance between the cost of and the return from migration. A second conclusion is that the estimated impact of immigration on wages and unemployment is found to be quantitatively small.

These results suggest that the surge of migration which has followed—in fact, preceded and possibly contributed to hasten—the collapse of communism in Eastern Europe, and was most dramatically observed in Germany, is now receding. Barring new crises, immigration into Europe is unlikely to reach a scale large enough to exert first order effects at the aggregate level. This conclusion needs to be qualified, however. The labor force is far from homogeneous. Particular categories of labor, industries and regions stand to be more affected than others. The policy response, in turn, may well have first-order effects.

A theme well recognized in the literature is the duality between labor mobility and trade.[1] In theory, under assumptions that do not seem too farfetched, trade should lead to factor price equalization, thereby removing one prime reason for migration. In practice, the recent literature on growth and convergence increasingly confirms Baumol's diagnostic that we observe "convergence clubs": groups of countries that converge within their own club but not with the other clubs. In particular, poor countries at best do not seem to catch up, and at worst fall increasingly behind. Thus income differentials may well be increasing, not fading away. This sharpens the background for debates on trade policy: the indirect link running from trade to jobs via immigration has be taken into consideration when evaluating the direct link between trade and the labor market. The paper closes with implications for labor market policies.

II   Immigration: The Size of the Problem

Immigration has dramatically increased in Europe in recent years. The collapse of communism has been prompted and followed by spectac-

---

[1] For a good introduction, see Razin and Sadka (1992).

ular movements of populations. Table 1 shows that the proportion of foreign population, which in most European countries had remained stable, sometimes even slightly declining, during the eighties, has increased markedly since 1989. The increase is particularly strong in Austria and Germany, an indication that, indeed, political changes in Eastern Europe play an important role. This is confirmed for Germany in Figure 1, which displays total immigration as well as the inflows of ethnic Germans from either the GDR or the other communist block countries (including the USSR).

While these numbers are arguably large, it would be easy to exaggerate the issue. Table 2 presents the stock of foreigners as a percentage of the total population.[2] Three lessons emerge from this table. First, there is a considerable disparity across seemingly similar European countries. The proportion of foreign workers varies from very low percentages such as 1.5 percent in Italy to 9.2 percent in Belgium and a maximum of 17.1 percent in Switzerland. Second, the most dramatic increases occurred much earlier as is made clear by the available 1950 data. The earlier build-up that took place during the growth years of the 1960s did not then raise fears of unemployment and low wages. Third, the literature on European labor market has not considered so far immigration as an important factor. For example, the large collaborative efforts at explaining European unemployment collected in Layard et al. (1991) and Dreze and Bean (1990) do not ever mention immigration. Either these authoritative works have missed something important, or immigration is not playing a significant role in European labor markets and the numbers in Table 2 corresponding to the latest wave of immigration are quantitatively insignificant.

III Aggregate Effects

The preceding remarks concern the (im)plausibility of significant macroeconomic effects of immigration; yet, in principle, direct estimates are preferable. The conclusion that seems to emerge from a survey of existing empirical results is that there is at best limited evidence that immigration hurts labor markets.

---

[2] It should be noted that these numbers most probably understate the size of the foreign population because of illegal immigration. Most of the conclusions drawn from the table are not affected by this observation.

Table 1. Increase in Foreign Population (% per year).

	Austria	Belgium	Denmark	Germany	Italy	Netherlands	Sweden	Switzerland	U.K.
1982	1.2	0.6	1.2	0.8	8.2	1.7	-2.1	1.7	–
1983	-9.2	0.0	1.0	-2.8	6.2	1.1	-2.1	0.0	–
1984	-2.3	0.8	3.5	-3.8	5.9	1.1	-1.6	0.7	–
1985	1.1	-5.7	8.6	0.3	4.7	-1.1	-0.5	0.8	8.1
1986	1.5	0.8	9.7	3.1	6.4	2.8	0.6	1.7	5.1
1987	2.6	1.1	6.2	2.6	27.1	4.2	2.6	2.4	1.0
1988	5.5	0.7	4.3	-3.0	12.8	5.4	5.0	2.8	-1.0
1989	8.0	1.4	6.1	7.9	-24.0	2.9	8.3	3.4	-0.5
1990	28.1	2.7	6.6	8.2	59.3	7.9	6.1	5.8	-4.9
1991	23.9	2.0	5.5	12.2	14.8	5.8	2.1	5.7	1.6

Notes: For Italy, regularizations occurred in 1987–1988 and 1990. Germany includes eastern Germany in 1991.
Source: OECD (1993).

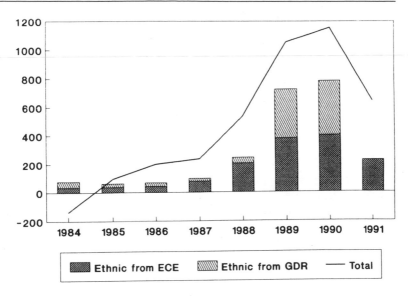

Figure 1. Immigration into Germany (net flows, thousand per year).
Source: OECD (1994).

In principle, under fairly general conditions, immigration is expected to raise, not to reduce, income per capita.[3] Basically, immigration increases a scarce resource, labor. Once labor has become more plentiful, it is expected that the stock of capital *per native worker* will rise as the capital stock per available labor (both natives and new immigrants) returns to its steady-state value. Other reasons advanced in the literature to justify the presumption that immigration actually raises the natives' income include excess demand for labor (starting from a situation of full employment), a better utilization of private and public capital resulting from the flexibility and abundance of new immigrants, various sources of increasing returns (such as learning by doing, and endogenous technological change proportional to population size), and better allocation of labor. A number of studies also mention positive Keynesian demand effects.

One way or another, the foregoing reasoning assumes that immigrant labor is a complement to the indigenous labor force. If, on

---

[3] This point is made very elegantly in Freeman (1993).

Table 2. Percentage of Foreign Population (% of total population).

	Austria	Belgium	Denmark	Germany	Italy	Netherlands	Sweden	Switzerland	U.K.
1950	–	4.3	–	1.1	–	1.1	–	6.1	–
1981	3.9	9.0	2.0	7.5	0.6	3.8	5.0	14.3	–
1982	4.0	9.0	2.0	7.6	0.6	3.8	4.9	14.4	–
1983	3.6	9.0	2.0	7.4	0.7	3.8	4.8	14.4	–
1984	3.6	9.1	2.1	7.1	0.7	3.9	4.7	14.4	2.8
1985	3.6	8.6	2.3	7.2	0.7	3.8	4.6	14.5	3.1
1986	3.6	8.6	2.5	7.4	0.8	3.9	4.7	14.7	3.2
1987	3.7	8.7	2.7	7.6	1.0	4.0	4.8	14.9	3.2
1988	3.9	8.8	2.8	7.3	1.1	4.2	5.0	15.2	3.2
1989	4.2	8.9	2.9	7.7	0.9	4.3	5.3	15.6	3.2
1990	5.3	9.1	3.1	8.2	1.4	4.6	5.6	16.3	3.2
1991	6.6	9.2	3.3	7.3	1.5	4.8	5.7	17.1	3.1

Source: Years 1981–1991, see Table 1. Year 1950: Razin and Sadka (1992).

the contrary, foreign labor is a substitute for, not a complement of, domestic labor, we would expect to observe negative effects on wages and/or unemployment. Similarly, adverse effects are expected to follow from a worsening of the terms of trade if domestic output rises and faces inelastic world demand, from heavier taxation of the population if immigrants consume a high quantity of public goods (education, health, welfare, etc.), and from the congestion and other costs of absorbing an additional and different population. Overall, therefore, on theoretical grounds, the effects of immigration on the labor market are ambiguous.

The empirical literature does not resolve this ambiguity. Most work attempts to detect immigration effects on growth and income per capita as well as on wages and employment. Most of the existing literature deals with the United States, a country that has had high immigration for more than a century. The majority of the studies find no clear adverse effects on growth and per capita output (sometimes they are even found to be positive), and the effects on aggregate wages and employment are found to be small or insignificant (see, e.g., Simon [1989], Altonji and Card [1991], and the summary of recent research in Freeman [1993]).

The literature faces several problems. First, there is the "Gold Rush" simultaneity problem: immigration tends to occur in waves, sometimes (but not always) in response to fast growth in the recipient country or region. This effect, which tends to produce positive correlations between wages or employment and immigration, can be easily accounted for, at least in principle. Second, there is the "Ghetto problem": immigrants from the same country or area tend to agglomerate in the same cities or regions, so that important local effects may be swamped by aggregate measures. This has led reseachers to study the effects of immigration at the local or industry level, and yet there is no evidence that cities with large immigration flows face lower wages or more unemployment than other cities.[4] Another problem concerns timing: positive effects are mostly expected in the long run and must be balanced against those shorter-run negative effects (which are linked to wage and/or price rigidities) that are prominent in the minds of those

---

[4] There is some evidence (see Filer, 1992) of reduced internal migration towards cities facing large international immigration. This might play an equilibrating role and explain the lack of international immigration effect at the local level. But then one would expect to detect an aggregate effect.

who fear immigration. This is why studies or particular (dramatic) events are of great interest, a point to which I will return shortly.

The evidence reported so far is for the United States. Unfortunately, work concerning Europe has been very limited until recently. Recent reviews of the rare studies conducted before the latest wave of European immigration can be found in Zimmerman (1994) and OECD (1993). A reading of these surveys tends to confirm the results found with respect to the United States, namely that the effects of immigration on the recipient economy are ambiguous, since there are reports of small positive and negative effects. The OECD survey reports just one strongly dissenting study by Blattner and Sheldon (1989), which detects a negative effect on output per capita in Switzerland.

The recent wave of immigration from Eastern Europe has led to a new research effort in Europe. Initially, there were widespread expectations that the elimination of the extremely severe border controls put in place and harshly enforced by the communist regimes—powerfully symbolized by the Berlin wall—would result in large migrations. It was common to liken the former East–West divide to the Rio Grande. Why such expectations have failed to materialize has given rise to some theoretical work reemphasizing older truths such as the high costs of migration (Wyplosz, 1994) or the role of uncertainty (Burda, 1993; Faini, 1993), while Faini and Venturini (1994) have noted that low incomes in the country of potential out-migration may prevent would-be migrants from actually undertaking the trip for lack of sufficient savings. As a result, they predict a hump-shaped relationship between out-migration and a country's income. This would mean that migration from the East to Western Europe might emerge later on as savings are accumulated in the East.

At the empirical level, and returning to the question of effects of migration on native workers' wages and employment, the rare new studies produced so far have focused, as is appropriate, on the German-speaking countries, which have experienced the largest inflows. The studies seem to confirm the results found in the United States. Pischke and Velling (1994) fail to detect any ambiguous or strong effects of the recent wave of immigration to Germany. Winter-Ebmer and Zweimüller's (1994) findings for Austria are similar.

Another approach has been to conduct case studies of particular waves of immigration, because they allow us to isolate migration from other contemporaneous trends such as business cycles, technological change, or changes in labor market regulations. For the United States, Card (1990) has looked at the effects of the sudden immigration from Mariel, Cuba. For Europe, Hunt (1992) looks at the wave of immigration into France that immediately followed the accession of Algeria to independence after a long and painful war. This episode, although not linked to postcommunist migrations, is particularly interesting to study for two main reasons. First, because it deals with a clearly exogenous migratory movement unrelated to any economic consideration: irrespective of individual economic situations, practically all the ethnic French population left Algeria in a matter of weeks. Second, such a spectacular shock bears more than a resemblance to the elimination of the Iron Curtain between Eastern and Western Europe, particularly between Eastern and Western Germany. Working with detailed regional data, Hunt is able to focus on areas where immigration is concentrated (southern France and the Paris area) and track down detailed local labor market effects. Her micro results largely confirm results from aggregate studies that attempt to link labor markets directly to immigration: she finds deceptively small elasticities of wage and employment response to immigration.

Such studies face the criticism that local or partial equilibrium analysis may fail to capture indirect channels. Using explicitly general equilibrium models, Williamson has studied two cases of "mass migration": from Ireland to Great Britain in 1820–1850 and to the United States in the late 19th century. He reports a decline of real wages in the receiving country of 1.4 percent per decade in the first case, and of 2.5 percent per decade in the second case (reported in Hatton and Williamson, 1994, p. 35). It is difficult to get excited by such small numbers.

In the end, it is probably safe to conclude that the aggregate effects of migration are negligible. This conclusion corresponds to the generally modest size of the phenomenon as documented in the previous section. For the occasional bursts of migration triggered by particular political events, both theory and empirical evidence predict small positive long-run effects and small short-run negative effects.

IV   Job and Worker Heterogeneity

The above conclusion that immigration is unlikely to matter much is based on aggregate reasoning and data. However, the literature on immigration has long emphasized the fact that immigrant workers, whether they are qualified or not, compete mainly for the less-well-paid jobs (see Todaro, 1969; Borjas, 1987; Borjas, Freeman, and Katz, 1991). In parallel, the literature on labor markets and unemployment has increasingly focused on the heterogeneity of jobs and people (see Davis and Haltiwanger, 1990; Burda and Wyplosz, 1994). Bringing the two observations together leads to renewed emphasis on the differential effects of migration on various categories of jobs and workers.

It is to be expected that, if indeed immigrant workers are mostly taking up less qualified jobs, they will bid down wages of the less skilled workers or increase unemployment in that category. This corresponds to the substitutability hypothesis. The complementarity hypothesis, instead, implies that immigrants bring with them (possibly low) skills in short supply at home and thus increase the productivity of higher-skilled domestic workers. If, realistically, we narrow down the category of population to be affected by immigrant workers to the low-skilled end of the population, it is not possible anymore to take solace at the smallness of the effects reported in the previous section. For example, if we assume that immigrant workers compete only with the lower decile of the distribution of skills, the numbers in Table 2 ought to be multiplied by a factor of ten. They become far from trivial and cannot be summarily dismissed anymore.

The empirical literature on this issue is, again, mostly based on U.S. data. In that case, a typical finding (see, e.g., Hatton and Williamson, 1994) is that immigration has at the same time a negative effect on the wages of the less skilled domestic workers (substitutability) and a positive effect for higher skills (complementarity). Yet, these effects are generally found to be small and of a short-run nature. Furthermore, a number of studies report no statistically significant effect at all. Table 3, borrowed from OECD (1993), is representative of these findings. For the United States and its particular segmentation of the population, it suggests a small overall substitution effect, with cases of complementarity with females and, possibly, black males. The few existing European studies reach qualitatively similar conclusions.

V Trade and Immigration

The deep links between trade and migration have been recognized for a very long time. The relevant point of departure here is the factor price

Table 3. Effect on native wages of an additional 10% influx of immigrants.	lower bound	upper bound
All nationals	−0.2	
White males	−0.2	−0.1
Black males	−0.3	0.5
Females	0.2	0.5
Young blacks	−0.1	
Young hispanics	−0.3	0.2

Source: OECD (1993).

Notes: These are estimates based on an analysis carried out by the OECD. In some cases it provides point estimates, in other cases upper and lower bounds.

equalization theorem: it is a fairly robust result of trade theory that free trade leads towards the equalization of factor rewards. The link with immigration is obvious. If migration responds primarily to income differentials, free trade will eliminate its root cause. In this sense trade and migration are substitutable ways of achieving the same result, the equalization of factor rewards. Put differently, migration occurs either because trade is not free and other factors of production do not move, or move insufficiently, or because trade is not delivering factor price equalization.

The process of European integration offers an appropriate testing ground for this issue. Looking at the European experience is also potentially useful for the question at hand since it leads us to focus on the way labor market institutions interfere with labor mobility. The question is whether, as European integration has been progressing, labor mobility has increased or not. Less migration is predicted by trade theory. More mobility is predicated upon a number of factors such as legislation explicitly designed to facilitate intra-European migration and the fact that firms are increasingly operating across all of Europe and setting up subsidiaries. For France and Germany, Table 4 shows the percentage of selected groups of foreigners in the total foreign population. Trade theory obviously wins: the proportion of European nationals living in France and Germany has declined.[5] The observations concerning the recent entries into the Common Market,

---

[5] Comparing with Table 2, it is possible to see that the decline is not only relative but also absolute.

Table 4. Foreign Population by Country of Origin (% of total foreign population).

France			
	1975	1982	1990
EC	54.3%	42.9%	36.5%
Portugal and Spain	36.5%	29.5%	24.1%
North Africa	32.3%	38.7%	38.7%

Germany		
	1981	1990
EC	32.8%	28.4%
Spain and Portugal	6.2%	4.2%
Greece	6.5%	6.4%
Yugoslavia and Turkey	47.2%	44.4%

Source: OECD (1993).

Table 5. Exports of Goods to the EC (% of total exports).

	1975	1981	1990
Greece	51.4%	43.9%	56.4%
Portugal	53.8%	56.7%	73.8%
Spain	47.9%	45.9%	69.0%

Source: European Economy (1994).

Greece (1981), Portugal and Spain (1986), are surprising, however. While, as expected from trade theory, the number of Spaniards and Portuguese working in France and Germany has quickly declined, this evolution clearly started prior to these countries' accession to the EC. As for Greece, there is no tendency for a decline in Germany, the main recipient country. Table 5 elucidates the puzzle: Greece has hardly reoriented its external trade towards the EC, while Portugal actually anticipated EC accession by reorienting its trade. Thus for a number of reasons not pursued here,[6] Greece has failed to take advantage of its entry into the Common Market, while trade effects have taken hold in the Iberian peninsula from the early 1980s onwards.

---

[6] For an exposition of Greece's conflictual relationship with market principles during this period, see Alogoskoufis (1995).

As already noted, factor price equalization may still occur in the presence of trade impediments as long as some factors are mobile.[7] In the canonical two-factor model, it is generally enough that capital be fully mobile to achieve wage equalization. In practice, a large number of countries have removed the most obvious restrictions to capital mobility over the last decade, so that there should be by now a visible tendency towards factor price equalization. This is certainly not found to be happening universally and, in fact, trade theory provides a large number of cases where indeed factor price equalization need not occur (full specialization, factor reversals, the presence of traded goods).

Another largely unrelated body of rapidly growing empirical literature, triggered by the new growth Romer–Lucas theory, explores the same issue from a different angle.[8] For our purposes, its main relevance is the large amount of empirical work recently generated around the theme of (per capita income) convergence. Most results in this tradition confirm the existence of what Baumol (1986) has called "convergence clubs": countries that converge into groups while the groups diverge from one another. The lesson here is that wage differentials, and the associated incentive to migrate, are not universally declining despite the perception of higher capital mobility, spreading transfers of technology and continuous progress in reducing trade barriers.

Using the methodology developed in the new growth literature, it is possible to return to the theme of factor price equalization. Under constant returns, in the standard two-factor model, equality of the capital-labor ratio implies equality of factor prices. Thus testing for a tendency towards factor price equalization can be turned into testing for convergence of the capital-labor ratios. Bernard and Durlauf (1991) suggest the following approach: for x and y to converge, a necessary condition is that x minus y be stationary (and, in addition, its mean

---

[7] For a useful graphical review of the conditions under which this happens in various models of trade, see Eichengreen (1990, Appendix A).

[8] This literature asks whether countries may fail to converge in the presence of technology transfers and financial integration. Irrespective of trade links and labor mobility, but assuming that financial markets are well integrated, classical growth theory predicts convergence unless there exist nondecreasing returns to scale. In this literature, failure to converge is ascribed to nondecreasing returns to scale such as externalities in knowledge.

and variance converge towards zero). Equivalently, x and y must be cointegrated with a cointegrating coefficient of unity.

Table 6 below presents results of convergence tests concerning the capital-labor ratios (in logs, approximated by the investment-labor ratio) over the period 1960–1989. We consider a number of country groupings: the European Union (EU), also broken down into the North and the South (Italy, Greece, Spain, Portugal), the four South-East Asian newly industrialized countries (NICs) (Korea, Taiwan, Singapore and Hong Kong), and four groups of developing countries based on the World Bank classification. Cointegration is only found for one pair: the EU (only its northern component) and the four East Asian NICs. For the other groups, the absence of cointegration and the fact that the convergence coefficient is not significantly different from zero indicates that convergence is not happening.[9]

As noted above, cointegration is only a necessary condition for convergence. Unfortunately, cointegration tests are known to have a very low power: if convergence is under way, but not complete, the difference between the capital ratios are continuously shrinking which may be misinterpreted by the test as a case of nonstationarity. It is interesting therefore to pay attention to the value and evolution of the cointegration coefficient. For the pair EU–Asia the cointegrating coefficient is different from one and not moving towards unity. This later finding suggests quite reasonably that these two groups are converging (so that the difference between their capital-labor ratios is stationary) but have not yet converged so that the two ratios are not yet equal.[10] For the other groups, the coefficients are changing over time and while they mostly move to the "right" side of unity[11] the other results do not

---

[9] The convergence coefficient is usually overlooked in stationarity tests as most authors emphasize the behavior of the disturbance term in the equation $Dz_t = a - bz_{t-1} + A(L)z_t + e_t$, where $z = y - x$. Consider however the following simple example. Let z follow the deterministic convergent process $z_t = rz_{t-1} + u_t$, where u is white noise. Then we have $Dz_t = -(1-r)z_{t-1} + u_t$ and the convergence coefficient $(1-r)$ is estimated as b in the stationarity test for z. If x and y have not yet converged, z may fail to be found stationary but a significantly positive convergence coefficient is indicative that convergence is under way.

[10] The cointegrating regression has $\log(K/L)_t$ on the left-hand side and $\log(K/L)_{t-1}$ on the right-hand side: the fact that the coefficient is less than unity suggests that the ratio is growing more slowly in the EU and in South-East Asia.

[11] See the previous footnote.

Table 6. Convergence Tests, 1960–1989.

	All EU Asia	North EU Asia	South EU Asia	North South EU	Groups 1 and 4	Groups 2 and 4	Groups 3 and 4	Groups 1 and 3	Groups 2 and 3	Groups 1 and 2
Cointegration	yes	yes	no	no	no	no	no	no	no	no
Convergence coefficient	−0.09*	−0.09*	−0.04	−0.06	0.00	0.00	0.00	0.00	0.00	0.00
Cointegrating coefficient										
Subsample 1	0.52*	0.50*	0.75*	0.67*	1.22*	0.93*	0.84*	1.47*	1.10*	1.31*
Subsample 2	0.57*	0.57*	0.47*	1.12*	0.92*	1.44*	1.36*	0.60*	1.00*	0.58*
Chow Test	accept	reject	reject	reject	reject	reject	reject	reject	accept	reject

Source: Neven and Wyplosz (1994).

Notes: Convergence coefficient is b in regression: $z(t) - z(t-1) = a - bz(t-1) + A(L)(z(t) - z(t-1))$. Cointegrating coefficient is calculated over two samples (1960–1974 and 1975–1989). Chow-Test: accept or reject the null hypothesis that coefficients are equal across subsamples, an asterisk indicates that the coefficient is significant at the 5% confidence level. World Bank Groups:

1. Richest developing countries.
2. Intermediate richer.
3. Intermediate poorer.
4. Poorest.

support the view that convergence is occurring. The only exceptions may be the two parts of the EU and the two intermediate groups (group 2 and 3) of developing countries.

Why is convergence of capital-labor ratios and, therefore, factor price equalization not happening, then? Explanations abound, of course.[12] A key explanation, relevant to the issue at hand, is that human capital does not travel well. While technologies and capital (financial and physical) can move fairly freely and quickly, the skills required to operate new technologies efficiently on a large scale seem to be crucially missing in large segments of the developing world. If human capital is a required input, this would be enough to impair the convergence process.[13] This interpretation of the lack of convergence and equalization of immobile factor prices implies that mobility of labor, a factor substitutable for the combination of physical and human capital, is the unavoidable channel for factor price equalization when serious impediments to trade exist. Thus trade protection feeds immigration pressures.

However, trade restrictions are unlikely to be the only explanation of the observed pattern of migrations in Europe. The reason for skepticism is that the argument assumes that migration is directed by income differentials. As it turns out, the empirical literature generally fails to find incomes, or income differentials, as an explanatory variable for migration. This has led many authors to emphasize either the role of unemployment or the existence of very sizable fixed costs of migration.[14] In particular, most waves of migration are historically linked to dramatic events, wars, famines, crises, which act like trigger mechanisms, overpowering the fixed costs.[15] This is the case of the recent wave

---

[12] For an extensive survey emphasizing trade theory, see Leamer (1992).

[13] One can imagine that physical and human capital are complements in the production function so that, contrary to Heckscher–Ohlin theory and more in line with Ricardian trade theory, the effective production functions differ across Baumol–type clubs of countries.

[14] For an application of costs of migration to migration between Eastern and Western Europe, see Wyplosz (1994). Hatton and Williamson (1994) report success in finding that relative incomes explain migration, but they still accept the view that migration costs may be "prohibitive."

[15] Burda (1993) has developed a model exhibiting this kind of mechanism using Dixit's (1989) fundamental intuition that it pays to wait in the presence of uncertainty. He shows how this model may help understand the pattern of migration from East to West Germany.

of migration in Europe, clearly linked to upheavals in Eastern Europe. Once the situation settles, as it seems to be doing by now, fixed costs are likely to reemerge as an irresistible barrier for most candidates.[16]

There are two reasons why this conjecture may be erroneous. First, the rate of unemployment has often been found to be a significant explanatory variable of migration: in the source country it acts as an incentive to look for places where jobs are more easily found; in the recipient country, the rate of unemployment can be seen as a crude but important measure of the probability of finding a job. Thus an alternative explanation of the slowdown of migration from Eastern to Western Europe could be the recession that has gripped most of the West soon after the end of communism in the East. Once the recession is over and unemployment declines in the West, migration might surge again, revealing a deeper trend than is currently suspected. The second reason for rejecting complacency is offered by Faini and Venturini (1993), who find that it is low incomes and the absence of accumulated savings (in convertible currencies) which act as a temporary barrier to large-scale migration. Paradoxically, therefore, once successful growth in the East provides citizens with the resources necessary to finance a move to the West, we could see a second wave of migration.

VI Policy Implications

The review of our understanding of migration leaves us with few certainties, but a number of fairly robust conclusions:

1. In quiet periods, at least in Europe, migration is a phenomenon more akin to a small relentless process than to large overpowering waves. The spurt that occurred after 1989 is likely to be over. The flow from Eastern Europe may now revert to a trickle, unless deep political crises trigger new waves.[17]

---

[16] In the aftermath of the collapse of communism, opinion polls in several Eastern and Central European countries showed that a large proportion of the population considered "living abroad" as a reasonable option. More recent polls now indicate that less than 5 percent of respondents entertain this view.

[17] This does not rule out other waves following new crises. For example, it is conceivable that radical integrists come to power in North Africa, or that wars erupt on the fringes of the former Soviet Union, not to mention continuing tribal strife in Africa.

2. There is fairly strong evidence of an unemployment-immigration tradeoff. Importantly, this link does not reflect causality from immigration to unemployment but the other way round.

3. The role of relative wages on the migration decision is less well established. In any case, the fixed costs of migration are likely to be considerable.

4. Trade and migration are not close substitutes. Wide income differentials between Europe and much of the rest of the (often highly populated and with fast demographic growth)[18] world are likely to remain despite progress on trade integration.

5. The effects of migration on wages and unemployment are theoretically ambiguous and empirically tenuous. There is some evidence of beneficial effects in the long run and of some adverse effects in the short run, especially on the less-skilled segments of the population.

These observations suggest the following implications regarding policies towards unemployment in Europe:

1. Unemployment policies should not be shaped with immigration in mind. Conversely, labor market considerations should not be used as a fig leaf to justify policies towards immigration based on other considerations.[19]

2. Economic measures towards immigration are likely to be of little practical effect because they are dwarfed by the fixed costs of migration and are irrelevant in the face of dramatic political events. Yet, there is a widespread perception in the public at large that immigration can be dealt with and is closely intertwined with the unemployment issue. Efforts at educating the public, e.g., pointing out that immigration has mostly beneficial effects in the long run (see Zimmermann, 1994), are unlikely to succeed against deep-seated fears. What is needed, therefore, is to deal with appearances.

3. One widely accepted solution (among economists) to mass unemployment is the lowering of labor costs, especially for less skilled jobs.

---

[18] On the links between migration and demographic trends, see Zimmermann (1994).

[19] Or the ideas advanced by Freeman (1993)—that the receptivity to immigrants can be analyzed along the lines used to analyze segregation—must be developed to form a coherent set of economic arguments.

This could be seen as reducing simultaneously unemployment and immigration. Such an approach requires caution, however. First, labor costs may be reduced without decreasing take-home pays (by reducing overhead costs), thus leaving immigration unaffected. Second, if take-home wages are reduced, the effect on migration is empirically uncertain, in any case very small. Third, care must be taken not to have public opinion interpret the reduction in low-skill wages seen as a consequence of competition from immigration.

4. The apparent lack of mobility of human capital (yet to be empirically confirmed) remains a source of lasting income differentials. These differentials provide incentives to migration of low-skilled workers and offer an argument against trade liberalization. Encouraging out-migration of skilled labor from the developed countries may significantly raise the returns from technology transfers while slowing down the process of substitution of skilled for unskilled labor that is often considered as one source of unemployment in Europe.

5. As always, immigration is more likely to have earlier beneficial effects the more flexible wages and prices are. First best considerations call for increased wage flexibility but they need to be carefully balanced by issues such as the perceived need for some degree of equality and the unavoidable inefficiencies of labor markets.

6. Particular categories of labor, industries and regions stand to be more affected by immigration than others. If, at least in present value terms, immigration is Pareto-improving, political difficulties can, in principle, be avoided with effective transfers from the winners to the losers. This raises a number of familiar difficulties, including the distortionary effects of taxation and the disincentive effects of transfers. Given that immigration effects are of a small order of magnitude, one has to verify that the solution is not worse than the problem.

Furthermore, as Tables 1 and 2 show, the extent of migration pressure differs sharply from one country to another. The recent waves that originated in Eastern and Central Europe affected primarily Germany and Austria. The subsidy component of any tax and transfer scheme is bound to create difficulties within the EU: friction among states or an expansion of the Commission's controversial redistributive actions. It is important to ascertain that the policy response to a temporary second order disturbance does not have lasting negative first order effects.

Bibliography

Alogoskoufis, G. 1995. "The Two Faces of Janus." Forthcoming in *Economic Policy* 20.

Altonji, J., and D. Card. 1991. "The Effects of Immigration on the Labor Market Outcomes of Natives." In: J. Abowd and R. Freeman (eds.), *Immigration, Trade and Labor*, pp. 201–234. Chicago: University of Chicago Press.

Baumol, W. 1986. "Productivity Growth, Convergence and Welfare: What the Long-Run Data Show." *American Economic Review* 76:1072–1085.

Bernard, A.W., and S.N. Durlauf. 1991. "Convergence of International Output Movements." NBER Working Paper No. 3717. Cambridge, Mass.: NBER.

Blattner, N., and G. Sheldon. 1989. "Foreign Labour, Growth and Productivity: The Case of Switzerland." In: I. Gordon and A.P. Thirlwell (eds.), *European Factor Mobility*.

Borjas, G. 1987. "Self-Selection and the Earnings of Immigrants." *American Economic Review* 77:531–553.

Borjas, G., R. Freeman, and L. Katz. 1991. "On the Labor Market Effects of Immigration and Trade." NBER Working Paper No. 3761, Cambridge, Mass.: NBER.

Burda, M. 1993. "The Determinants of East–West Migration: Some First Results." *European Economic Review* 37:452–461.

Burda, M., and C. Wyplosz. 1994. "Gross Worker and Job Flows in Europe." *European Economic Review* 38:1287–1326.

Card, D. 1990. "The Impact of the Mariel Boatlift on the Miami Labor Market." *Industrial and Labor Relations Review* 43:245–257.

Davis, S., and J. Haltiwanger. 1992. "Gross Job Creation and Destruction: Microeconomic Evidence and Macroeconomic Implications." *NBER Macroeconomic Annuals*, pp. 123–168.

Dixit, A. 1989. "Entry and Exit Decisions Under Uncertainty." *Journal of Political Economy* 97:620–638.

Dreze, J., and C. Bean. 1990. *Europe's Unemployment Problem*. Cambridge, Mass.: MIT Press.

Eichengreen, B. 1990. "One Money for Europe? Lessons from the US Currency Union." *Economic Policy* 10:118–187.

Faini, R. 1994. "Migration in the Integrated EC." Forthcoming in P. Haaparanta and J. Kiander (eds.), *Expanding European Regionalism: The EC's New Members*. Cambridge, Mass.: Cambridge University Press.

Faini, R., and A. Venturini. 1994. "Migration and Growth: The Experience of Southern Europe." CEPR Discussion Paper No. 964. London: CEPR.

Filer, R. 1992. "Immigrant Arrivals and the Migratory Pattern of Native Workers." In: G. Borjas and R. Freeman (eds.), *Immigration and The Work Force: Economic Consequences for the United States and Source Areas*. Chicago: University of Chicago Press.

Freeman, R. 1993. "Immigration from Poor to Wealthy Countries: Experience of the United States." *European Economic Review* 37:452–461.

Giersch, H. (ed.). 1994. *Economic Aspects of International Migration*. Berlin, Heidelberg: Springer-Verlag.

Hatton, T.J., and J.G. Williamson. 1994. "International Migration and World Development: A Historical Perspective." In: H. Giersch (ed.), *Economic Aspects of International Migration*. Berlin-Heidelberg: Springer-Verlag.

Hunt, J. 1992. "The Impact of the 1962 Repatriate From Algeria on the French Labor Market." *Industrial and Labor Relations Review* 45:556–572.

Layard, R., S. Nickell, and R. Jackman. 1991. *Unemployment, Macroeconomic Performance and the Labour Market*. Oxford: Oxford University Press.

Leamer, E. 1992. "Testing Trade Theory." NBER Working Paper No. 3957. Cambridge, Mass.: NBER.

Neven, D., and C. Wyplosz. 1994. "Trade Effects on European Labor Markets." Unpublished paper.

OECD. 1993. *Trends in International Migration*. Annual Report. Paris: OECD.

Pischke, J.S., and J. Velling. 1994. "Wage and Employment Effects of Immigration to Germany: An Analysis Based on Local Labor Markets." CEPR Discussion Paper No. 935. London: CEPR.

Razin, A., and E. Sadka. 1992. "International Migration and International Trade." NBER Working Paper No. 4230. Cambridge, Mass.: NBER.

Simon, J.L. 1989. *The Economic Consequences of Immigration*. Oxford: Basil Blackwell.

Todaro, M. 1969. "A Model of Labor Migration and Urban Unemployment in Less Developed Countries." *American Economic Review* 59:138–148.

Winter-Ebmer, R., and J. Zweimüller. 1994. "Immigration and the Earnings of Young Native Workers." CPER Discussion Paper No. 936. London: CEPR.

Wyplosz, C. 1994. "Migration from the East: The Role of Reform and Capital Mobility." In: H. Siebert (ed.), *Migration: A Challenge for Europe*. Tübingen: Mohr.

Zimmermann, K.F. 1994. "Some General Lessons for Europe's Migration Problem." In: H. Giersch (ed.), *Economic Aspects of International Migration*. Berlin, Heidelberg: Springer-Verlag.

Foreign Trade, Wages, and Unemployment

Richard N. Cooper

World trade has increased about twice as rapidly as world output during the past two decades. Most countries have both become more open
with respect to imports and have seen a sharp growth in imports (and
hence exports as well). Phased trade liberalization agreed on during the
Kennedy and Tokyo multilateral trade negotiations (completed in 1975
and 1987, respectively) contributed to this result, as did the enlarge-
ment of the European Community from six to twelve members and the
inauguration of the U.S.-Canada free trade area in 1989. But it was
driven also by structural developments in the world economy, notably
the great reduction in practical barriers to communication among
national markets. Developing countries during this period have become
major exporters of manufactured goods, which now account for over
half of their nonoil exports.

During the same period, unemployment rose substantially in European countries, from low single-digit rates in the early 1970s to high
single-digit or even double-digit rates in the early 1990s. Table 1 reports
unemployment rates in six European countries and the United States.
The steady increase in unemployment rates in all European countries
over the two decades is noteworthy. The high rates in 1993 are partially
explicable in terms of a European recession, which occurred two years
earlier in Britain and the United States. But the rates for 1990 are
notably higher than those a decade earlier, which in turn were higher
than the low rates of 1970. Much of the growth in unemployment was
accounted for by females, far higher than their share in the labor force.
And the rates in 1990, following a period of strong growth in the late
1980s, were the lowest for the decade (1991 saw the lows for Germany
and the Netherlands).[1] Furthermore, on a comparative basis the rates

---

[1] Throughout this paper, "Germany" refers to West Germany.

Table 1. Unemployment Rates (percent).

	1970	1979	1990	1993[b]
United States	4.8	5.8	5.4	6.9
France	2.5	5.9	8.9	11.6
Germany	0.8	3.2	4.9	7.3
Italy	3.8	5.2	7.0	11.3
Netherlands	1.3	5.4	7.5	6.2
Spain	2.4	8.5	15.9	21.7
United Kingdom	2.6[a]	4.0	5.8	10.3

[a]1971.
[b]Mid-year, seasonally adjusted.
Source: Layard, Nickell, and Jackman (1994, Table A3), and *Economist*.

for Britain and Italy are somewhat understated because of their failure to include new entrants to the labor force (on an OECD standardized basis, Britain's unemployment rate was 6.8 percent and Italy's was 10.3 percent in 1990).

Although the United States also experienced increased import competition, it did not experience a rise in unemployment. However, wage dispersion in the United States increased markedly during this period, and in particular the real wages of low-skilled individuals actually declined, even while average real compensation was rising.

Is it possible, or likely, that the increased import competition resulted in higher wage dispersion in the United States—and in Britain, where a similar phenomenon can be observed—while being manifest in Europe as higher unemployment because of differences in how labor markets function there? In particular, what part of the relative decline in the wages of unskilled workers in the United States can be plausibly attributed to increased imports from developing countries well endowed with unskilled labor? And to what extent were similar pressures in Europe translated into higher unemployment? These are the questions this paper will address.

There are at least four channels through which increased import competition might affect unemployment. The first is macroeconomic in character: imports might be so competitive that the trade balance deteriorates and leads to a decline in aggregate output, leading in turn to higher unemployment.

The other three are structural in character. Even with no change in the trade balance we might observe a sharp increase in import penetration (and a corresponding increase in exports, both relative to GDP), leading to the need to reallocate resources from the production of nontradables to the production of tradables and, among tradables, from the production of import-competing goods to production for export. If the market for labor does not function smoothly and quickly, this required transformation might lead to higher "structural" unemployment, insofar as labor released from production of import-competing goods or nontradables is not quickly reemployed in production for export.

Second, even without increased import penetration on average, worldwide changes in the structure of comparative advantage might be such as to require substantial reallocation of resources, including labor, among the tradable sectors, from sectors with stiff import competition to sectors with new export opportunities. Again, if the labor market does not function smoothly and quickly, structural unemployment will increase, this time among workers in sectors subject to new foreign competitive pressures.

Finally, the nature of increased foreign competition may be such as to push down the rewards to particular factors of production, and if those factors cannot be reabsorbed smoothly and quickly in other sectors, they will go underutilized. In particular, if foreign competition is focused especially in goods produced with unskilled labor, continuing full employment of such labor will require a fall in its relative wage. If because of downward rigidity in wages (e.g., due to minimum wage legislation or conventions) such wages cannot fall, labor will become unemployed. Or if the reservation wage of unskilled labor exceeds its new lower market-clearing wage (e.g., because of unemployment compensation or welfare entitlements), unemployment will rise or some unskilled labor will withdraw from the labor force—in either case leading to a fall in employment of unskilled labor.

This paper examines briefly all four channels by which foreign competition might lead to increased unemployment, drawing on data from Britain, France, Germany, Italy, the Netherlands, and Spain, as the six largest economies in Europe, along with the United States for comparison. Since European unemployment rose especially in the 1980s, the focus will be on that decade; but some of the underlying trends predate that decade, so earlier trends must also be examined. For simplicity,

Table 2. Net Exports of
Goods and Services
(percent of GDP)[a].

	1970	1978	1990
United States	0.0	−1.2	−1.2
France	0.1	1.3	0.0
Germany	2.1	2.9	6.8
Italy	−0.8	0.6	−0.4
Netherlands	−1.7	0.0	4.7
Spain	−0.9	0.7	−3.4
United Kingdom	0.8	1.1	−2.6

[a]Figures exclude net receipts of factor income.
Source: IMF, *International Financial Statistics.*

comparisons will be made between 1970, 1980, and 1990, or closely
related dates when those are misleading for one reason or another (e.g.,
the exceptionally high oil prices in 1980), or data are not available.

I Macroeconomic Factors

The first channel identified above, the macroeconomic channel, can
be easily dismissed, both on theoretical and on empirical grounds. On
empirical grounds, only two of the seven countries in fact experienced
significant worsening of their international balance on goods and services between 1978 and 1990 (1980 not a good year for comparison
because of exceptionally high oil prices, starting in 1979, leading to
large temporary current account deficits in all countries except Britain,
an oil exporter); see Table 2. Spain experienced a significant expenditure boom in the late 1980s, based in part on foreign capital inflows,
which would cause a deterioration in the balance on goods and services
without depressing domestic economic activity. Britain, with a deterioration of 3.7 percentage points of GDP, thus is the one instance where
a case might be made that deteriorating international competitiveness
led to increased unemployment. (Of course, once Spain's boom subsides, that country also might be left with wage levels that are internationally uncompetitive at an unchanged exchange rate.)

During the period 1970–1978, the current account positions of all
the European countries improved, and during the 1980s that of Germany and the Netherlands improved by four percentage points or

more, suggesting that external demand was a strong stimulus to output and employment in those countries.

Higher current account deficits usually signify booms, which reflect high domestic demand, high growth in output, and strong demand for labor. When they reflect lack of competitiveness, i.e., a growth in imports (or decline in exports) despite weak domestic demand, that can and should be corrected these days by a depreciation of the currency, to restore the joint possibility of internal and external equilibrium. Britain and Italy found themselves in this situation in 1992. Britain entered the European Monetary System in 1990 at what was widely viewed at the time as an overvalued exchange rate, and Italy maintained an unchanged exchange rate against the German mark and other EMS currencies from early 1987 despite higher domestic inflation. The lack of competitiveness in both countries was presumably eliminated, at least temporarily, by the currency depreciations of late 1992. The Spanish peseta also depreciated during 1992–1993.

Thus, unemployment arising from this source can be attributed to poor macroeconomic and exchange rate policy, rather than to an autonomous increase in competition from imports.

II   Increased Foreign Trade

The relative importance of foreign trade has increased in all our countries over the past two decades, measured, for example, by the ratio of exports to GDP (that is what is relevant for the structure of output and employment). But the rise occurred most rapidly during the 1970s; it slowed noticeably in all countries except Germany during the 1980s, and actually reversed itself significantly for Britain (whose exports in 1980 were temporarily inflated by the high oil prices of that year) and marginally for Italy and the United States. Thus, the pressure for structural change from an increase in foreign trade was much greater during the 1970s than during the 1980s, and any increase in frictional unemployment should have occurred then. If the relative growth in exports ceases, but remains high, structural unemployment from this source should stop rising, and then should gradually decline as workers are reabsorbed into employment, except when the attractions of not working exceed those of returning to work.

Table 3. Share of Exports in GDP (percent)[a].

	1970	1980	1990
United States	5.3	10.2	9.9
France	15.8	21.5	23.1
Germany	22.6	28.4	36.2
Italy	14.8	19.9	19.2
Netherlands	44.8	52.5	54.4
Spain	13.5	15.8	17.2
United Kingdom	22.3	27.1	23.4

[a] Export of goods and services in the national accounts.
Source: IMF, *International Financial Statistics.*

Table 3 reports the export/GDP ratio for 1970, 1980, and 1990. Despite the rise in relative importance of exports, employment in the nontrade sectors (i.e., most services) in these countries rose more rapidly than employment in manufacturing and agriculture. Indeed, employment in manufacturing declined in all the European countries during the 1980s, reflecting growth in productivity. So labor resources did not have to be shifted to the tradable sector to accommodate the rising relative importance of exports; trade-induced structural change did not seem to be disruptive at this level.

Trade could create structural disturbances in the labor market even if import penetration and export/GDP ratios do not increase. This could occur if the pattern of comparative advantage, and hence the commodity structure of trade, is changing more rapidly than domestic markets for labor can comfortably accommodate, giving rise to increases in frictional unemployment as import-displaced labor requires time to find jobs in the expanding export sectors.

A crude measure of such structural change is the dispersion of changes in export/sales ratios across economic and especially manufacturing sectors. In particular, the standard deviation of changes in export/sales ratios across 22 manufacturing sectors offers a rough but concrete measure of the degree of structural change that has occurred through foreign trade. The baseline hypothesis here is that foreign and domestic demand grow at the same pace, sector by sector, leaving export/sales ratios unchanged even though sectors may be growing at different rates. Table 4 reports such statistics for several countries, along with the mean increases in export/sales ratios. The latter (in

Table 4. Dispersion of Changes[a] in Ratio of Exports to GDP, 1970–1989.	1970s	1980s
United States	3.8 (4.2)	3.2 (0.3)
France	5.5 (6.7)	6.4 (4.8)
Germany	10.6 (5.3)	9.6 (10.4)
Italy	12.6 (5.3)	9.2 (0.8)[b]
Netherlands	10.0 (9.6)	8.6 (7.6)[c]
United Kingdom	18.3 (11.9)	20.5 (1.9)[c]

[a] Standard deviation of changes in export/GDP ratios across 2-digit manufacturing industries between 1970 and 1980 and between 1980 and 1989. Mean changes in parentheses.
[b] 1980–1987.
[c] 1980–1988.
Source: Calculations from OECD STAN database for industrial analysis.

parentheses) confirm what was stated above, that except for Germany the relative growth of exports of manufactures was considerably more rapid during the 1970s than during the 1980s. The dispersion around these average increases in the 1980s was about the same as in the 1970s, modestly higher for France and the United Kingdom (where unemployment increased by only 43,000 over the period covered, to 1989), modestly lower for the other countries.

As with total import penetration and export/GDP ratios, increases in unemployment should be associated with increased dispersion; at a constant dispersion, frictional unemployment should remain unchanged, provided workers continue to seek work. Structural changes in the commodity composition of trade would have to intensify to explain *increases* in unemployment. Thus a rapidly changing structure of international comparative advantage is not plausibly an important source of increased frictional unemployment during the 1980s, although this factor may have played some role in all the countries during the 1970s, a possibility that is not examined here.

III Trade-Induced Pressures on Factor Prices

International trade theory in the Heckscher–Ohlin framework, with its focus on relative factor endowments, suggests that increased imports

Table 5. Imports of Manufactures from Developing Countries (billions of dollars).

	Total[a]		TAF[b]	
	1980	1990	1980	1990
United States	31.0	129.3	8.8	36.1
France	4.5	15.9	1.3	5.7
Germany	8.8	32.8	1.8	14.0
Italy	3.4	12.6	0.8	2.9
Netherlands	1.9	6.1	0.8	1.7
Spain	0.6	4.5	0.1	1.0
United Kingdom	5.0	18.8	2.0	5.6

[a] SITC 5–8.
[b] Textiles, apparel, and footwear (SITC 65 + 84 + 85).
Source: United Nations, *Commodity Trade Statistics.*

from countries well endowed with unskilled labor should lead to reduced wages for unskilled labor in the rich countries. Imports of manufactured goods from developing countries into Europe and North America, especially light manufactures such as clothing, shoes, and toys, increased sharply during the 1980s. Imports of all manufactured goods from developing countries into the OECD area increased by more than 13 percent a year in dollar value over the period 1980–1992, compared with an overall growth of 7.6 percent in the value of world trade in manufactures over the same period. In 1990 they accounted for over 4 percent of U.S. consumption of manufactured goods, up from 2 percent in 1980, and over 3 percent in the European Community, up from $2\frac{1}{2}$ percent. (Table 5 reports increased imports of manufactured goods from developing countries into the seven countries under examination here.) Can we attribute to these imports some portion of Europe's increased unemployment by adapting the simple Heckscher–Ohlin analytical framework with its assumption of full employment?

Much work has been done for the United States recently on the impact of import competition on increased wage dispersion during the 1980s, with the general conclusion that such impact has been small (Bound and Johnson, 1992; Revenga, 1992; Lawrence and Slaughter, 1993; Sachs and Shatz, 1994). This paper will supplement that work by focusing especially on unskilled labor, and hence on workers in textiles, apparel, and leather—the largest employers of unskilled labor in manufacturing—and on retail trade, the largest employer of unskilled labor among services. The analysis suggests that increased import competition from low wage countries can account for 10 percent of the relative decline in wages of U.S. unskilled workers during the 1980s. This number is not negligible, but it suggests that most of the explanation lies elsewhere.

The United States is believed to have a high degree of wage flexibility compared with some European economies; pressures that call for a decline in relative wages to assure full employment of unskilled labor may result in unemployment if for a variety of reasons the relevant wages do not decline. In particular, "rigidities" in the European labor market, either on the side of demand for labor or with respect to labor supply, might translate downward pressure on wages of unskilled workers into higher unemployment there. On the analysis here, however, it turns out that increased import competition from low-wage countries can explain only a small portion of Europe's higher unemployment.

IV The United States

Much analysis of the American labor market has taken the ratio of nonproduction to total workers in each industry to be an adequate measure of the degree of skill of the labor force in each industry (Lawrence and Slaughter, 1993; Sachs and Shatz, 1994). That might be so. But the argument runs that imports of goods produced by unskilled labor in developing countries such as Mexico or China have led to a depression in the wages of *unskilled* labor in the United States. Why not, then, look directly at unskilled labor, instead of at a very rough proxy for labor quality? Many production workers are in fact highly skilled, and many nonproduction workers do not have high skills.

An inspection of the wage profile of U.S. labor suggests that unskilled workers in manufacturing are concentrated in just a few industries: apparel ($7.05 per hour per production worker in early 1993), leather-working ($7.49), meat-processing, and to a lesser extent textiles ($8.81).[2] These compare with an average wage of $11.62 an hour for production workers in all manufacturing, and $13.82 an hour in the

---

[2] From U.S. Department of Labor, *Employments and Earnings*. This wage profile can also be observed in European countries. See Eurostat (1993), Table 3.41.

primary metals industry. Apparel workers accounted for 6.9 percent of the 12.34 million U.S. production workers in manufacturing in 1992 (down from 7.6 percent in 1980), textile workers for 4.7 percent, and leather- and meat-processing workers together for around three percent—altogether 1.88 million workers or about 15 percent.

Thus we will look closely at textile, apparel, and leather—TAL for short—industries with a high ratio of unskilled workers for which data are readily available. If wages of U.S. unskilled workers are being lowered by foreign trade with developing countries, the focus would have to be in these industries (low-skill meat-processing—slaughterhouses—is mainly a nontradable activity). We will compare 1980 with 1990, covering the decade of the 1980s, when wage growth was especially low and the drop in real wages of unskilled workers especially pronounced. The year 1980 involved a small recession, and the year 1990 involved a downturn during the fourth quarter; the overall unemployment rate was 7.0 percent in 1980 and 5.4 percent in 1990, rising to 6.7 percent in 1991. (The year 1980, however, experienced exceptionally high world oil prices, and that makes 1980 a bad year for comparison of overall trade levels and ratios—the value of world trade in fuels fell by 2.7 percent a year during 1980–1990. What follows will focus on trade in manufactured goods.)

U.S. imports of textiles and apparel grew rapidly throughout the 1980s, by 10 and 14 percent a year, respectively, in dollar value. Of course, the value of world trade in all manufactured goods also grew rapidly, by 8.3 percent a year between 1980 and 1990 in dollar value, and 5.7 percent in volume, twice the real growth of 2.9 percent in world manufacturing production. World trade in textiles grew a bit more slowly at 6.5 percent and clothing more rapidly at 10.2 percent. Thus U.S. imports of these products grew more rapidly than world imports. Imports of manufactured goods into North America from non-OECD regions grew at 14.1 percent a year, and, by 1992, imports from these regions accounted for 38 percent of U.S. imports of manufactured goods, up from 26 percent in 1980 (data from GATT, 1993).

The U.S. economy also grew during this period: the value of manufacturing output increased by 4.4 percent a year over the decade. Imports grew more rapidly, however, and imports from developing countries still more rapidly. By 1992 imports of manufactured goods from developing countries by value accounted for about 5.5 percent of U.S. consumption of manufactured goods, up from around 2 percent in 1980.

By 1992, imports of textiles from non-OECD countries accounted for 58 percent of total U.S. imports of textiles and 6 percent of apparent U.S. textile consumption. The corresponding figures for apparel were 92 percent and 28 percent.

Production of textiles grew throughout this period, by nearly 95 percent in (value-added) value and by six percent in volume; the corresponding figures for apparel were 95 percent and a mere 3.3 percent—this while total U.S. manufacturing was growing about 133 percent in value and 39 percent in volume.

The slow increase in production of textiles and apparel was reflected in employment. Total U.S. employment in manufacturing declined by 6 percent—1.2 million workers—between 1980 and 1990. Employment in TAL fell by 20 percent over the same period. In all, 40 percent of the decline in employment in manufacturing was in textiles, apparel, and leather, versus a 14 percent share of those sectors in 1980. Thus employment in manufacturing declined in general, reflecting a sharp increase in productivity over the decade, but employment in textiles and especially apparel fell even more, even though productivity in those two sectors grew considerably more slowly than in all of manufacturing.

Can these developments explain the increased wage dispersion in the United States over this period, and in particular the fact that wages of unskilled workers grew more slowly than the average wage, and even of the average wage of all production workers? Indeed, the wage of unskilled workers fell in real terms, by 10 percent, measuring price increases by the consumer price index for all urban consumers.

At this point it is tempting to introduce the Stolper–Samuelson theorem, which observes (under a number of assumptions) that trade liberalization will lead to a decline in the real wage of the factor of production used intensively in the sectors that compete with the increased imports. Imports of textiles and apparel increased substantially, absolutely and as a share of U.S. consumption, coming mainly from developing countries with lots of unskilled labor, and these sectors rely heavily on unskilled labor in the United States. Total labor content is relevant, not just labor directly employed by the sector; the main supplier to apparel is the low-skill textile sector, and the main supplier to textiles is the agricultural sector (for natural fibers) and the chemical sector (for synthetic fibers), plus machinery. Value-added in apparel is a higher ratio of the value of shipments than is typical for manufacturing, implying lower-than-average reliance on material inputs (but textiles is higher); and payroll is about 44 percent of value-added in both sectors, compared with 40 percent for all manufacturing (with only furniture and fabricated metal products being—modestly—higher), implying a lower-than-average reliance on capital.

The key assumptions underlying the Stolper–Samuelson theorem are that products be homogeneous with their production subject to constant returns to scale, that product and factor markets be competitive (implying prices reflect costs and each factor earns its marginal product), and that each product use intensively in its production a particular factor of production over the relevant range of prices. It is a long-run equilibrium theory, in that it focuses on relationships after both the structure of output and the techniques of production have been fully adapted to the initiating change, but assumes that the same products are produced both before and after the change.

Under these assumptions, there is a one-to-one relationship between commodity prices and factor prices, and between factor prices and factor-use ratios (techniques of production, K/L) in each of the commodities, as shown in Figure 1. There TAL is the industry that uses

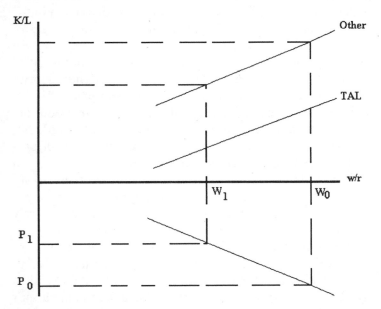

Figure 1. Relation between Commodity Prices, Factor Prices, and Techniques of Production.

unskilled labor intensively, relative to "Other" industries. w/r is the relative wage of unskilled labor, and p is the relative price of TAL goods, increasing from the origin.

The Stolper–Samuelson theorem presupposes that increased import competition, whatever its source (lower trade barriers, improved competitiveness abroad), leads to relatively lower prices for the import-competing goods. Indeed, it is the lower prices that compel the factor used intensively in those sectors to accept lower rewards, even in terms of the cheaper imports (through the so-called magnification effect, named by R.W. Jones [1979]). That is the force of the theorem. In Figure 1, p_0 declines to p_1 and restoration of equilibrium requires both a drop in the relative wage, from w_0 to w_1, and a relative increase in the use of unskilled labor in *both* industries (a drop in K_i/L_i, $i =$ TAL, other industries), indicated only for "Other" industries in Figure 1.[3]

Before we can apply Stolper–Samuelson as an explanation, therefore, we need to ask whether the relative prices of textiles and apparel in the United States fell over the 1980s. Here it is domestic prices, not import prices, that are relevant, since rewards to domestic factors of production are influenced by (in Stolper–Samuelson, determined by) the prices received for their production. Domestic prices are of course assumed to be related to the prices of competing imported goods. But a number of questions have been raised about the quality of import prices (see Sachs and Shatz, 1994). Since domestic prices are relevant anyway, we should look at them directly. Moreover, the domestic prices we should inspect are the prices of value-added in the sectors in question, not the output prices, since the latter will also reflect changes in prices of material inputs, fibers in the case of textiles and apparel. The substantial drop in oil prices over the decade suggests that the relative prices of petroleum-based synthetic fibers might have fallen, and that is indeed the case. Cotton prices, down 12 percent between 1980 and 1990, are also influenced by lower prices for fertilizer. Wages of

---

[3] The main findings of Lawrence and Slaughter (1993) that lead them to reject foreign trade as a major factor in explaining increased wage dispersion in the United States are that the relative prices of imported goods did not fall and that the ratio of skilled to unskilled labor (measured by the ratio of nonproduction to production workers) *rose* during the 1980s in most activities, whereas a relevant Stolper–Samuelson effect would have required a fall.

unskilled labor should be determined by the "price" of the activity of making textiles or apparel, i.e., the value-added prices.

What can we say about these prices, or, more accurately, the implicit deflators that represent the difference between growth in value and growth in volume of the value-added in textiles and apparel? They fell relative to the GDP deflator, but they rose relative to the deflator for all manufacturing, with textiles exceeding the latter by 15 percent and clothing by 14 percent over the decade. That is, the value-added prices of textiles and apparel increased relative to those of other tradable goods.[4] Insofar as factor prices are determined by the prices of tradable goods, therefore, as required by Stolper–Samuelson, the relative decline of wages for unskilled labor cannot be explained by the sharp increase in imports of textiles and especially apparel.

But maybe factor prices, particularly the price of unskilled labor, are not determined by the prices of tradables after all; only influenced by the patterns of trade. What is striking about the use of unskilled labor in the U.S. economy is that, while textiles and apparel use around 1.5 million unskilled workers, many more—17 million—are used in retail trade, clearly an activity without competition from abroad, except indirectly through the relatively small purchases by travelers. U.S. average wages of production workers in retail trade, at $7.26 an hour in early 1993, were barely above those in apparel, and substantially lower than the average wage in textiles. Some categories of retail trade showed considerably lower wages than the lowest reported wage category of apparel manufacturing (children's dresses and blouses, at $6.36 an hour)—car-washing, at $6.09 an hour, and eating and drinking places at $5.34 an hour, a number whose interpretation is complicated by the practice of tipping, the results of which are not reported in the wage.

---

[4] The relative rise in prices occurred despite a relative decline in labor costs because of lower-than-average increases in productivity in textile and apparel production over the decade.

Allowance, in principle, should also be made for tradable services. Services accounted for about 21 percent of world trade in goods and services in 1992. But price data for services are notoriously poor. Developing countries in 1991 accounted for 15 percent of world exports of services, mostly tourism, compared with 20 percent of world exports of manufactured goods.

Is it possible that the wages of unskilled workers are determined by their employment in the apparel industry, and hence by world prices for apparel, as required by the Stolper–Samuelson theorem? It is possible (see Leamer, 1987), but highly unlikely, given three considerations:

1. Production workers employed in apparel are less than 5.1 percent of those employed in retail trade, and the figure rises only to 9.1 percent if textile and leather workers are included (down from 14.9 percent in 1980).
2. The apparel industry is not free from protection, not only by relatively high tariffs (which would not affect the argument if they stood alone) but also by quantitative restrictions negotiated with exporting countries, product by product, under the auspices of the Multifiber Agreement (MFA), whenever a country's exports grow rapidly. Thus classical competitive conditions may not be satisfied, although as the rapid growth of total apparel imports suggests, they are not wholly absent either.
3. Unskilled workers are probably the most mobile factor in the nation, moving easily from industry to industry, so more severe import competition will fall in the first instance on the rewards to skilled workers and capital that are specialized in the production of apparel or textiles.

The wages of unskilled workers are thus likely to be determined by the demand for such workers in the nontrading sectors of the economy, mainly retail trade but also including substantial demand for such workers in hotels and restaurants, health care, and elsewhere. Foreign trade sectors such as textiles and apparel contribute to such demand, and thus influence the wage without however determining it, as in the Stolper–Samuelson framework. Cheap foreign goods (e.g., shoes, clothing) appeal to some consumers, so domestic production declines relative to what it otherwise would have been. But other consumers prefer the higher quality, higher priced domestic goods, and continue to buy them at the previous prices. Such goods are not homogeneous, as required by the Stolper–Samuelson theorem. Firms under increased competitive pressures from imports have an incentive to cut their production costs, but also to improve the quality of their output with a view to preserving some of their sales. Domestic output will fall but domestic prices may not fall, as we have observed. The released labor gets absorbed into the general economy, albeit perhaps at lower wages.

If this is so, the release of unskilled workers from textile and apparel production during the 1980s surely put downward pressure on the wage, regardless of what happened to domestic prices of textiles and apparel, by reducing overall demand for unskilled labor—or, put alternatively, by increasing the supply of unskilled labor to the nontradable sectors. What magnitude is involved? That requires specifying a counterfactual scenario. A plausible one is that leather, textiles, and apparel would have shed proportionately as many production workers over the period 1980–1990 as were shed by all manufacturing. The number of production workers in manufacturing other than those three sectors declined by 3.9 percent. Applying this ratio to 1980 production worker employment in textiles, apparel, and leather suggests a decline in those sectors by 91,000 production workers. This compares with the actual decline by 478,000, or an "excess" decline by 387,000 workers, to be absorbed elsewhere in the economy. Employment of production workers in retail trade, hotels, and restaurants grew by 6,150,000 workers over this period of time, from 21.4 million to 27.5 million. Thus the excess supply from textiles, apparel, and leather amounted to 1.4 percent of 1990 employment in retail trade, hotels, and restaurants.

In 1980 the average wage in retail trade (our proxy for the wage of unskilled workers) amounted to 73.3 percent of the average hourly wage of production workers in the total private economy ($6.66); by 1992 the average retail wage had fallen to 67.4 percent of the average hourly wage of production workers in the total private economy ($10.58). If the release of "excess" workers from textiles, apparel, and leather, relative to the counterfactual of those sectors being typical of all manufacturing, is assumed to reduce the wages of unskilled workers by 5.9 percent of the average private sector wage of production workers (= 8.0 percent of their initial relative wage), the implied elasticity of demand for unskilled labor in the retail sector is 0.175 (= 0.014/0.08), which seems implausibly low.

This calculation assumes that all of the workers displaced from these three sectors were absorbed into the retail sector, i.e., that they did not withdraw from the labor force or become unemployed, an assumption that is plausible given the large size, wide geographic distribution, and considerable growth of the retail sector. At the reduced wage, some workers may however have withdrawn from the labor force. Such withdrawal would lower further the demand elasticity calculated above. For instance, if the elasticity of supply of unskilled labor is 0.1, the implied elasticity of demand calculated above would be only 0.075. Of course, release of unskilled workers from other manufacturing sectors would increase it.

This calculation imputes the entire reduction in relative wages of unskilled workers to their excess supply in textiles, apparel, and leather, implicitly in turn due to stiff import competition from developing countries in those sectors. It thus ignores the other various reasons why demand for unskilled labor might have declined, implicit in the general rise over the decade in the ratio of nonproduction workers, and why such adjustments might have fallen disproportionately on manufacturing sectors that use unskilled labor heavily.

The elasticity of demand for labor is determined not only by the possibilities for substituting unskilled labor for other factors of production—skilled labor and capital—but also by the increased demand for retail services induced by their lower cost. If we assume that retail purchases face a unitary elasticity of demand and that the wage bill averages 25 percent of retail sales, then a ten percent drop in wages in retail trade would increase the volume of sales by 2.5 percent, i.e., a derived demand elasticity for unskilled labor of 0.25.

Katz and Murphy (1992, p. 72) estimate, with assumptions in which they do not have high confidence, an economy-wide elasticity of substitution between college and high school graduates of 1.41. Thus a drop in the relative wage of high school graduates by ten percent would increase demand for them by 14 percent. Factor substitution and stimulus to total demand are additive considerations provided total expenditures remain unchanged, implying an elasticity of demand for unskilled labor on the order of $0.25 + 1.41 = 1.66$. If that is so, an increase in supply of unskilled labor by 1.4 percent would depress wages by 0.8 percent, or 10 percent of the observed decline. That leaves 90 percent of the decline to be explained by other factors.[5]

---

[5] Adrian Wood (1994) provides a substantially larger estimate of the impact of imports from developing countries on employment in the rich countries. His is a highly sophisticated analysis on the basis of weak data combined with thoughtful judgments. But it involves a serious methodological flaw. Wood uses production in developing countries to determine the labor content of their exports. He then adjusts these labor coefficients of developing countries to allow for more expensive labor in rich countries to estimate the labor that is displaced in the rich countries by imports from developing countries.

Wood neglects to allow for the likelihood, however, that the resulting high labor content, if paid rich country wages, would price most manufactured products

V   Application to Europe

The wage structure in Western Europe is similar to that in the United States: the lowest paid workers in manufacturing are in apparel, leather-working, and textiles; and, outside manufacturing, in retail trade, hotels, and restaurants. As in the United States, employment in the latter activities greatly exceeds those in the TAL industries. As in the United States, women are employed in a high proportion in the TAL industries within manufacturing, and in retail trade, hotels, and restaurants. And as in the United States, imports of textiles and especially clothing rose rapidly during the 1980s, by 8.1 and 9.4 percent a year, respectively, in dollar value, despite import restrictions under the Multifiber Agreement, and employment in the domestic TAL industries fell more rapidly than in manufacturing generally, while employment rose in retail trade.[6]

We can apply the same counterfactual assumption that we used for the United States: in the absence of increased imports from low-wage countries, employment in the TAL industries would have followed the course of employment in manufacturing generally, yielding the "excess" decline in TAL employment attributable to import competition from low-wage countries, which can then be related to employment in retail trade and to total unemployment.[7]

---

from developing countries out of the market completely, i.e., demand for those products would drop to zero. Consumers would instead buy substitutes made in the rich countries, of course using labor coefficients of the rich countries. Thus Wood greatly exaggerates the labor displacement by imports from developing countries. Modern technology may be available everywhere, as Wood assumes; but it is certainly not *used* everywhere, and it is the technology actually used that determines the high labor coefficients in developing countries on which Wood draws.

[6] Unlike in the United States, however, the value-added deflator for the TAL industries seems to have fallen slightly relative to all manufacturing, by 1.3 percent in France and 4.5 percent in Germany over the decade 1980–1990.

[7] Of course, in a general equilibrium framework we would also have to allow for the stimulus to exports of manufactured goods generated by higher imports of manufactures from low-wage countries. But we are assuming employment of unskilled workers in other manufacturing sectors is negligible, so increases in exports of their products would have a negligible direct effect on the demand for unskilled workers. Increases in real incomes would, however, increase retail sales, hence demand for unskilled labor into that sector.

Table 6. "Excess" Decline in Employment in Textiles, Apparel, and Leather, 1980–1990[a].

	Number ('000)	In Relation to 1990		Decline in Relative Wages of Unskilled Workers[d]	
		Total Unemployment	Employment in Retail Trade[b] (%)	War-ranted[c] (%)	Actual (%)
United States	387	5.6	1.4	0.8	8.0
France	136	6.2	3.6	2.2	1.3
Germany	249	13.2	5.5	3.3	6.6
Italy	8	0.2	0.2	0.1	10.0[e]
Netherlands	24	4.4	2.2	1.3	6.3
Spain	54	2.2	2.1	1.3	3.8
United Kingdom	44	2.8	1.0	0.6	6.6

[a] See text for calculations of "excess" decline in TAL employment.
[b] Including hotels and restaurants.
[c] By a demand elasticity of 1.66. See text.
[d] Retail trade for United States and Spain; apparel workers for other European countries.
[e] 1988–1991.
Source: Calculations using OECD, *Labor Force Statistics*; U.S. Department of Labor, *Employment and Earnings*; Eurostat, *Basic Statistics of the European Community*, 1993; ISTAT, *Compendio Statistica Italiano*, 1992, Banca de España, *Boletin Estadistico*, July 1986 and October 1992.

Table 6 sets out the results of these calculations. The first column shows the "excess" decline in TAL employment over the 1980s. The second column reports this as a share of total unemployment in 1990, a figure that ranges from 0.2 percent in Italy to 12 percent in the case of Germany. The third column shows the ratio of such "excess" decline in employment to total employment in the retail trade, hotel, and restaurant activities in 1990—the sector that would be expected to absorb most of those displaced from the TAL industries. The fourth column applies the elasticity of demand for unskilled labor of 1.66 used above for the United States to the European countries, indicating the decline in relative wages that would be required to reemploy the excess released labor in the retail sector, ranging from 0.1 percent in Italy to 3.3 percent in Germany. A final column reports the decline in relative wages that actually took place in apparel (average retail wages were not available for all European countries, but I assume comparable declines occurred there), relative to all manufacturing, over the 1980s. It suggests that, apart from France, wages fell sufficiently to absorb the excess labor released from the TAL industries. In particular, the relative wages of unskilled labor on this measure declined by more than 6 percent in four major European countries, compared with 8 percent in the United States. Thus on this line of reasoning, import competition from low-wage countries led to increased unemployment only in France among the seven countries. French (relative) wages for unskilled workers did not decline sufficiently to absorb the displaced labor, perhaps as a result of the highly centralized and structured wage bargaining that occurs there, or because of France's very high minimum wage.

Of course, the responsiveness of employment of unskilled labor to changes in wages may be different in European countries from the United States. In particular, the elasticity of substitution between skilled and unskilled workers might be lower, while the derived demand for labor in retail trade may be modestly higher. If the overall elasticity is 1.0 (instead of 1.66 used above), column 3 of Table 6 gives the "warranted" decline in relative wages of unskilled workers. The generalizations above continue to hold, although in this case over 80 percent (5.5/6.6) of the relative wage decline observed in Germany can be attributed to workers released from the TAL industries.

Two institutional factors may influence the responsiveness of employment, one affecting the demand for the labor, one the supply of labor. With respect to *demand*, if the decline in wages required to sustain reemployment of the displaced labor drops below a statutory or conventional minimum wage, the (legal) demand for labor becomes inelastic at that point and some displaced labor will remain unemployed. This factor may have been important especially in France, where, as noted above, the actual drop in the relative wage of unskilled workers did not reach that "required" to reemploy the labor. France has an exceptionally high minimum wage, 5,756 francs a month in early 1994, or over $6.40 an hour at an exchange rate of 5.3 francs per dollar. Heavy social charges in excess of 40 percent raise the wage to over $9 an hour for the employer, nearly twice what it was in the

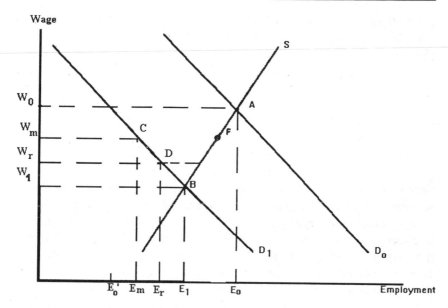

Figure 2. The Market for Unskilled Labor.

United States. One study suggested that the minimum wage did not generally affect French adult employment from the mid-1960s to the mid-1980s, but it did have a modest negative effect on youth employment (Bazen and Martin, 1991). An effort by the French government in early 1994 to reduce the minimum wage for young workers met strong political resistance and was abandoned.[8]

Figure 2 illustrates the point analytically. Suppose as a result of increased imports demand for unskilled workers (e.g., in the TAL industries) shifts downward from D_0 to D_1. The market-clearing wage will then drop from w_0 to w_1. At the lower wage, w_1, some workers will withdraw from the labor market (i.e., the supply schedule, S, is not

---

[8] Statutory minimum wages exist in the United States and Spain, but they are relatively low. A high minimum wage—63 percent of the median wage in 1992—exists in the Netherlands, but teenagers can be hired below that minimum. In Germany and Italy negotiated wages are extended by law to the rest of the economy, so wage minima are numerous and complex. The United Kingdom has no statutory minimum wage, although the Labour Party endorsed one in 1994.

completely vertical), but the lower wage will also increase the demand for labor on the new demand schedule, D_1, from E_0' to E_1. If, however, the new market-clearing wage, w_1, is below a statutory minimum wage, w_m, demand ends at the point C, employment will drop to E_m, and unemployment will rise by the segment CF.[9]

Labor *supply* will be influenced by the alternatives available to the displaced workers. In Europe these include unemployment compensation and social welfare payments. If the new market-clearing wage (w_1 in Figure 2) is too low, workers will voluntarily remain unemployed, or go onto welfare, rather than accept the lower wage, i.e., their reservation wage will exceed the wage that would reemploy the displaced workers. In terms of Figure 2, the supply schedule, influenced by unemployment compensation or social welfare entitlements, becomes horizontal at the reservation wage, w_r. In this case employment will drop from E_0 to E_r where the effective supply schedule crosses the new demand schedule at D. Whether the displaced workers are recorded as unemployed or as having withdrawn from the labor force depends on the precise reasons for the high reservation wage and the exact protocol for measuring unemployment, in particular whether able-bodied persons receiving welfare payments are counted as unemployed.

Unemployment compensation and social welfare entitlements vary from country to country, but some countries are very generous, both in terms of amount and in terms of duration. For example, in the mid-1980s unemployment benefits amounting to 80 percent of the last wage could be received for six months in Spain, followed by supplementary benefits of gradually declining amounts for another three years.[10] Benefits of 70 percent of the wage were available for $2\frac{1}{2}$ years in the Netherlands, followed by social benefits of a lower amount available for an indefinite period (Layard, Nickell, and Jackman, 1994, Table

---

[9] In 1983 the U.S. minimum wage was applied to Puerto Rico, a much lower wage market. The ratio of the minimum wage to the average wage became 63 percent, compared with 34 percent in the United States. Castillo-Freeman and Freeman (1992, p. 186) estimate that this change reduced employment in Puerto Rico by nine percent. The impact on the unemployment rate was not determinate, since some of the displaced workers withdrew from the labor force, and others migrated to the United States.

[10] In 1992 the initial "replacement ratio" was reduced to 70 percent followed by 60 percent thereafter. See Banca de Espana, *Monthly Bulletin*, Feb. 1994, p. 35.

A1). Generous amounts were also available in Germany and France. An unskilled metal worker with two children could receive through social assistance the equivalent of 95 percent of his after tax disposable income from employment in Germany, for instance, and an unmarried retail employee with one child could receive 82 percent of her disposable income from employment. Britain and the United States were less generous. In the United States, for instance, unemployment benefits amount to about half of previous pay and last only 26 weeks, unless extended by special legislation, as it normally is in periods of overall recession. U.S. reemployment rates have been shown to rise sharply after unemployment compensation is exhausted (Pedersen and Westergård-Nielsen, 1993).

Displaced workers may prefer to find new jobs initially, but if they cannot find a job soon they adapt their expenditures to the income available and reduce their search for a new job, which requires effort and is often psychologically disheartening. Except for France, most or all of the increase in unemployment in our six European countries between 1979 and 1990 was persons who were unemployed for more than one year.

On a cross-section analysis of 20 countries over 1983–1988, Layard, Nickell, and Jackman (1994, p. 82) estimate that a one-year increase in duration of unemployment benefits increases unemployment by 0.92 percentage points, and each ten-percentage-point increase in the "replacement rate" (i.e., the ratio of benefits to wage) raises unemployment by 1.7 percentage points, with a high degree of statistical reliability. Thus unemployment seems to be quite sensitive to public policies to mitigate its hardships—generous mitigation, not surprisingly, increases unemployment. Of course, the unemployment benefit payments also may contribute to aggregate demand, and thus may also to some extent increase the demand for labor through that channel. The magnitude of this effect, if any, will depend upon the overall fiscal policy of each country.

VI Conclusions

This paper has considered four different channels whereby foreign trade might influence employment: macroeconomic imbalance, increased trade penetration, accelerated change in the structure of comparative advantage, and impact on factor prices combined with factor price rigidities. It found none of these channels to be a significant influence on the substantial rise of European unemployment during the 1980s, although some marginal impact might be attributed to one or another channel in the case of particular countries. Increased imports of manufactured goods from low-income developing countries have plausibly put downward pressure on the relative wages of unskilled workers, accounting on rough estimate for about ten percent of the relative decline in the United States over the 1980s. But wage flexibility has been sufficient in most of the seven countries examined to prevent this downward pressure from translating into involuntary unemployment, the exception being France.

Bibliography

Bazen, S., and J. Martin. 1991. "The Effect of the Minimum Wage on Employment and Earnings in France, 1963–85." *OECD Economic Studies* 16 (Spring).

Bhagwati, J., and M.H. Kosters (eds.). 1994. *Trade and Wages*. Washington, D.C.: American Enterprise Institute.

Bean, C.R. 1994. "European Unemployment: A Survey." *Journal of Economic Literature* 32:573–620.

Bound, J., and G. Johnson. 1992. "Changes in the Structure of Wages in the 1980s: An Evaluation of Alternative Explanations." *American Economic Review* 82 (June): 371–392.

Castillo-Freeman, A.J., and R.B. Freeman. 1992. "When the Minimum Wage Really Bites: The Effect of the US-Level Minimum on Puerto Rico." In: G.J. Borjas and R.B. Freeman (eds.), *Immigration and the Work Force*. Chicago: University of Chicago Press.

Cline, W.R. 1987. *The Future of World Trade in Textiles and Apparel*. Washington, D.C.: Institute for International Economics.

Drèze, J.H., and C.R. Bean (eds.). 1990. *Europe's Unemployment Problem*. Cambridge, Mass.: MIT Press.

Ethier, W.J. 1984. "Higher Dimensional Issues in Trade Theory." In: R.W. Jones and P.B. Kenen (eds.), *Handbook of International Economics*, Vol. 1. Amsterdam: North-Holland.

Eurostat. 1993. *Basic Statistics*, 1993. Luxembourg.

GATT (General Agreement on Tariffs and Trade). 1993. *International Trade 1993: Statistics*. Geneva.

Gregory, M., and V. Sandoval. 1994. "Low Pay and Minimum Wage Protection in Britain and the EC." In: R. Barrell (ed.), *The UK Labour Market*. Cambridge: Cambridge University Press.

Jones, R.W. 1979. *International Trade: Essays in Theory*. Amsterdam: North-Holland.

Katz, L.F., and K.M. Murphy. 1992. "Changes in Relative Wages, 1963–1987: Supply and Demand Factors." *Quarterly Journal of Economics* 107 (February): 35–78.

Krugman, P. 1994. "Europe Jobless, America Penniless?" *Foreign Policy* 95 (Summer): 19–34.

Lawrence, R.Z. 1994a. "The Impact of Trade on OECD Labor Markets." Occasional Paper 45. Washington, D.C.: Group of Thirty.

Lawrence, R.Z. 1994b. "Trade, Multinationals, & Labor." June, processed.

Lawrence, R.Z., and M.J. Slaughter. 1993. "International Trade and American Wages in the 1980s: Giant Sucking Sound or Small Hiccup?" *Brookings Papers: Microeconomics* 2:161–226.

Layard, R., S. Nickell, and R. Jackman. 1994. *The Unemployment Crisis*. London: Oxford University Press.

Leamer, E.E. 1987. "Paths of Development in the Three-factor, n-Good General Equilibrium Model." *Journal of Political Economy* 85 (October): 961–999.

Levy, F., and R.J. Murnane. 1992. "US Earnings Levels and Earnings Inequality: A Review of Recent Trends and Proposed Explanations." *Journal of Economic Literature* 30 (September): 1333–1382.

Murphy, K.M., and F. Welch. 1992. "The Structure of Wages." *Quarterly Journal of Economics* 107 (February): 285–326.

OECD. 1993. *Employment Outlook*. July. Paris: OECD.

Pedersen, P.J., and N. Westergård-Nielsen. 1993. "Unemployment: A Review of the Evidence from Panel Data." *OECD Economic Studies* 20 (Spring): 65–114.

Pelkmans, J. 1993. "Opening Up the Euro-Market for Textiles." CEPS Paper No.54. Brussels: Center for European Policy Studies.

Revenga, A.L. 1992. "Exporting Jobs: The Impact of Import Competition on Employment and Wages in U.S. Manufacturing." *Quarterly Journal of Economics* 107 (February): 255–284.

Sachs, J.D., and H.J. Shatz. 1994. "Trade and Jobs in U.S. Manufacturing." *Brookings Papers on Economic Activity* 1:1–84.

Stolper, F.W., and P.A. Samuelson. 1941. "Protection and Real Wages." *Review of Economic Studies* 9 (November): 58–73.

Wood, A. 1994. *North–South Trade, Employment and Inequality: Changing Fortunes in a Skill-Driven World*. Oxford: Clarendon Press.

Unemployment and the Crisis of the German Model: A Long-Term Interpretation

Karl-Heinz Paqué

Germany
E24
J53
P17

This paper presents an account of the reasons why the so-called German model finds itself in a serious and persistent crisis. The main point of the paper is that there are powerful long-term forces changing the structure of the German economy in a way that is at odds with the egalitarian philosophy of German-style collective wage bargaining and the relevant provisions of the welfare state. With appropriate qualifications, the point may equally apply to other European countries with a similarly constructed set of "corporatist" labor market institutions.

In essence, the paper is no more than an evaluative survey of arguments that draws heavily on ideas and pieces of empirical evidence scattered in the relevant literature. It consists of three parts: Section I gives a definition of what the term "crisis" can and should mean with respect to a system of collective bargaining; Section II elaborates the main line of reasoning that underlies the diagnosis of a crisis; and Section III draws policy conclusions concerning whether and possibly how industrial relations and the welfare state could be adjusted to meet the emerging challenges without a complete dismantling of what is commonly known as the German model.

I Defining the Term "Crisis"

Applied to a system or practice of collective wage bargaining, the term *crisis* may have two different meanings, a positive and a normative one.

Thanks are due to the participants of this symposium—notably to Richard Freeman, Michael Burda, Richard Cooper, Patrick Minford, and Charles Wyplosz—for valuable comments. The author is also grateful to Alfred Boss for suggestions on an earlier draft of this paper.

In the *positive* sense, the system is in a crisis if an ever-increasing share of all wage agreements in an economy is determined outside the system, i.e., if the system is increasingly deserted by its traditional members and/or bypassed by fast-growing competition from nonmembers. In the *normative* sense, the system is in a crisis if its very functioning leads to a persistent violation of some generally accepted political, economic, or social goal that is impossible or at least very costly to redress by taking any compensatory policy measures.

In the positive sense, the German bargaining system has been remarkably stable over the almost half a century of post–World War II labor market history:[1] not only its constituent legal principles and institutional practices,[2] but also its main economic characteristics have survived quite different unemployment regimes. The basic system can be characterized as a model of regionalized industrial bargaining—involving regional negotiations and agreements between the relevant industrial union and employers' association in an industry, roughly speaking on the level of states (*Länder*). About a quarter of all collective agreements are concluded on a company basis; on the other hand, some industries like construction and printing have (quasi-)nationwide agreements. In theory, the existence of roughly 800 (sectoral and regional) bargaining districts and a large number of company-specific agreements allows for a high degree of structural wage flexibility, but the long-standing wage leadership of metal manufacturing in some major bargaining district (nowadays typically northern Baden-Württemberg) has secured a rather uniform growth of wages across sectors and regions.[3] Hence, though not formally centralized, the German bargaining system is—and has always been—highly synchronized.

Outsider competition with the system has remained very limited in the past: while the share of union members among employees never surpassed 40 percent over any longer period of time, it was, above all,

---

[1] With some minor qualifications, most national bargaining systems in continental European countries have remained quite stable over this period. For a rich survey of the relevant systems and their development over time in all major industrial countries, see the various contributions in Hartog and Theeuwes (1993).

[2] For details on these, see Paqué (1993a, pp. 214–224).

[3] For econometric evidence on the intertemporal stability of the relevant wage structure in Germany and its rigidity with respect to sectorally and/or regionally concentrated labor market shocks, see Paqué (mimeo) and Burda and Mertens (1994).

the high degree of organization among *employers* which ensured that most wage contracts in western Germany were the outcome of collective bargaining. A rough guess is that, in western Germany, about two-thirds of all employers are members of some employers' association, and that nine out of ten employees work on terms fixed in some collective agreement.[4] Basically, all the sectors of the western German economy—with the exception of parts of retail trade and household (and related) services, which employ a predominantly female labor force—have had collective agreements throughout the postwar period; thus the distinction between "unionized" and "nonunionized" sectors or firms, which is used in the literature on American labor markets as an analytical means to estimate "union relative wage effects" (see, e.g., Lewis, 1986), makes no real sense in the German context.

It is a most remarkable fact that neither the high unemployment of the early 1950s nor the rise of unemployment in the 1970s and early 1980s and its subsequent persistence at historically high levels has destabilized the system in the sense that many established or new firms found it profitable to quit or stay out of the employers' associations and hire unemployed persons at subcontractual wage levels. As there are, in principle, no major *legal* obstacles to doing this[5], there is at present no real reason to speak of a collective bargaining crisis in the positive sense mentioned above, at least not as concerns western Germany. For the eastern part of the country, the situation may become somewhat different in due course: with factual rates of under-employment of 20–30 percent (including various forms of hidden unemployment not counted in the official unemployment statistics),[6] outsider competition may reach new dimensions and thus pose a more serious threat to the stability of the system. Recent polls on the degree

---

[4] See Paqué (1993a, p. 217), who quotes estimates provided by the Federation of German Employers' Associations. Note that the statistical basis of these estimates is remarkably poor: no systematic polls or surveys are conducted on a regular or even occasional basis in order to verify the numbers.

[5] Under certain restrictive conditions, collective agreements can be extended to third parties by a declaration of the Federal Minister of Labor (for details, see Paqué, 1993a, pp. 218–220). However, there are good reasons to suspect that this legal option, which is rarely used in practice, has *not* been a decisive threat and thus cannot be held responsible for the conspicuous lack of outsider competition. I shall return to this matter below in Section III.

[6] See Paqué (1993b) for various measures of this kind.

of employer organization and on the frequency of subcontractual payment practices in eastern Germany seem to support such a conjecture.[7] For the time being, however, this remains a matter of speculation because the information provided by the polls is still very shaky.

In any case, any claim that there is a crisis in the collective bargaining system must be based mainly on normative, not on positive, grounds: while it is still essentially stable, the system may not be able to prevent, or may even lead to, persistent unemployment.

II   Structural Change and Unemployment in the Long Run

In the 1980s there was a boom in research into the causes of unemployment. In view of the stepwise increase of the unemployment rate that most European countries had experienced in the (then) recent past, the natural focus of this research lay first on the specific supply and demand shocks that led to the rise of unemployment, and then on the asymmetric forces that supported its persistence well after the relevant shock.[8] This research lacked what might be called a *historical dimension*: usually, the econometric testing grounds for subjecting the theories to empirical scrutiny were time series stretching back to no earlier than the 1960s, and cross-section and panel data of most recent vintage. The informational content of the important time-series dimension was thus restricted to basically two major historical events, namely, the two oil price hikes in 1973–1974 and around 1980, supplemented by the respective subsequent recessions in 1974–1975 and 1981–1983. This rather narrow focus gave the relevant research a high degree of empirical coherence and theoretical subtlety: crude early notions of "Keynesian" demand gaps and "neoclassical" wage gaps as explanations of unemployment gave way to more sophisticated theories of shock persistence and hysteresis as a consequence of physical capital shortage, of insider/outsider-wage determination, and of declining search intensity among the long-term unemployed.

---

[7] See DIW and IfW (1994, Table 1). Note, however, that the methodology of these polls does not ensure their being representative in a strict statistical sense.

[8] A by now classical example of the first type of research is Bruno and Sachs (1985); major examples of the second type—among them the seminal papers Blanchard and Summers (1986) and Lindbeck and Snower (1986)—are reprinted in Cross (1988) and Lindbeck and Snower (1988).

On the other hand, hardly any attempt was made to find more fundamental reasons, such as specific long-term trends in economic growth and structural change, for the observed facts. In my view, this rather narrow focus is most unfortunate because it may stand in the way of a more comprehensive assessment of the deeper challenge that is associated with the observed changes in labor market regimes, say, from the 1950s and 1960s to the 1970s and 1980s (and beyond). In the following subsections, I present such an assessment.

A   The Emergence of Unemployment

Historically, the perception that unemployment is a well-defined economic phenomenon and a social and political problem is closely linked to the twin process of industrialization and urbanization. Although it is difficult to identify the precise periods of time and geographical places in which unemployment first emerged and was understood in the modern sense of the term as *involuntary idleness*, it is probably a good guess to locate its birth in the course of the 19th century in the leading industrializing countries, i.e., in Britain and the United States, and somewhat later in Germany and its western neighbors France, Belgium, and the Netherlands. A well-known historical case study on the matter (Keyssar, 1986) comes to the uncontroversial conclusion[9] that in a particular region—the state of Massachusetts—unemployment in the modern sense became a fact of social life during the rapid urban and industrial growth that took place between, say, the first and the last quarter of the 19th century. With respect to the reason for the emergence of unemployment, it is worth recalling the words of a prominent economic and social historian:

At the beginning of the nineteenth century, industrial work ... was combined in close geographic and institutional proximity to domestic work and agriculture. It tended to be done in small household-based workshops or put out to farmers. Thus, when industrial activity was slack, industrial workers simply shifted to farm tasks or household maintenance; when demand picked up, they shifted back to industrial activity. In the course of the century, however, work moved off the farms and out of the household into factories that were separated socially, geographically, and institutionally. When factory work fell off, workers could not

---

[9] See the approving review by Piore (1987).

therefore easily shift. They were without a job and finding something else to do involved a distinct effort, a recognizable period of time and social space. That space came to be referred to as unemployment. (Piore, 1987, p. 1839)

Hence the emergence of unemployment in the modern sense can be traced back to a specific form of structural change that can best be described in a two-sector model of an economy consisting of a primary sector ("agriculture") and a secondary sector ("manufacturing"). In this model of stylized "industrialization," an (exogenous) technical progress leads to a sharp rise in capital intensity, labor productivity, and the wage in the secondary sector. Because of the specific characteristics of production in that sector, however, the wage rise goes along with a sharp rise in the costs of intersectoral mobility, a cost that consists of all pecuniary, as well as all social and psychological, costs of moving to a different region and adjusting from a rural to a fast-growing urban environment. It is the rise in the mobility cost that tends to make the reallocation of labor between the two sectors largely irreversible, a form of definite one-way migration. While the prospect of a permanently and substantially higher wage in manufacturing employment makes it profitable for workers to incur the cost of moving from agriculture to manufacturing, layoffs in manufacturing do not lead to a symmetrical movement back to agriculture: in an era of long-term "industrialization," layoffs will by definition be cyclical, so that workers can expect to be back in (comparatively well-paid) manufacturing employment within a relatively short period of time, which they can survive in a state of "waiting," i.e., of genuine unemployment.

Analytically, one may thus say that unemployment in the modern sense of the term presupposes the existence of at least one sector that pays relatively high wages and that is reasonably well separated from the rest of the economy by a barrier posed by the high costs of inter-sectoral mobility. As long as this sector does not exist, there can only be an "underutilization" of labor in the sense that the workers would switch to different, better-paid jobs if these were available. Even this idea of "underutilization" has its narrow limits: it only makes sense if the alternative jobs can realistically be considered to define the standard of normal employment and the taking of inferior jobs to be a temporary deviation; if "underutilization" is permanent, however, it becomes a mere euphemistic description of (relative) poverty. In fact, when taking a historical perspective of the labor market, one may describe the very process of industrialization in the 19th century as the transformation of the economy from a state of "poverty-cum-full-employment" into a state of "prosperity-cum-unemployment," with unemployment here meaning temporary involuntary idleness.[10]

For Germany—as for all other countries that industrialized during the 19th century—most of that century remains a statistical blank space with respect to the actual extent of unemployment in the modern sense. Only for the time after 1887 is some information available, namely, figures on unemployment among union members. They indicate that, by today's standards, full employment prevailed in Germany at least until World War I, with an average unemployment rate of roughly 2.4 percent for union members in 1887–1913 and brief cyclical peaks of 6–7 percent in two recessions (1892, 1901).[11] In terms of a "modern" definition of unemployment, i.e., in terms of the share of unemployed persons in the total labor force, these numbers probably mean an average unemployment rate of not much more than 1 percent and recession peaks of 3–4 percent, which comes close to the conditions of the 1960s, the decade generally regarded as the "golden age of full

---

[10] In this respect, there is a strong parallel in the emergence of unemployment between 19th-century Europe and America, on the one hand, and the Third World today on the other: in developing countries, the only usable definition of unemployment one can make applies only to the highly urbanized regions, where there is no easy substitution between agricultural and industrial work. Typically, migrants from rural areas who realize that well-paid work can be found in urban centers crowd into the slums of fast-growing cities, "waiting" for the opportunity to find a relatively well-paid industrial job. Qualitatively, this is the same process that occurred in 19th-century Europe and America; however, due to its quantitative dynamics—notably the extremely fast and apparently self-reinforcing pattern of migration from rural to urban areas—the process seems to lead, on average, to somewhat higher equilibrium unemployment rates in the Third World today than was the case in 19th-century Europe and America. All this is highly conjectural because the relevant statistical information is very poor indeed. For an empirical survey of unemployment in developing countries, see Turnham and Eröcal (1990).

[11] Own calculation with data from Mitchell (1981, p. 175), whose figures for 1903–1913 are based on official union statistics published by the Imperial Statistical Office in its annual yearbooks (Statistisches Reichsamt, various issues), and for 1887–1903 on estimates by Kuczynski (1962, p. 260; 1967, p. 315), who also uses union records as the basis for his calculations. See also Hentschel (1983, p. 104) and Faust (1982, p. 257).

employment."[12] Hence, while unemployment became a phenomenon separate from poverty during the industrialization of the German economy, it remained a purely *cyclical* phenomenon, with no traces of persistence over longer periods.[13]

Why was this so? Seen from a bird's-eye view, a combination of two reasons stands out. First, there were only very modest systems of unemployment insurance that were run by various unions for their members and partly subsidized on a rather small scale by some local governments. While they provided a bare minimum of short-term emergency aid to alleviate the effects of unemployment on living standards, they certainly did not lay the economic ground for any extended phases of job search. Hence, finding a job quickly after being laid off remained of existential importance to the vast majority of

---

[12] As proxies for the economy-wide unemployment rate, the figures on unemployment among union members are likely to reflect two biases that pulled in opposite directions. The upward bias was constituted by union membership having been almost exclusively restricted to the industrial work force, which was that part of the labor force with the highest incidence of unemployment in the modern sense (as argued in the text above). The downward bias was constituted by union membership, within the industrial work force, having contained a disproportionately high share of skilled labor that usually had a lower rate of unemployment than unskilled labor. Given the large share of agricultural employment in the German economy still present at the outset of the First World War (38 percent in 1913 according to the national accounts provided by Hoffmann [1965, p. 205]), it is reasonable to assume that the upward bias dominated the downward bias. An estimate by Maddison (1991, Table C 6, p. 260) of unemployment as a share of the total labor force for Germany in the 1920s (see Table 1 of this paper's appendix) indicates that the unemployment rate of union members usually overstated that of the total labor force by slightly more than 100 percent. If this is assumed to hold for imperial times as well, the relevant average unemployment rate was roughly 1 percent.

[13] Despite the statistical lacunae, casual historical evidence indicates that this statement is also true for the two decades before 1887. After the *Gründerzeitboom* following German unification, there was a sharp business downturn in the mid-1870s, which led to a hefty increase in emigration and, according to one very crude estimate, to a rise of the unemployment rate up to 20 percent (Mottek, 1966, p. 102). However, time-series data on unemployment in selected groups of union members (notably printers) indicates that, by 1880, unemployment had apparently reached more or less the known level after 1887; other indicators point in the same direction. For details, see Kuczynski (1962, pp. 262–263).

workers.[14] Second, the forces of structural change as driven by the income elasticities of product demand, technological progress, and newly emerging patterns of international trade were pulled in a direction that favored a smooth labor market adjustment. Notably, the fast growth in employment in industry at the expense of (low-productivity) agriculture and high-productivity branches like iron and steel, metal manufacturing, electrical engineering, and the chemical industry ensured that structural change proceeded "voluntarily": workers—skilled and unskilled—who were forced to change jobs because of a spell of unemployment were likely to find a better paid alternative somewhere else in the economy fairly soon. In this respect, industrial growth led to a potential *revaluation* of the labor force that could be transformed into wage increases by a competitive labor demand pull, even without resort to collective bargaining, which still played only a minor role in wage determination.

B Collective Bargaining and Unemployment Insurance

The interwar period brought two important institutional innovations: collective wage bargaining and compulsory unemployment insurance. The decisive "displacement effect" from a basically free labor market to a collective bargaining system on a broad scale took place during the First World War, but the organizational roots on the unions' and the employers' side can be traced back to the 1890s, partly even back to the 1860s.[15] During the first half of the 1920s, the legal framework and the "culture" for today's industry-based bargaining was laid. Although most unions were still crafts-based, in the major branches of industry a bargaining system that was factually industry-based began

---

[14] On union-run unemployment insurance schemes in imperial times, see Risch (1983, pp. 176–196). Although the schemes varied greatly between different unions with respect to contribution and benefit rules, they were all very modest by modern standards. Official union statistics show that, in the 10-year period 1904–1913, roughly one-half of all unemployed union members received benefits; in the same period, the average duration of a completed spell of unemployment was about 17 days, with very little variation over time (own calculations with data from Statistisches Reichsamt [various issues]).

[15] On the history of collective bargaining in imperial times, see Moses (1982, Vol. I).

to emerge. For example, metal workers, who at times accounted for up to 30 percent of all union members in the Weimar republic, were organized in the "German Metal Workers Union" (the predecessor of the IG Metall and at the time already the largest single industrial union in the world), which was founded in 1891 as an industrial union and carried out its collective bargaining consistently on an industry-wide basis. The backbone of this union (as of all others) was skilled workers, who made up about two-thirds of the membership, but actual negotiations covered all skill groups (including unskilled and semiskilled workers). Formally, there were still many different crafts associations or unions within any industry, but they were usually united under special cartel arrangements (e.g., in the branches related to metal manufacturing the so-called *Metallkartell*) which delegated their right to conclude collective agreements to the relevant "leading" industrial union (e.g., the German Metal Workers Union).[16] Hence the eventual formal move from crafts-based to industry-based unions, which took place after World War II, was no longer of fundamental economic importance as a step towards the more encompassing organization of collective bargaining in the sense popularized by Olson (1965, 1982).[17]

A state-run compulsory unemployment insurance system was introduced by law in 1927. Although the structure of benefits it provides has repeatedly been adjusted in detail, the basic design of this insurance system has remained unchanged until today (disregarding, of course, the Nazi period): contributions are collected by means of a payroll tax, half of which is paid by employers, the other half by employees, with the government standing ready as a lender of last resort in case of high deficits, benefits are based on a specified share of any particular recipi-

---

[16] On the structure of the Metal Workers Union, see Hartwich (1967, pp. 65–72).

[17] See Paqué (1994, pp. 11–26) for a detailed discussion of the "Olson thesis" that there was a deep institutional break concerning the influence of interest groups between the German economy of the 1920s and that of the 1950s. The only major institutional innovation in collective bargaining after World War II was the removal of compulsory arbitration as the means of last resort for resolving a bargaining conflict, which was part of the Weimar labor market constitution (and which was used quite often in practice). Whether the relatively bad industrial relations of the 1920s were the cause or the consequence of the poor record of compulsory arbitrations remains a matter of controversy that deserves more economic research. For a detailed historical account of how the system worked, see Bähr (1989).

ent's terminal net wage—depending, above all, on his or her family status, but are usually well above 50 percent—for a limited period, originally 26 weeks—with further benefits being provided on a means-tested basis according to standard welfare criteria.[18]

In view of the persistent growth of industrial employment that had been going on for some decades, these institutional innovations appeared to be well justified on economic grounds. With the benefit of hindsight, an economic case for their introduction at the time could have read like the following paragraphs.

Collective bargaining.   Broadly speaking, theory and empirical evidence suggest that German-style collective bargaining involves two departures from wage setting in a free labor market, namely, that there is a greater monopolistic rent due to cartelization (the "union wage effect") and that employed insiders have greater market power vis-à-vis unemployed outsiders (the "group membership effect").[19] The union wage effect involves social costs in terms of lower employment and, ceteris paribus, higher unemployment levels compared with a free labor market. In turn, the group membership effect may involve benefits *or* costs in terms of employment because it tends to increase the persistence of (unexpected) exogenous shocks to the labor market, which may be positive or negative.[20] In view of the four-decade-long experience of fast growth of industrial employment at the expense of agriculture (i.e., the "voluntary" structural change from a low- to a high-wage sector), the economic observer towards the end of imperial times (one equipped with modern theory!) might have reasonably

---

[18] For details on the system at the time of its introduction and on adjustments in later decades, see Hentschel (1983, pp. 111–118, 198–201).

[19] The first effect receives its theoretical rationale from standard monopoly union models (see Farber, 1986; Oswald, 1986), the second one from insider/outsider models (see, e.g., Blanchard and Summers, 1986; Lindbeck and Snower, 1986).

[20] Note that we do not consider the "standard" benefits of unionism in terms of a stronger "voice" of workers on the plant level and in the political process that may lead to higher productivity on the job and lower labor turnover (see Freeman and Medoff [1984], who apply ideas on "voice" to American unionism, vs. Hirschman [1970], who deals with "exit"). For our case, these benefits are irrelevant because we do not see a plausible reason why they should have varied greatly over time (as we argue the costs have) between, say, the early 1920s and today.

argued in favor of introducing collective bargaining: "expecting" the pattern observed in the past to continue, she would have assumed that industrial employment would continue to see a positive stochastic trend (i.e., a random walk with upward drift)[21] whose labor market effect would be made persistent precisely via the collective bargaining that transformed outsiders (notably former agricultural workers) into insiders. Given the observed size of the positive shocks in the past, this type of benefit may well have been deemed to overcompensate the employment cost of a union monopoly rent.

Unemployment insurance. Similarly, providing more generous unemployment benefits may be viewed as a reasonable means to bring the length and breadth of the average job search closer to the social optimum: under the expected circumstances of long-term structural change from (low-wage) agriculture to (high-wage) manufacturing (regardless of cyclical fluctuations in industrial employment), if temporarily unemployed persons were to engage in a more thorough and careful evaluation of new job options (and hence in a longer job search), this would likely incur a social benefit by increasing the efficiency of labor reallocation, and this increase in efficiency would outweigh the cost of longer average unemployment spells.

There have been basically three distinct historical testing periods for these two pillars of the German labor market institutions: the period of the Weimar republic (excluding the years of Nazi rule), the postwar period up to 1973, and the two decades thereafter. For the analysis of the link between long-term trends of structural change and equilibrium unemployment, the Weimar period was, unfortunately, too short and too subject to violent cyclical fluctuations in economic activity that had their roots outside the labor market: the time span between the stabilization program in late 1923 (following four years of inflationary chaos at full employment) and the onset of the Great Depression in 1929 covered just one business cycle with a very sharp rise and fall of industrial production and employment. If anything, the statistics point towards an equilibrium unemployment rate that appears to be higher than it was in imperial times: in the peak boom year 1928, 8.4 percent of all union members and roughly 3.8 percent of the labor force were

---

[21] Univariate time-series tests for the period 1875–1913 show that the log of industrial employment appears to follow a stochastic trend of order one.

still unemployed (see Table 1 of the Appendix). However, it remains totally unclear to which rate of unemployment the economy would have converged in the longer run had there not been the Great Depression and the subsequent rise of the Nazi command economy. Hence, while the labor market in the Weimar Republic raises a host of interesting historical issues,[22] it hardly adds any insight to the questions at hand.

C   The "Good-Weather" Period 1948–1973

The two and a half decades that followed the West German currency reform of 1948 brought a somewhat belated, but almost perfect vindication of the positive economic scenario that provides the economic rationale for the institutional innovations of the 1920s. Due to the postwar influx of roughly ten million ethnic German refugees from Eastern Europe, the postwar German economy started off with an unemployment rate of 8–10 percent in 1949/1950; within ten years, however, the rate had come down to 1 percent (and below), where it stayed until 1973, with just one very brief interruption in the recession year 1967, when it temporarily peaked at an annual average of around 2(!) percent.

In terms of structural change, the first half of these two and a half decades can be regarded as the straight continuation and final conclusion of the industrial growth that had been the hallmark of imperial times. With some minor qualifications, all of what has been said above about workers "voluntarily" shifting sectors in imperial times applies equally to the 1950s. Again, income elasticities of product demand, technical progress, and above all a newly emerging pattern of international trade—this time driven by the fast-growing intraindustrial division of labor within the nascent European Community—allowed a

---

[22] There is in particular the important hypothesis put forward by Borchardt (1979) and James (1986) and contested by Balderston (1993) that the Weimar economy suffered from inherent weaknesses (including uncooperative unions) that damaged its international competitiveness and made it particularly vulnerable to severe cyclical shocks like the subsequent Great Depression. For an evaluation of this controversy with a view to the labor market, see Paqué (1994a, pp. 39–52).

further forceful expansion of employment in virtually all branches of manufacturing, with high-productivity investment goods branches like mechanical and electrical engineering, metal manufacturing, and, most of all, the production of vehicles standing out in terms of output and employment expansion. And again, agricultural workers—in 1950 still roughly one-quarter of the total labor force—stood ready to accept relatively well-paid industrial jobs on offer, and so did the unemployed, many of them highly mobile refugees who were crowded in the agrarian north of the country and who, when necessary, moved quite easily to the growing industrial heartlands of western and southern Germany.[23]

In these circumstances of fast industrial expansion, the institutions of collective bargaining and unemployment insurance were likely to have the positive effects described above. There can hardly be any doubt that growth performance repeatedly surpassed prior expectations, so that former outsiders could be enfranchised and subsequently exert a moderating influence on wage growth,[24] collective bargaining thus helped to move the labor market to a state of "overfull employment" that might have been beyond reach under free market conditions. Besides, the unemployment insurance system is likely to have worked smoothly in the envisaged sense of allowing an efficient reallocation of labor from low- to high-productivity uses simply because the incentive for overlong search activity remained small in view of the emerging high-wage job options.

The second half of the period—from the early 1960s to 1973—"conserved" the state of the labor market reached by the late 1950s. With industrial employment staying roughly constant and the domestic labor force shrinking for demographic reasons, the decline in agricultural employment was accommodated rather easily. Moreover, given the persistent state of overfull employment, foreign workers took over the role of a supplementary labor force to fill industrial job slots, now mainly in the lower-skill segments that were left open by upwardly mobile domestic workers. Given the large and cyclically variable wage

---

[23] For a detailed account of structural change in the West German economy of the 1950s, see Giersch, Paqué, and Schmieding (1992, Section 3.A.) and for details on the intraindustry pattern of growth, see Paqué (1994a, pp. 31–33).

[24] On the link between unexpected positive shocks and the actual decline of real unit labor costs in the 1950s, see Paqué (1994a, pp. 34–37).

drift as well as the elasticity of the labor force gained through the cyclical "buffer stock" of foreign workers, the German labor market of the 1960s had probably the maximum flexibility that can realistically be achieved within the constraints of a collective bargaining system.[25]

D   The "Bad Weather" Period since the Mid-1970s

In the last two decades, the state of the western German labor market has changed decisively and lastingly for the worse: from an average share of unemployment in the total labor force of 0.9 percent in 1960–1974 to 3.4 percent in 1975–1981 and 5.4 percent in 1982–1993. And there is no realistic prospect of any significant improvement in the years to come. At no time in the last twelve years did the unemployment rate fall below 4 percent, not even towards the end of the very powerful unification boom in 1991, when it reached 4.2 percent—far above the boom time levels of the 1960s, though still relatively low by the contemporaneous standards of most other European countries.[26] Historically, the last two decades are by far the longest period of unemployment ever experienced in Germany; if the short and erratic record of the 1920s is disregarded, they are in fact the *only* period in German history of persistent noncyclical unemployment.

Much has been written about the actual reasons for the stepwise rise of unemployment and its subsequent persistence.[27] There is now general agreement that, after two major recessions that followed severe supply-side shocks, the labor markets in most western European countries have *dualized*: part of the previously laid-off labor force soon found its way back into employment while a smaller part remained as a

---

[25] For a more detailed account of the West German labor market in the 1960s, see Giersch, Paqué, and Schmieding (1992, pp. 126–139). Note that the period 1960–1973 presents a major unsolved puzzle: while the long persistence of overfull employment may still be explained by positive "ratchet effects" within insider/outsider models, the sudden and extremely sharp wage increases in and after 1970 remain a mystery that no econom(etr)ic model has been able to account for in a convincing fashion.

[26] Note, however, that most of these countries also had higher unemployment rates than Germany in the 1960s, so that the extent of the *relative worsening* over time is in fact quite similar (see Table 1 in the appendix).

[27] See footnote 8 above.

kind of sediment of long-term unemployment that lacked the (poten-tial) productivity to be reintegrated at the then prevailing wage level. Matters of controversy in the literature have been the deeper reasons for the dualization: some have identified wage setting as the culprit, because it was insider-oriented with respect to unions and/or efficiency-oriented with respect to employers, others regarded a skill atrophy or decline of motivation of the outsiders in the course of the unemploy-ment spell as the decisive factor.[28]

At least for the case of West Germany, both of these reasons run into some difficulties. Insider-oriented and efficiency-oriented wage setting does not square nicely with the fact that, by historical stan-dards, the ten-year period after 1983 was *neither* a period of poor employment growth *nor* one of a rise in labor costs: in the period 1983–1993, employment grew at an annual rate of 1 percent, faster than at any time since the 1950s, creating a total of almost 3 million new jobs and thus allowing the rapid integration of the baby-boom generation and many immigrants from eastern Europe; and aggregate real labor costs (however measured) declined slowly and continuously from 1983 until the onset of the forceful unification boom in 1990, just as they had for the last time in the 1950s (see Paqué, mimeo, pp. 12–33). In turn, skill atrophy (or the like) in the course of the unemployment spell raises the question why it could not be observed in a period with a similar labor market disequilibrium: while long-term unemployment has un-doubtedly been high since the mid-1980s, it was even higher in the early 1950s, but at that time, it did not lead to a permanent dualization of the labor market.[29] Apparently, there is something missing in both theories that helps to distinguish between "good" and "bad" outsiders.

Once again, the key to the puzzle may lie in the change in the trend in industrial employment: in the first half of the last twenty years (1973–1983), industrial employment shrank—and then with two million

---

[28] The former standpoint is taken, e.g., by Lindbeck (1993), the latter by Layard, Nickell, and Jackman (1991). Note, however, that both sides would certainly concede that there is some truth in both views.

[29] In September 1953, when the only special survey on long-term unemployment in the early postwar period was held in West Germany, 32.3 percent of all jobless men and 22.4 percent of all jobless women had been unemployed for at least two years; since the mid-1980s, the corresponding figures are 15–18 percent for men and 14–16 percent for women. See Paqué (mimeo, p. 66).

industrial jobs lost, it stagnated in the second half (1983–1993), though its share in the economy-wide total continued to decline; in turn, employment in trade and services grew at a fairly constant rate throughout the twenty-year period. Hence, while the brunt of the job losses in the first half hit industrial workers disproportionately, the subsequent employment growth took place exclusively in the service sectors. If industry is, on average, the sector that pays the highest "premium" for physical work, this structural change meant a *devaluation* of the market value of unskilled labor and of everything in workers' skills that is sector-specific to industry. If, in addition, there was a trend towards "servicification" in industry itself—meaning that physical routine work is replaced by machine activity that is supervised and serviced by a smaller number of better-skilled workers—then the respective devaluation becomes even more dramatic. Data on changes in employment disaggregated by skill levels and branches of economic activity strongly support the view that structural change in the last twenty years has gone in these directions.[30]

Given these trends, there are likely to be "good" outsiders and "bad" outsiders. The good ones are typically those who have up-to-date job qualifications, preferably in a professional service job, who are newcomers (and thus do not yet carry the "scars" of industrial work), and who can be expected to adjust flexibly and with high motivation to the new working environment. Obviously, young labor market entrants—notably the many who have successfully finished an apprenticeship of two to four years—are at a clear advantage in these respects. Also, the immigrants of the late 1980s, who mainly came from eastern Europe, are still relatively good candidates. In turn, former industrial workers are at a competitive disadvantage, in particular when they are older or physically handicapped or have no formal vocational or professional training. In addition, they tend to have higher reservation wages because they held rather well-paid industrial jobs before and because they are granted more generous support by the unemployment insurance system, which makes particularly the duration of benefit payments depend on the accumulated length of all prior spells of employment (see below in Section III).

By and large, the structural statistics of unemployment in West Germany over the last twenty years strongly confirm this picture: in-

---

[30] See Paqué (1994b, pp. 197–198, notably Table 45).

sofar as the required data is available, it shows for this period that unemployment, notably long-term unemployment, has become increasingly prevalent, for example, among unskilled (versus skilled) labor, among wage workers (versus salaried employees), and among persons who are older or physically handicapped.[31] In fact, by the early 1990s, about 80 percent of all long-term unemployed persons were above the age of 55 and had a physical handicap and/or no vocational or professional training.[32]

In general, these trends in the labor market apparently did *not* lead to a corresponding wage differentiation that might have eased the reintegration of the disadvantaged outsiders: insofar as there is wage data disaggregated by the relevant structural characteristics, it indicates a high degree of structural rigidity over the last twenty years. In particular, there has not been any widening of the wage difference between high-skill and low-skill workers as in the United States.[33] The reason for this high degree of structural wage rigidity is very likely to be found in collective bargaining, combined with a rather generous system of unemployment benefits. With structural change drastically devaluing the human capital of part of the economy's outsiders, there is little incentive for the bargaining cartel to sacrifice insider interests and allow for a substantial wage differentiation that would be to the disadvantage of those insiders who share traits with those outsiders (e.g., unskilled and/or older workers). This is all the more so because the unemployment insurance system is set up so as to allow long periods of low-intensity job search.[34]

E   Will the "Weather" Improve Again?

If one searches for the deeper "exogenous" reasons for the drastic devaluation of unskilled labor in West Germany and other industrial countries over the last twenty years, two major forces come to mind:

---

[31] For statistical details, see Paqué (1994b, pp. 204–213).

[32] See Paqué (mimeo, p. 143a, Table 3.16, based on unpublished data provided by the Bundesanstalt für Arbeit).

[33] See OECD (1993) for data on the 1980s, and Paqué (1994b, pp. 204–214) for the last twenty years.

[34] For crucial details of the system, see Section III below.

globalization and *technological progress*. The former means that a growing group of newly industrialized and developing countries have reached a level of industrialization, technical standards, and labor skills that allow them to compete successfully in the markets for labor- and (physical-)capital-intensive production and increasingly also in the lower market segments of human-capital-intensive goods. The latter means that technological progress in industry has been labor-saving in the sense that it has remained persistently profitable to replace manpower by modern (physical) capital equipment. Which of the two forces has dominated is a matter of dispute[35] that appears to be most relevant to certain major issues in trade policy vis-à-vis the Third World, but much less so for a speculative assessment of future trends in the labor market. After all, the speed and the shape of technological progress is itself to a large extent the (endogenous) outcome of a competitive race on all levels—encompassing growing intraindustry trade within and between industrial countries as well as growing inter-industry trade between industrial and developing countries. Hence the process of globalization in a broader sense—meaning the worldwide trend towards the integration of product and service markets, which in turn is fueled by the (technology-induced) decline of transportation and communication costs—may well be the true driving force behind the secular changes in virtually all labor markets in Western industrial countries.

For the future, it is hard to imagine a change or a significant slow-down in this trend towards globalization in the broadest sense, not least because the major population giants of the Third World—notably China and India—are now embarking on the path that a few much smaller Asian countries have gone down during the last three decades. Hence, if anything, the process is likely to speed up and will further accentuate structural change in the rich countries: industrial employment will continue to shrink notably in terms of low-skill jobs, service employment—in the upper "professional" segment and in the lower

---

[35] See the antagonistic views of Wood (1994), who regards the increasing North–South trade as decisive, and Freeman (1994, as quoted in *The Economist* of April 2, 1994), who holds that the driving force must have been technological change because, in the Western countries, the import share of developing and newly industrialized countries is still too small to explain any dramatic effect on the labor market.

"low-productivity" segment—will tend to grow.[36] For former industrial workers, the upper segment will, in general, be beyond reach and
the lower segment will be unattractive.

In this sense, the long historical period of "voluntary" structural
change that involved the growth of a sector with high wages for
unskilled labor and thus an almost automatic trend towards more
equality of incomes may have come to an end by the 1970s. For
a country like Germany, this is having quite dramatic consequences
for the viability of its labor market institutions: while the quality of
its labor force is continually improving as a result of "generational
exchange"—older, on average less-skilled workers leaving and younger,
on average better skilled ones entering the labor force—there seems to
be no safeguard in the system to make sure that this "natural" adjustment is proceeding fast enough to avoid extended phases of high search
(or better, structural) unemployment.

For such external conditions, collective bargaining and the German-
style welfare state do not appear to be well equipped: as the viability
of a pay-as-you-go system of old-age insurance depends crucially on
whether the population is growing or shrinking, so the viability of
"egalitarian" collective bargaining combined with generous welfare
state provisions depends crucially on whether structural change, by
itself, has egalitarian implications or not. If not—and provided the
problem of chronic unemployment is to be tackled seriously—some
major reforms of the "German model" will be unavoidable.

III   Some Guidelines for Reforming the "German Model"

From the analysis above, it follows that a return to full employment in
(western) Germany, as well as probably in many countries of the
European Union, would require a quite substantial reduction in the
unit labor cost that firms incur when hiring formerly unemployed and
especially long-term unemployed persons. In principle, there are two
nonexclusive ways to accomplish this intermediate aim: (1) raise the

---

[36] There is also an "industry-close" middle segment of services like transportation
and wholesale trade, which is similar to industry in terms of the skill intensity of
work and the level of wages. Unfortunately, it is also that part of the service
sector that tends to shrink or at least stagnate.

potential labor productivity, and (2) lower the prospective wage of the idle work force.

A   Raising Labor Productivity

Once there is persistent unemployment, a policy of improving the potential productivity of jobless persons is basically constrained to the use of two instruments: (re)training measures and work creation schemes. Since the early 1980s, both instruments have been used quite extensively in western Germany. In the most recent seven-year period 1987–1993, an annual average of 170,000 unemployed persons participated in (re)training measures and almost 100,000 in work creation schemes, so that, arithmetically, almost every seventh unemployed person was matched at any point in time by one person in any of these programs.[37]

It is extremely difficult to evaluate these programs in terms of their costs and benefits because the lack of appropriate control groups prohibits any precise estimate of the extent to which the likelihood of an unemployed person finding a job is increased by his or her participating in a program. So far, the available empirical evidence is far from unambiguous, but it does indicate that the programs improve the chances of the unemployed becoming reintegrated into the labor market, though possibly only by a relatively small margin.[38] Whether this justifies the cost of publicly organizing or subsidizing the private organization of the programs—on top of paying unemployment benefits—remains a completely open question.

In any case, the programs are, by design, not well-suited to resolving a large-scale unemployment problem resulting from structural change: usually, they can only provide new qualifications "in the neighbor-

---

[37] Own calculations based on data published in Bundesanstalt für Arbeit (various issues). After German unification, both types of programs were used even more extensively in the eastern part of the country, where, in the peak year 1992, more than 800,000 persons either participated in retraining or in work creation schemes while 1.2 million were unemployed.

[38] See Hofbauer and Dadzio (1987) and Kasparek and Koop (1991) on retraining measures and Schmid, Krömmelbein, Klems, and Gaß (1993) on work creation schemes.

hood" of old skills, so that many of the structural deficiencies of long-term unemployed persons—complete lack of skills and formal education, physical handicaps, and above all age—are not remedied. In a way, it is precisely these deficiencies that limit the scope for (re)training in the first place, so that labor market programs remain typically focused on the more flexible part of an economy's stock of under-utilized manpower and human capital. In fact, the basic rationale for (re)training has always been to smooth the intraindustry movement of workers from one job to another—a kind of skill updating—rather than to open the door for a reintegration into the labor market.[39]

B   Lowering the Wage

In a country like Germany where wage setting is dominated by collective bargaining, the change in the wage level and structure that would be required to achieve a permanent reduction of unemployment should ideally be initiated at the bargaining table by unions and employers' associations. As argued above, however, the experience of the last two decades has shown that the dominance of insider interests generally prevents the long-term victims of structural change from having any significant influence on the bargaining outcome. Given the group rationality of the behavior of both unions and employers' associations in terms of insider/outsider wage and efficiency wage considerations, it is not obvious how the outcome could be affected by macroeconomic policy.[40]

---

[39] This is also the author's interpretation of the Swedish labor market programs: these programs were successful as long as there still was enough job creation in industry due, above all, to the hefty two-step devaluations in the early 1980s, a classical case of beggar-thy-neighbor demand policy, which cut Sweden off from the continental recession-cum-industrial-shrinkage. However, with the unemployment rate now being in the range of 8–9 percent and no macroeconomic "emergency exit" available, the labor market programs appear to be hopelessly overburdened as a prime policy instrument to restore full employment. For a similar view, see Lindbeck (mimeo).

[40] Some early proponents of the hysteresis view of European unemployment made a strong plea for engineering a nonanticipated macroeconomic demand expansion to "enfranchise" the outsiders (see, e.g., Blinder, 1988). However, if it is correct that the remaining "hard core" of noncyclical unemployment is the long-term consequence of structural change rather than just the consequence of cyclical bad luck, such an expansion would be useless, if not counterproductive.

Therefore, apart from moral suasion, which also has obvious limits,[41] the only major policy options available are changes in the institutional background against which collective bargaining operates, which in essence consists of two major elements, the labor market constitution and the unemployment benefit system. One such change would necessarily be to change the *labor market constitution* to remove all of the legal or political obstacles preventing outsiders from competing with the collective bargaining cartel. In particular, this would mean that the option of declaring a collective agreement "generally binding" should once and for all be closed to the government—at best by simply repealing the relevant legal rule (Section 5 of the Tarifvertragsgesetz). This is a necessary condition to save future outsider competition from being strangled by government action on behalf of insider interests; however, it is by no means a sufficient condition to create this competition as some of the principles upon which the welfare state is based stand in its way (see below). At present, the rule is used very seldom, apparently because outsider competition is not a powerful threat to collective agreements anyway.

In any case, it would be of paramount importance to reform the *unemployment benefit system*. To aid the reader in understanding the

---

[41] In Germany, moral suasion has a long tradition going back to the so-called calls for moderation regularly issued by the first minister of economics, Ludwig Erhard, in the 1950s and later institutionalized in the "concerted action" of government, employers, and unions in the later 1960s and the early 1970s. At its best, the concerted action succeeded in tying up package deals consisting of short-run macroeconomic policy shifts and wage moderation that were useful for stabilization purposes; the benefit that accrued to the unions from their participating in the concerted action consisted of representing themselves as an essential, reliable, and responsible (political) partner in a successful macroeconomic operation. This benefit could be expected to accrue in the short run— usually within no more than one phase of the business cycle—and to be politically well visible to a general public that was very open to ideas of demand management. (For details, see Giersch, Paqué, and Schmieding, 1992, pp. 139–154.) In today's fight against long-term unemployment, there are no such benefits to be had for the unions: the fruits of the fight concern merely fringe group and they will accrue only after a prolonged adjustment process that tends to blur the link between the unions' goodwill and the outcome in the eyes of the public. Hence the incentives for the union leadership to sacrifice membership interests for the uncertain and remote political benefit of a "compact for wage flexibility and employment" are likely to be minimal.

practice and consequences of the current system and thus the starting point for reform, I will present some institutional details below; they concern, above all, replacement ratios, replacement periods, and rules of job acceptability.

At present, the system provides so-called unemployment pay (*Arbeitslosengeld*), which is financed by unemployment insurance contributions, and which amounts to 60 percent of the terminal net wage (67 percent for persons with at least one child) for roughly 12–32 months, depending on age and length of prior employment.[42] When unemployment pay runs out, it is replaced by so-called unemployment aid (*Arbeitslosenhilfe*), which is granted for the remaining—possibly indefinite—spell of unemployment on a means-tested basis, and which amounts to 53 percent of the terminal net wage (57 percent to persons with at least one child),[43] with a lower ceiling implicitly defined by standard supplementary welfare payments (*Sozialhilfe*), which is also granted on a means-tested basis to persons not registered as unemployed (whether they work or not). In the seven-year period 1987–1993, an annual average of one-third of all unemployment benefit recipients received unemployment aid, the other two-thirds received unemployment pay.[44] Note that, during the time of unemployment, any recipient of unemployment support ("pay" or "aid") remains a member of the public health, pension, and accident insurance systems, provided she was previously a member (which is usually the case); the person's contributions to the system are made in part by the unemployment insurance system, and in part are simply discontinued, with the benefits remaining the same as during his or her last spell of employment.[45]

---

[42] These replacement ratios apply since the beginning of 1994. Until 1993, the relevant ratios were 63 and 68 percent respectively. Special rules apply to persons with very short periods of prior employment. For details, see Section 106 of the Arbeitsförderungsgesetz (AFG).

[43] For details, see the AFG (Section 136). Until 1993, the replacement ratios were 56 and 58 percent, respectively.

[44] Own calculations based on data published in Bundesanstalt für Arbeit (various issues). By comparison, the numbers for the low-unemployment seven-year period 1967–1973 are 14 percent unemployment aid and 86 percent unemployment pay, which at that time was still more strictly limited to one year.

[45] See the AFG (Sections 155–166) for the (very complicated) details.

The legal framework for the rules on "job acceptability" (*Zumutbarkeit*) is provided in a special "job acceptability directive" (*Zumutbarkeits-Anordnung*), which is of great practical importance. In particular, it stipulates[46] that a job need not be accepted by an unemployed person

• if the wage is (1) below the level fixed in collective agreements or commonly paid in the region for this type of work, or (2) below the level of the unemployment aid she receives, or (3) below the level of the unemployment money she receives unless this is unusually high by the standard of the region in which this standard applies, or
• if taking the job would significantly worsen his or her chances of finding a job identical or similar to the one she held before becoming unemployed, or
• if the skill level required for the job is significantly below the skill level required for the job she held before becoming unemployed, with the criteria for the acceptable "downgrading" of the person becoming looser, the longer the unemployment spell, or
• if the workplace is not located within an acceptable distance from home, with a commuter time of 150 minutes (round-trip) being the standard maximum of acceptability for a full-time job.

By all common-sense standards, this unemployment benefit system—as defined by its replacement ratios, the time spans for which benefits are granted, and the various criteria of acceptability—is very generous. Economically, it is almost tailor-made to invite extended job searches, notably in those cases where the unemployed person was a (well-paid) industrial worker for some time who has relatively little chance of finding a comparative job in due course. While his manpower may be drastically devalued due to the shrinkage of industry, he is highly subsidized, first by the working population and then by the taxpayer, to stand in the queue at the gates of the high-productivity sector. Even if indefinitely unsuccessful in his search, he will receive unemployment aid of at least 53 percent of his terminal wage provided he passes the means test, which he will usually do because the definition of "need" is in practice invariably tied to his prior living standard, which is typically linked to the relatively high wage he used to earn. In no circumstances can he be forced to accept low-productivity service jobs that fall below

---

[46] See the AFG (pp. 342–347, Zumutbarkeits-Anordnung, Sections 2 II, 3, 4, 5 I, 6 I, 8–12 I, all with further legal details).

the 53 (57) percent threshold of his historical wage, which thus defines the long-term lower limit of his reservation wage; and even if the prospective wage is higher, the job may be unacceptable for one of the other broadly defined reasons. As a consequence, the growth of a low-productivity service sector is severely hampered: as many job offers in the lower wage segment can simply be disregarded by a large part of the unemployed, no such offers will be made by rational employers, so that a whole potential segment of the economy (well known in the United States) remains nonexistent or relatively small.

For collective bargaining, the system as it stands has two straight-forward ramifications. First—and quite obviously—the induced low search intensity of the unemployed reduces outsider competition from the labor supply side. Second, the rule that unemployed persons need not accept a job offered by any firm at a wage below the contractual minimum narrows the effectively available labor supply for non-organized employers, thus checking the outsider threat from the labor demand side as well. Hence the unemployment insurance system provides strong indirect support to the wage cartel, thus impeding the necessary reorientation of bargaining outcomes.

How could the system be sensibly reformed to reduce the incentives for overextended job searches without undermining the philosophy of the "German Model," or, for that matter, the "European Model" (see Emerson, 1988), of the welfare state? If one of the basic principles of this philosophy can be seen to consist in the providing of all citizens who have lost their jobs with a minimum of subsistence that is not intolerably far below their prior standard of living, then a kind of minimalist reform of the German system could take on a shape similar to that described in the following.

As always, unemployed persons would receive contribution-financed unemployment pay, at the replacement ratios prevailing in the present system, though preferably for a somewhat shorter period of time, ranging, say, from 6 to 15 months, depending primarily on the age of the person (as is the case now). During this period of time, the criteria for job acceptability would remain the same as in the present system, i.e., the unemployed person would still be free to search exclusively "in the neighborhood" of her prior wage and job experience, and to turn down any job for which she would be substantially overqualified and thus considerably underpaid. If she were still unemployed after 6–15 months, she would be entitled to receive tax-financed unemployment aid, again with today's replacement ratios applying. While receiving unemployment aid, however, the person would *no longer* be entitled to turn down *any* job offer at whatever wage or working conditions, provided she is physically able to do the job. On the other hand, she would be entitled to receive financial compensation for any net income loss incurred by taking the job: if the wage for the job is below the level of unemployment aid she obtains at the time of the offer, she would receive a government *matching grant* that makes up for the difference, or preferably even more than makes up for the difference in order to give the person a stronger incentive to consider lower-wage jobs during her search. The rationale for this matching grant is basically the same as the rationale for various employment subsidy schemes that have recently been put forward (see, e.g., Phelps, 1994; Snower, 1994): if the philosophy of the welfare state requires that part of the devaluation of manpower and human capital that occurs during the course of structural change be "socialized", then it should be done by subsidizing *states of employment* and not states of (long-term) unemployment.[47]

Subsidizing a relatively small part of total employment is somewhat more complicated than providing benefits to a well-defined group of

---

[47] Note that, to a very limited extent, there already exist employment subsidy schemes in Germany. Within the general framework of labor market programs, employment subsidies may be granted to firms for hiring long-term unemployed persons above 55 years of age on an unlimited contract basis. If granted, the subsidies usually amount to 50 percent of the relevant contractual minimum wage; they are paid for a maximum of three years, with the rate of subsidization declining to 40 percent in the second year and 30 percent in the third year. Under very restrictively defined circumstances, the subsidy may even be higher and paid for a longer period of time (for details, see the AFG, Sections 97–99). Although no empirical assessment of how well this rule works is available, the general impression is that it has played only a marginal part and has not led to a significant differentiation of labor costs. The reasons for this are probably twofold. First, the subsidy is granted only for a fixed term, which may not be long enough to compensate the employer for the disadvantage of being committed in the longer run to a worker who is underqualified. Second, the subsidy has the character of an ad hoc offer that job centers make to firms for a single person only if funds are available, rather than the character of a reliable rule that signals potential employers a once-for-all change in the costs of this particular type of labor. Employment subsidies other than the ones provided by this scheme are provided to commercial firms (1) for jobs whose output is in the public interest (AFG, Sections 91 and 96), which in practice rarely happens; and (2) for on-the-job training of labor market fringe groups (FdA-Anordnung, Sections 19–23).

registered unemployed persons. Four issues here deserve particular attention: (1) the time horizon of employment subsidization and its costs, (2) the lack of incentives for job change within the low-wage segment of the labor market, (3) the potential for joint abuse by employer and (prospective) employee, and (4) the basis for assessing future unemployment benefits and old-age pensions.

1. To be a valuable instrument to create a market for low-productivity labor on unlimited contracts, it is important that the matching grant also be given for a long, preferably an *unlimited*, period of time. At first glance, this seems to imply an unbearable burden for the government budget because the average length of time that a formerly long-term unemployed person would spend in (subsidized) employment should be many times longer than the average length of time that the person would have otherwise spent in (fully financed) unemployment; what the government saves in unemployment aid would thus be vastly over-compensated by what it has to spend on matching grants. However, at second glance, this seemingly plausible argument is largely unfounded because it neglects the incentive to accept a high-wage job—i.e., a job with a wage above the critical threshold of unemployment aid—and this incentive should work *equally* well in both systems: each (unsubsidized) job that is attractive enough to a person for him to leave a state of long-term unemployment is also attractive enough for him to leave a state of (subsidized) employment because, by nature of the subsidization scheme, the reservation wage of the same person is likely to be the same in both cases. Only if one assumes that the costs of changing jobs are higher than the costs of taking up a job after a spell of unemployment (or if one makes some other equally implausible "biased" assumption)[48] could the above argument claim more than prima facie plausibility. Hence, if anything, the matching grant scheme is likely to be the fiscally cheaper system because, at roughly the same number of government subsidy recipients, the matching grant per person is lower than the respective unemployment aid.

---

[48] For example, the assumption that the search intensity of long-term unemployed persons is higher than that of employed persons receiving the same net income, so that the latter is less likely to "notice" the better-paid job opening. Given the notoriously low search intensity that could be empirically observed for long-term unemployed persons in the past, this assumption is very implausible indeed.

2. Nevertheless, the matching grant system has a labor allocation problem of its own *within* the newly created segment of low-wage labor, i.e., of labor paid less than the unemployment aid threshold. Competition for low-wage labor may drive up its market wage and thus open up better-paid, but still low-wage, job slots not only for those who still remain among the ranks of the long-term unemployed, who have no free choice anyway, but also for those who have found a job and are receiving a matching grant; however, the latter have no pecuniary incentive to change jobs or to ask for higher pay, at least as long as the market wage being offered does not rise above the wage plus matching grant that they currently receive.

There are basically two potential (nonexclusive) ways to deal with this problem. The first and probably most foolproof way is to make payment of the matching grant contingent upon the readiness of a subsidized employee to accept any better-paid job (and conversely to reject any worse-paid job) or, alternatively, to negotiate a higher wage with his current employer. Practically, this could be done by leaving the subsidized employees registered at the public job centers, subjecting them to a code of job acceptability similar to the one to which the unemployed are subjected, and possibly by authorizing private commercial employment agencies—since such agencies are now no longer prohibited in Germany—to watch the labor market for superior low-wage job alternatives open to the subsidized employees. The second way would be to give low-wage employees a stronger search incentive, e.g., by reducing the matching grant by less than the realized wage gain. However, such a strategy has its natural limits because it also gives some "perverse" incentives: it would become attractive to deliberately start with the worst-paid job and then move up by changing jobs so as to "privatize" part of the self-created potential for social gains; and after this has been accomplished, there would also be an unwelcome incentive to stay in the range of subsidized employment instead of searching for unsubsidized jobs that pay wages above the unemployment-aid threshold. This is why the private gains would have to remain within reasonably narrow bounds and be allowed to accrue only for a very limited period of time, say a few months after a job change.

3. There is a possibility that a potential employer and an employee could form a cartel at the expense of the government: in private

arrangements, they may agree to set the wage below the person's marginal product so as to maximize the share of the person's income that is covered by the matching grant. Again, the remedy lies in the fact that the demand side engages in competitive bidding for low-wage labor: if, for whatever reason, an employer-employee cartel sets the wage well below the market level, then it is very likely that the respective employee will find a better-paid job in due course, which will push the wage up again, thus leading back to the solvable problem of making subsidized labor move from worse- to better-paid jobs (see 2 above).

Similarly, it has been argued—and is allegedly supported by empirical evidence—that there tend to be large deadweight losses involved in employment subsidy schemes because, typically, a large part of all employers who cash in on subsidies for hiring long-term unemployed persons would have hired them anyway; also, there is supposed to be a strong substitution effect because employers have an incentive to replace unsubsidized workers with subsidized ones, thus in effect reducing labor costs at the expense of the taxpayer without increasing employment.[49] Even if one were to accept this empirical evidence, which is based, for the most part, on rather small case studies that have many conceptual problems, it is hard to see how the malappropriation of subsidies could be more than a short-term problem within the matching grant system proposed here: if, as this evidence seems to suggest, long-term unemployed persons are indeed relatively good substitutes for employed workers, then competitive pressures will push up their wages in the way described above and thus reduce the extent of subsidization.

4. A technical problem of economic significance is the question of how to calculate future unemployment benefits (and also pension rights) if a person spends part of his working life in subsidized low-wage employment. Currently, all future claims against the social security system are kept at the level defined by the terminal *gross* income, no matter how long the unemployment spell; depending on the particular characteristics of the case, the cost of this generous rule is borne by different communities of insured people or by the taxpayer. If one wants to

---

[49] See the survey on various empirical studies of employment subsidy schemes in OECD (1993, pp. 63–64); see also *The Economist* of July 16 and August 20, 1994.

continue this practice within the matching grant system, one simply has to supplement the matching grants with social security payments that just ensure that the person concerned can keep her prior level of entitlements. Economically, however, this may lead to odd situations, notably for the unemployment insurance system, because it would imply an absurdly high replacement ratio for persons laid off from subsidized low-wage employment.[50] Hence some phasing out of the "historical" value of the demands on the social security system will have to be made, and there is a wide array of possible models with which to accomplish this, models ranging from a gradual downward adjustment to an immediate cut in contributions and future claims down to a level that corresponds to the low wage. This would also reestablish some incentive for the employee to be hired at the highest possible wage because, in the end, this wage will be important for her future claims against the social security system, notably her pension after retirement.

Bibliography

Bähr, J. 1989. *Staatliche Schlichtung in der Weimarer Republik*. Berlin: Colloquium Verlag.

Balderston, T. 1993. *The Origins and Course of the German Economic Crisis 1923–1932*. Berlin: Haide & Spener.

Blanchard, O., and L.H. Summers. 1986. "Hysteresis and the European Unemployment Problem." *NBER Macroeconomic Annual* 1:15–78.

Blinder, A.S. 1988. "The Challenge of High Unemployment." *American Economic Review* 78:1–15.

Borchardt, K. 1979. "Zwangslagen und Handlungsspielräume in der großen Wirtschaftskrise der frühen 30er Jahre: Zur Revision des überlieferten Geschichtsbildes." *Jahrbuch 1979*. Munich: Bayerische Akademie der Wissenschaften.

Bruno, M., and J.D. Sachs, 1985. *Economics of Worldwide Stagflation*. Oxford: Basil Blackwell.

Bundesanstalt für Arbeit. Various issues. *Amtliche Nachrichten der Bundesanstalt für Arbeit–Jahreszahlen*.

Burda, M., and A. Mertens. 1994. "Locational Competition versus Cooperation in

---

[50] For example, a person with at least one child would still receive unemployment pay to the amount of 67 percent of his or her "historical" net wage, i.e., about 15 percent more than her new terminal net income (wage plus matching grant).

Labor Markets: An Implicit Contract Reinterpretation." Paper presented at the Kiel Week Conference on Locational Competition in the World Economy, 22–23 June.

Cross, R. (ed.). 1988. *Unemployment, Hysteresis and the Natural Rate Hypothesis.* Oxford: Basil Blackwell.

Deutsches Institut für Wirtschaftsforschung (DIW), Berlin, and Institut für Weltwirtschaft (IfW). 1994. "Gesamtwirtschaftliche und unternehmerische Anpassungsprozesse in Ostdeutschland. 10. Bericht." Kiel Discussion Papers No. 231. Kiel: Kiel Institute of World Economics.

The Economist. 1994. "Schools Brief: Workers of the World, Compete." April 2, pp. 79–80 (European edition).

The Economist. 1994. "Long-term Unemployment: Paying for Jobs." July 16, pp. 34–39 (European edition).

The Economist. 1994. "Economics Focus: No Free Lunch for the Jobless." August 20, p. 55 (European edition).

Emerson, M. 1988. *What Model for Europe?* Cambridge, Mass.: MIT Press.

Farber, H.S. 1986. "The Analysis of Union Behaviour." In: O. Ashenfelter and R.G. Layard (eds.), *Handbook of Labor Economics*, Vol. 2, pp. 1039–1089. Amsterdam: North Holland.

Faust, A. 1982. "Arbeitsmarktpolitik in Deutschland. Die Entstehung der öffentlichen Arbeitsvermittlung 1890–1927." In: T. Pierenkämper and R.H. Tilly (eds.), *Historische Arbeitsmarktforschung. Entstehung, Entwicklung und Probleme der Vermarktung von Arbeitskraft*, pp. 253–273. Göttingen: Vandenhoeck & Ruprecht.

Freeman, R.D. 1994. "Is Globalization Impoverishing Low-skill American Workers?" Cambridge, Mass.: Harvard University (mimeo).

Freeman, R.D., and J.L. Medoff. 1984. *What Do Unions Do?* New York: Basic Books.

Giersch, H., K.-H. Paqué, and H. Schmieding. 1992. *The Fading Miracle. Four Decades of Market Economy in Germany*. Cambridge: Cambridge University Press.

Hartog, J., and J. Theeuwes (eds.). 1993. *Labour Market Contracts and Institutions. A Cross-National Comparison.* Amsterdam: North Holland.

Hartwich, H.H. 1967. *Arbeitsmarkt, Verbände und Staat 1918–1933*. Berlin: de Gruyter.

Hentschel, V. 1983. *Geschichte der deutschen Sozialpolitik 1880–1980*. Frankfurt am Main: Suhrkamp.

Hirschman, A.O. 1970. *Exit, Voice and Loyalty. Responses to Decline in Firms, Organizations, and States.* Cambridge, Mass.: Harvard University Press.

Hofbauer, H., and W. Dadzio. 1987. "Mittelfristige Wirkungen beruflicher Weiterbildung." *Mitteilungen aus der Arbeitsmarkt- und Berufsforschung* 20:129–141.

Hoffmann, W.G. 1965. *Das Wachstum der deutschen Wirtschaft seit der Mitte des 19. Jahrhunderts.* Berlin: Springer.

James, H. 1986. *The German Slump*. Oxford: Clarendon Press.

Kasparek, P., and W. Koop. 1991. "Zur Wirksamkeit von Fortbildungs- und Umschulungsmaßnahmen." *Mitteilungen aus der Arbeitsmarkt- und Berufsforschung* 24:317–333.

Keyssar, A. 1986. *Out of Work: The First Century of Unemployment in Massachusetts*. Cambridge: Cambridge University Press.

Kuczynski, J. 1962. *Die Geschichte der Lage der Arbeiter unter dem Kapitalismus*. Vol. 3. Berlin (East): Akademie-Verlag.

Kuczynski, J. 1967. *Die Geschichte der Lage der Arbeiter unter dem Kapitalismus*. Vol. 4. Berlin (East): Akademie-Verlag.

Layard, R.G., S. Nickell, and R. Jackman. 1991. *Unemployment. Macroeconomic Performance and the Labour Market*. Oxford: Oxford University Press.

Lewis, H.G. 1986. "Union Relative Wage Effects." In: O.C. Ashenfelter and R.G. Layard (eds.), *Handbook of Labor Economics*, Vol. 2, pp. 1139–1181. Amsterdam: North Holland.

Lindbeck, A. 1993. *Unemployment and Macroeconomics*. Cambridge, Mass.: MIT Press.

Lindbeck, A. Mimeo. "The Crisis of the Swedish Model."

Lindbeck, A. and D. Snower. 1986. "Wage Setting, Unemployment and Insider-Outsider Relations." *American Economic Review* 76:235–239.

Lindbeck, A. and D. Snower. 1988. *The Insider-Outsider Theory of Employment and Unemployment*. Cambridge, Mass.: MIT Press.

Maddison, A. 1991. *Dynamic Forces in Capitalist Development*. Oxford: Oxford University Press.

Mitchell, B.R. 1981. *European Historical Statistics 1750–1975*. Second edition. London: Macmillan Press.

Moses, J.A. 1982. *Trade Unionism in Germany from Bismarck to Hitler 1869–1933*. Vol. 1. London: Prior.

Mottek, H. 1966. "Die Gründerkrise. Produktionsbewegung, Wirkungen, theoretische Problematik." *Jahrbuch für Wirtschaftsgeschichte* No. 1:51–128. Berlin: Deutsche Akademie der Wissenschaften.

OECD. 1993. *Employment Outlook*. Paris: OECD.

Olson, M. 1965. *The Logic of Collective Action. Public Goods and the Theory of Groups*. Cambridge, Mass.: Harvard University Press.

Olson, M. 1982. *The Rise and Decline of Nations. Economic Growth, Stagflation and Social Rigidities*. New Haven: Yale University Press.

Oswald, A. 1986. "The Economic Theory of Trade Unions: An Introductory Survey." In: L. Calmfors and H. Horn (eds.), *Trade Unions, Wage Formation and Macroeconomic Stability*, pp. 18–51. Hampshire: Macmillan Press.

Paqué, K.-H. 1993a. "Living with Tight Corporatism. The Case of Germany." In: J. Hartog and J. Theeuwes (eds.), *Labour Market Contracts and Institutions. A Cross-National Comparison*, pp. 209–232. Amsterdam: North Holland.

Paqué, K.-H. 1993b. "East/West-Wage Rigidity in United Germany: Causes and Consequences." Kiel Working Papers No. 572. Kiel: Kiel Institute of World Economics.

Paqué, K.-H. 1994a. "The Causes of Slumps and Miracles. An Evaluation of Olsonian Views on German Economic Performance in the 1920s and the 1950s." CEPR Discussion Paper No. 981. London: Centre for Economic Policy Research.

Paqué, K.-H. 1994b. "Wachsende Ungleichgewichte am Arbeitsmarkt." In: H. Klodt, J. Stehn et al., *Standort Deutschland: Strukurelle Herausforderungen im neuen Europa*. Tübingen: Mohr.

Paqué, K.-H. Mimeo. *Structural Unemployment and Real Wage Rigidity in Germany*.

Phelps, E.S. 1994. "Low-wage Employment Subsidies versus the Welfare State." *American Economic Review, Papers and Proceedings* 84(2): 54–58.

Piore, M.J. 1987. "Historical Perspectives and the Interpretation of Unemployment." *Journal of Economic Literature* 25:1834–1850.

Risch, B. 1983. *Alternativen der Einkommenspolitik*. Kieler Studien 180. Kiel: Kiel Institute of World Economics.

Schmid, A., S. Krömmelbein, W. Klems, and G. Gaß. 1983. "Neue Wege der Arbeitsmarktpolitik: Implementation und Wirksamkeit des Sonderprogramms." *Mitteilungen aus der Arbeitsmarkt- und Berufsforschung* 2:236–252.

Snower, D.J. 1994. "Converting Unemployment Benefits into Employment Subsidies." *American Economic Review, Papers and Proceedings* 84(2): 65–70.

Statistisches Reichsamt. Various issues. *Statistisches Jahrbuch für das Deutsche Reich*.

Turnham, D., and D. Eröcal. 1990. "Unemployment in Developing Countries. New Light on an Old Problem." Technical Papers 22. Paris: OECD Development Centre.

Wood, A. 1994. *North–South Trade, Employment and Inequality*. Oxford: Clarendon Press.

Appendix

Table 1. Unemployment as a Percentage of the Total Labor Force, 1920–1993.

	Australia	Austria	Belgium	Canada	Denmark	Finland	France	Germany	Italy	Japan	Netherlands	Norway	Sweden	Switzerland	U.K.	U.S.
1920	4.6	—	—	—	3.0	1.1	—	1.7	—	—	1.7	—	1.3	—	1.9	3.9
1921	5.9	—	6.1	5.8	10.0	1.8	2.7	1.2	—	—	2.6	5.6	6.4	—	11.0	11.4
1922	5.5	—	1.9	4.4	9.5	1.4	—	0.7	—	—	3.2	5.2	5.5	—	9.6	7.2
1923	4.9	—	0.6	3.2	6.5	1.0	—	4.5	—	—	3.3	1.3	2.9	—	8.0	3.0
1924	5.5	5.4	0.6	4.5	5.5	1.2	—	5.8	—	—	2.6	0.3	2.4	—	7.1	5.3
1925	5.6	6.3	0.9	4.4	7.5	2.0	—	3.0	—	—	2.4	3.4	2.6	—	7.7	3.8
1926	4.6	7.0	0.8	3-0	10.5	1.6	1.2	8.0	—	—	2.1	10.4	2.9	—	8.6	1.9
1927	5.2	6.2	1.1	1.8	11.0	1.5	—	3.9	—	—	2.2	11.3	2.9	—	6.7	3.9
1928	6.4	5.3	0.6	1.7	9.0	1.5	—	3.8	—	—	1.6	7.6	2.4	—	7.4	4-3
1929	8.2	5.5	0.8	2.9	8.0	2.8	1.2	5.9	1.7	—	1.7	5.4	2.4	0.4	7.2	3.1
1930	13.1	7.0	2.2	9.1	7.0	4.0	—	9.5	2.5	—	2.3	6.2	3.3	0.7	11.1	8.7
1931	17.9	9.7	6.8	11.6	9.0	4.6	2.2	13.9	4.3	—	4.3	10.2	4.8	1.2	14.8	15.8
1932	19.1	13.7	11.9	17.6	16.0	5.8	—	17.2	5.8	—	8.3	9.5	6.8	2.8	15.3	23.5
1933	17.4	16.3	10.6	19.3	14.5	6.2	—	14.8	5.9	—	9.7	9.7	7.3	3.5	13.9	24.7
1934	15.0	16.1	11.8	14.5	11.0	4.4	—	8.3	5.6	—	9.8	9.4	6.4	3.3	11.7	21.6
1935	12.5	15.2	11.1	14.2	10.0	3.7	—	6.5	—	—	11.2	8.7	6.2	4.2	10.8	20.0
1936	9.9	15.2	8.4	12.8	9.5	2.7	4.5	4.8	—	—	11.9	7.2	5.3	4.7	9.2	16.8
1937	8.1	13.7	7.2	9.4	11.0	2.6	—	2.7	5.0	—	10.5	6.0	5.1	3.6	7.7	14.2
1938	8.1	8.1	8.7	11.4	10.5	2.6	3.7	1.3	4.6	—	9.9	5.8	5.1	3.3	9.2	18.8

Table 1. Cont.

	Australia	Austria	Belgium	Canada	Denmark	Finland	France	Germany	Italy	Japan	Netherlands	Norway	Sweden	Switzerland	U.K.	U.S.
1950	1.5	3.9	5.0	3.6	4.0	1.0	2.3	8.2	6.9	1.9	2.8	1.2	1.7	0.0	2.5	5.2
1951	1.3	3.5	4.4	2.4	4.6	0.3	2.1	7.3	7.3	1.7	3.2	1.5	1.6	0.0	2.2	3.2
1952	2.2	4.7	5.1	2.9	5.8	0.4	2.1	7.0	7.8	1.9	4.9	1.6	1.7	0.0	3.0	2.9
1953	2.5	5.5	5.3	2.9	4.4	1.5	2.6	6.2	8.1	1.7	3.5	1.9	1.9	0.0	2.6	2.8
1954	1.7	5.0	5.0	4.5	3.8	1.0	2.8	5.6	8.3	2.2	2.3	1.8	1.8	0.0	2.3	5.3
1955	1.4	3.6	3.9	4.3	4.5	0.4	2.4	4.3	7.0	2.5	1.5	1.6	1.8	0.0	2.1	4.2
1956	1.8	3.4	2.8	3.3	5.1	2.2	1.8	3.4	8.7	2.3	1.0	1.9	1.6	0.0	2.2	4.0
1957	2.3	3.2	2.3	4.5	4.9	2.2	1.4	2.9	7.0	1.9	1.5	2.1	1.7	0.0	2.4	4.2
1958	2.7	3.4	3.3	6.9	4.5	2.2	1.6	3.0	6.0	2.0	3.0	3.3	2.0	0.0	3.0	6.6
1959	2.6	3.1	4.0	5.8	3.1	2.1	1.9	2.0	5.2	2.2	2.1	3.2	1.8	0.0	3.0	5.3
1960	2.5	2.3	3.3	6.8	2.1	1.4	1.8	1.0	3.9	1.7	1.2	2.3	1.7	0.0	2.2	5.4
1961	2.3	1.8	2.5	7.0	1.9	1.2	1.5	0.7	3.4	1.4	0.9	1.8	1.5	0.0	2.0	6.5
1962	2.2	1.9	2.1	5.8	1.6	1.3	1.4	0.6	2.9	1.3	0.9	2.0	1.5	0.0	2.8	5.4
1963	1.8	2.0	1.7	5.4	2.1	1.5	1.3	0.7	2.5	1.2	0.9	2.4	1.7	0.0	3.4	5.5
1964	1.6	1.9	1.3	4.3	1.2	1.5	1.1	0.6	3.9	1.2	0.8	2.1	1.6	0.0	2.5	5.0
1965	1.5	1.9	1.5	3.6	1.0	1.4	1.3	0.5	5.0	1.1	1.0	1.7	1.2	0.0	2.2	4.4
1966	1.7	1.7	1.6	3.3	1.1	1.5	1.4	0.6	5.4	1.3	1.4	1.6	1.6	0.0	2.3	3.7
1967	1.8	1.8	2.3	3.8	1.2	2.9	1.8	1.7	5.1	1.3	2.8	1.5	2.1	0.0	3.4	3.8
1968	1.7	1.6	2.7	4.4	1.6	3.9	2.1	1.2	5.3	1.2	2.5	2.2	2.2	0.0	3.3	3.5
1969	1.7	2.0	2.1	4.4	1.1	2.8	2.3	0.7	5.2	1.1	1.8	2.1	1.9	0.0	3.0	3.5
1970	1.6	1.4	1.8	5.6	0.7	1.9	2.4	0.6	4.9	1.1	1.6	1.5	1.5	0.0	3.1	4.9
1971	1.8	1.3	1.7	6.1	1.1	2.2	2.6	0.7	4.9	1.2	2.3	1.5	2.5	0.0	3.8	5.9
1972	2.6	1.2	2.7	6.2	0.9	2.5	2.8	0.8	6.3	1.4	3.9	1.7	2.7	0.0	4.0	5.5
1973	2.3	1.1	2.7	5.5	0.9	2.3	2.7	0.8	6.2	1.3	3.9	1.5	2.5	0.0	3.0	4.8
1974	2.6	1.3	3.0	5.3	3.5	1.7	2.8	1.6	5.3	1.4	4.4	1.5	2.0	0.0	2.9	5.5

Table 1. Cont.

	Australia	Austria	Belgium	Canada	Denmark	Finland	France	Germany	Italy	Japan	Netherlands	Norway	Sweden	Switzerland	U.K.	U.S.
1975	4.8	1.8	5.0	6.9	4.9	2.2	4.0	3.6	5.8	1.9	5.9	2.3	1.6	0.4	4.3	8.3
1976	4.7	1.8	6.4	7.1	6.3	3.8	4.4	3.7	6.6	2.0	6.3	1.8	1.6	0.7	5.6	7.6
1977	5.6	1.6	7.4	8.0	7.3	5.8	4.9	3.6	7.0	2.0	6.0	1.5	1.8	0.4	6.0	6.9
1978	6.2	2.1	7.9	8.3	8.3	7.2	5.2	3.5	7.1	2.2	6.2	1.8	2.2	0.3	5.9	6.0
1979	6.2	2.1	8.2	7.4	6.0	5.9	5.9	3.2	7.6	2.1	6.6	2.0	2.1	0.3	5.0	5.8
1980	6.0	1.9	8.8	7.4	6.9	4.6	6.3	3.0	7.5	2.0	6.0	1.6	2.0	0.2	6.4	7.0
1981	5.7	2.5	10.8	7.5	10.3	4.8	7.4	4.4	7.8	2.2	8.5	2.0	2.5	0.2	9.8	7.5
1982	7.1	3.5	12.6	10.9	11.0	5.3	8.1	6.1	8.4	2.4	11.4	2.6	3.2	0.4	11.3	9.5
1983	9.9	4.1	12.1	11.8	11.4	5.4	8.3	8.0	8.8	2.6	12.0	3.4	3.5	0.9	12.4	9.5
1984	8.9	3.8	12.1	11.2	8.5	5.2	9.7	7.1	9.4	2.7	11.8	3.1	3.1	1.1	11.7	7.4
1985	8.2	3.6	11.3	10.4	7.3	5.0	10.2	7.2	9.6	2.6	10.6	2.6	2.8	0.9	11.2	7.1
1986	8.0	3.1	11.2	9.5	5.5	5.3	10.4	6.4	10.5	2.8	9.9	2.0	2.7	0.8	11.2	6.9
1987	8.0	3.8	11.0	8.8	6.9	5.0	10.5	6.2	10.9	2.8	9.6	2.1	1.9	0.7	10.3	6.1
1988	7.2	3.6	9.7	7.7	7.2	4.5	10.0	6.2	11.0	2.5	9.2	3.2	1.6	0.6	8.5	5.4
1989	6.1	3.1	8.1	7.5	7.8	3.4	9.4	5.6	10.9	2.3	8.3	4.9	1.4	0.5	7.1	5.2
1990	6.9	3.2	7.2	8.1	8.0	3.4	8.9	4.8	10.3	2.1	7.5	5.2	1.5	0.5	6.8	5.4
1991	9.5	3.5	7.2	10.2	8.7	7.5	9.4	4.2	9.9	2.1	7.0	5.5	2.7	1.1	8.7	6.6
1992	10.7	3.6	7.9	11.2	9.3	13.0	10.3	4.6	10.5	2.2	6.8	5.9	4.8	2.5	9.9	7.3
1993*	10.9	4.8	9.1	11.1	10.1	17.8	11.6	5.3	9.4	2.5	8.2	6.0	7.4	4.5	10.2	6.7

Source: 1920–1938, 1950–1989: Maddison (1991, pp. 262–265, Table C.6), 1990–1993: OECD, *Economic Outlook* (various issues), *preliminary.

Part III
Current Policy Issues

Reforming the Welfare State in Western Europe

Roland Vaubel

As economists, we know that we do not know, and cannot know, the desirable degree and pattern of redistribution. But we agree on procedures: redistribution is desirable if it is voluntary—either in the form of private charity or by way of government transfers based on a general consensus. As economists, we know that giving may be in the interest of the giver and that, owing to externalities or economies of scale, collective giving may be more efficient than individual giving. As long as collective giving is voluntary, it is a Pareto improvement. The same is true for social insurance and social regulation. There is much scope for such a Paretian social policy that makes nobody worse off.

By contrast, if redistribution, insurance or regulation is imposed by the state even though a consensus is lacking, we can no longer be sure that the benefits will outweigh the costs because it is not possible to compare the cardinal utilities of different persons in a scientific way. Thus, as economists, we would have more confidence in the welfare state if social policy measures required qualified rather than simple majorities. This is the case for a procedural reform.

However, even if social policy is not based on a broad consensus, the economist has an important contribution to make. He can take the degree and pattern of governmental redistribution as given and inquire whether it could be brought about at a lower cost. Do the governments of Western Europe use efficient instruments to reach their redistributive targets? Which instruments would be less or even least costly? This is the question that will concern us in the following sections.

I shall distinguish between social insurance, social regulation, and explicit transfers (including public policy towards private charity). I shall argue that social insurance can be made more efficient by enlarging the scope for choice and competition and that such a reform would also assist in reducing unemployment. The aims of social regulation can be achieved more efficiently by other means (except for requiring citizens to carry insurance that provides coverage equivalent to the social minimum). The tax and transfer system is the most efficient instrument of redistribution. But in the Europe of today, it is not used in a consistent and incentive-compatible way. Its faults have contributed to the present unemployment.

I   Social Insurance: Choice and Competition

The reform of social insurance cannot be discussed without reference to the theoretical arguments that are usually adduced to justify present-day social insurance. Three justifications are prominent in the literature: the moral hazard created by the social minimum, adverse selection due to asymmetric information, and economies of scale in the provision of insurance. The first two are based on externality theory.

If the individual citizen can rely on government or private charity to obtain the social minimum in an emergency, he or she will have an insufficient incentive to save or insure for, or avoid, such emergencies, so that the general taxpayer will face a negative externality. The indiscriminate guarantee of a nonrepayable social minimum is like insurance that generates moral hazard. This inefficiency can be eliminated by requiring citizens to have some type of actuarily fair insurance. If a person is unable to pay the insurance premium, the government would provide it (e.g., as part of the social minimum under a negative income tax).

This justification has three important implications for the reform of social insurance:

1. If the government establishes public insurance, it must charge actuarily fair premia to eliminate moral hazard.
2. The required insurance coverage need not exceed the social minimum.
3. If the government establishes public insurance, every citizen must be free to contract out, i.e., to buy the required insurance coverage from the insurance company of his or her choice.

Adverse selection prevails when insurance companies repeatedly fail to recognize the bad risks among their clients. In these circumstances, the good risks will tend to demand too little insurance, and the market for insurance may break down even though insurance would be efficient if information were symmetric. Under asymmetric information, there is a presumption that too little insurance is demanded and supplied. Requiring citizens to have insurance is a possible remedy. However, as long as the government does not possess the missing information either, it cannot know what would constitute optimal insurance coverage. Moreover, the optimal coverage depends on risk aversion, which differs between individuals and is not known to the government. With adverse selection, the optimal insurance coverage may exceed the social minimum. But by requiring excessive insurance coverage, the government may make matters worse than they were without intervention. Even if the government collected the missing information about individual risks (which it does not) and if it did so more efficiently than the private insurance industry ever could, it would not be justified in requiring citizens to have insurance; it would merely have to supply its superior information to the private insurance market.

Public provision of insurance might be justified if, owing to the law of large numbers and the central limit theorem, insurance was a natural monopoly good. In this case, competition between private insurance companies should have a tendency to destroy itself. This is not borne out by the evidence. In Germany, for example, there are at least 20 private suppliers of insurance for most categories of risk even though the regulatory authorities permit, and sometimes even encourage, mergers between insurance companies.

To summarize, requiring citizens to carry insurance with coverage equivalent to the social minimum can be justified. But there is no convincing case for the governmental provision of such insurance, let alone a government monopoly. If the government continues to offer insurance coverage but freely permits contracting out, the public insurance must not be exempt from the taxes and regulations that private insurance providers are subject to.

Since efficiency requires choice and competition between insurance providers and since competing insurance providers do not redistribute voluntarily, efficient redistribution can only be effected by other means. As we shall see, the redistributive targets that governments have pursued with social insurance, are most efficiently attained with an appropriate tax and transfer system. Persons who suffer from chronic illness or who have many children, for example, could receive a special tax allowance or transfer. The tax and transfer system is also a more efficient instrument of redistribution because it can be better targeted to need as measured by income and wealth. Since the "means test" is implemented by the tax authorities, it is strictly confidential, and since it is required for income tax purposes anyway, it does not cause additional information or transaction costs.

I will now apply these general considerations separately to the three main branches of European social insurance: health insurance, unemployment insurance, and insurance for old age.

A   Health Insurance

Requiring citizens to have insurance coverage equal to the social minimum implies that each citizen must purchase health insurance (including old-age care) that ensures that his income net of health expenditure will not fall below the social minimum. In other words, the maximum deductible that he may agree to is the difference between his after-tax income and the social minimum. Within these limits, he could choose any type of coinsurance, proportional or otherwise. If, owing to illness, his net income falls short of the social minimum, the insurance contract must provide for the difference.

In the same vein, employers would no longer be obliged to offer sickness pay, if they added the per capita cost of sickness pay to the wage. Workers could use the wage increase to obtain the mandatory insurance coverage from an insurance provider of their choice, and each could pick the combination of sickness pay, coinsurance, and premium that conforms to his or her risk aversion. The pooled regression in the Appendix shows that the introduction of waiting days and a reduction of the replacement ratio would significantly reduce absenteeism. Thus, by reducing moral hazard, coinsurance would reduce the premium by more than the amount of the coinsurance. The individual employer, it is true, may have a comparative advantage in controlling for moral hazard, notably shirking. However, if, as a result, he can provide sickness pay to his workers at a lower cost than an external insurance provider could, he will do so voluntarily to avoid the wage increase.

The Western European health insurance systems do not conform to these liberal criteria. Choice of and competition between insurance providers are least restricted in Switzerland, but only one-third of the population is required to have insurance. In both respects, Switzerland is similar to the United States, and in both countries, there are political initiatives to oblige more people to have insurance. Unfortunately, the proposed reforms would also increase the regulation of, and redistribution by, the health insurance system. To the extent that they rely on additional employers' contributions, they would raise the cost of labor and make for higher unemployment. In Switzerland, such initiatives have repeatedly been rejected in referenda.

The international comparisons published by the OECD and other organizations focus on the size of health expenditure, its composition and financing, and the extent of coinsurance. Such quantitative data tell us little or nothing about whether choice and competition are restricted and whether people get what they want. A low ratio of health expenditure to GDP is—as the British National Health Service and the German spending caps show—not necessarily a sign of efficiency. Procedural, not structural, criteria have to be used.[1]

B Unemployment Insurance

Many people believe that unemployment insurance cannot efficiently be provided by private competitive suppliers. Private unemployment insurance has never been widespread. Commercial unemployment insurance providers have tended to be short-lived, and, in the absence of government intervention, the insurance offered by trade unions has hardly ever been demanded by a majority of workers.[2] In many West

---

[1] The most relevant, but a very imperfect, quantitative proxy of choice and competition is the share of private expenditure in total health expenditure. In 1987, it exceeded 30 percent in Portugal (39%), Switzerland (32%), and Austria (32%) but it fell short of 10 percent in Norway (1%), Luxembourg (8%), and Sweden (9%). The unweighted average of the West European countries (20%) amounts to only one-third of the private share in the United States (source: OECD Health Data File).

[2] Before World War I, several German trade unions provided unemployment insurance to their members but participation was fairly limited. In 1906, for example, only 7 percent of German workers had such insurance. As the unions gained members and, by 1919, could even extend their minimum wages to non-

European countries, governments have raised participation in union-supplied unemployment insurance by subsidizing it and opening it for nonmembers. In one form or other, this so-called Ghent System is still practiced in Denmark, Finland, and Sweden.

Thus, to judge from historical experience, private unemployment insurance is clearly feasible but, in the absence of large subsidies, voluntary participation tends to be low. The most likely reasons are adverse selection and the moral hazard that is generated by social assistance and is inherent in unemployment insurance. But participation cannot be low if each worker is obliged to purchase insurance from an insurance provider of his choice. The required insurance coverage could be confined to a lump-sum benefit that is equal for all (as in the United Kingdom, Ireland, and Sweden)—the social minimum. The choice of additional insurance, the time profile of benefits, behavior-related coinsurance, credit components, top-up payments for recipients who accept lower-paid work, options to convert benefits into wage subsidies, experience-rated contributions, etc., could all be left to the market.

In a recession, private unemployment insurance providers may not be able to raise their premia from the employed by a margin that is sufficient to pay the guaranteed benefits to the unemployed, nor may they be able to borrow in the market. Like private health insurance companies now, they might have to be obliged to accumulate considerable reserves. The reserve fund would have to be sufficient to weather a severe and protracted recession. The reserves could be individually earmarked and repayable at retirement (like the mandatory savings accounts that Schanz [1895] has proposed as a protection against unemployment). By drawing on these reserves in recession, private, like public, unemployment insurance would act as a built-in stabilizer of aggregate demand. In boom times, however, by accumulating its reserves, private insurance would tend to be a more effective built-in stabilizer than public unemployment insurance, which tends to raise benefits when revenue from contributions is plentiful.

---

members, they lost their fear of underbidding and their interest in supplying unemployment insurance. The state unemployment insurance that was introduced by a center-right coalition government before the election of 1927 has enjoyed a legal monopoly ever since. Private suppliers—even of supplementary insurance—have been prosecuted.

Clark (1954, p. 25) and Hayek (1960, p. 302) have suggested that labor unions or employers' associations, or both, should contribute to the financing of unemployment insurance to the extent that their wage bargains have caused unemployment. By internalizing the cost of unemployment with them, we could reduce their temptation to set excessive wages. Such a tax on the generation of unemployment is preferable to a tax-based incomes policy because the government does not know the wage level that is consistent with full employment. The search for market-clearing prices and wages should be left to the private sector. Both tax schemes, however, suffer from an identification problem: which part of total unemployment are unions and employers' associations to be blamed for? Not all unemployment is of a classical nature. There is considerable evidence that some part of it is voluntary. Moreover, there can be Keynesian unemployment caused by macroeconomic disturbances that unions and employers' associations could not anticipate. Is there a simple and reasonable rule for apportioning responsibility?

It seems to be a stylized fact that macroeconomic policy shocks affect output with a lag of about one year and employment with a lag of about two years, and that the lag from wage adjustment to employment is about two years. Thus, if there is, say, a permanent negative shock in year t, labor and employers could react to it in year $t+1$ and restore full employment by year $t+3$. If the shock is transitory, i.e., confined to year t, the return to full employment in $t+3$ is even automatic. In this stylized world, unions and employers' associations would only be responsible, and only be held responsible, to the extent that unemployment persisted beyond $t+2$. If there were only one shock in t, they could not be liable in $t+1$ and $t+2$, nor would they have to contribute in $t+3$ if they adjusted wages in $t+1$. The general implication is that they ought to be responsible to the extent that the current unemployment rate had already prevailed a year ago.

There are two complications, however. The first is that negative shocks may be serially correlated. During the Great Depression, a series of cumulative contractionary monetary shocks occurred over almost four years. Thus, it may be reasonable to extend the reference period of our rule to, say, five years (which is also the maximum electoral cycle for European parliaments). The second complication is that some unemployment is purely frictional or even voluntary. It has to be deducted. It could be approximated as, say, the lowest ten-year average of the unemployment rate during the last two or three decades.[3] With these modifications, unions and/or employers' associations would be obliged to finance the mandatory unemployment benefits to the extent that the current unemployment rate among the insured had already prevailed in each of the five previous years minus the lowest ten-year unemployment rate over the last two or three decades. Even so, internalization would probably remain incomplete because, in most cases, the welfare cost of classical unemployment is likely to exceed the cost of the unemployment benefit, i.e., the social minimum. Like all rules, this one, too, would not be perfect, but it seems to be better than no rule at all.

There remains the question of whether labor unions, employers' associations, or both ought to be liable. Since both sides would have to finance the compensation payments by raising their membership fees, the assignment of responsibility would affect their relative bargaining powers. Clearly, the built-in stabilization effect on employment would be stronger, the larger the share of the compensation to be paid by the side that is primarily interested in raising wages. Notwithstanding the theory of efficiency wages, this is the union side.

If responsibility for unemployment is to be assigned exclusively to individual trade unions, there is the question of who pays for unemployed entrants to the labor market. The burden could be spread over the unions in accordance with the share of the employed that is covered by each wage bargaining agreement. Alternatively, the scheme could be confined to those who are unemployed because they have been dismissed from their jobs. However, mere experience-rating of this sort would fail to deal with the insider-outsider problem.

C   Old-Age Insurance

In Western Europe, all governments require their citizens to be enrolled in the old age insurance schemes run by the respective social insurance monopolies. In the United Kingdom, however, some portion of the

---

[3] In Germany, the average unemployment rate in 1964–1973 was close to one percent. To allow for a possible increase in voluntary unemployment and the pace of structural change, the addition of another percentage point would afford a reasonable safety margin.

required insurance protection may be purchased from the private sector. The contracting-out option was introduced by the Labour government in 1978 and extended by the Conservative government in 1983. It is widely used.

In several European countries, e.g., the United Kingdom, the Netherlands, Belgium, and several Scandinavian countries, the basic pension provided by the state is the same for everyone. Except for the United Kingdom, these countries finance their basic pensions from general tax revenue. With respect to moral hazard, such a tax-financed state pension scheme is not different from social assistance. Moreover, any social insurance for old age that operates on a pay-as-you-go basis is subject to severe moral hazard because, under a pay-as-you-go system, the positive external effects of raising children are not internalized individually. In Western Europe, all public insurance systems for old age are pay-as-you-go systems, but in several countries some funded private insurance is also mandatory.

Samuelson (1958) and Diamond (1965) have tried to justify the pay-as-you-go system on the grounds that, with an infinite time horizon, it brings about a lower and more appropriate savings rate. Others have objected that (1) it may not reduce the savings rate owing to inter-generational utility interdependence (Barro, 1978), that (2) the savings rate has already been excessively reduced by capital taxation (Feldstein, 1977), and that (3) to assume an infinite time horizon is a dubious way of extending the budget constraint. One does not need these objections, however, in order to invalidate Samuelson's original argument. As he points out, the pay-as-you-go system is equivalent to government debt. Thus, government debt is at least as effective (or, according to Barro, ineffective) in bringing about Samuelson's optimal savings rate as the pay-as-you-go principle for social security can ever be. But government debt is theoretically more efficient (or, according to Feldstein, less inefficient) in doing so because, unlike pay-as-you-go, it does not require a governmental insurance monopoly. (Of course, both pay-as-you-go and deficit financing may be undesirable because, as public choice theory shows, they encourage excessive government spending and may bring about a *sub*optimal rate of capital accumulation.)

If choice and competition among actuarially fair private insurance providers is more efficient than the state monopoly, the transition from pay-as-you-go to a funded system can be a Pareto improvement for all generations. As Buchanan (1968) has suggested, the pay-as-you-go system could be transformed into a funded system by converting all public pension liabilities into transferable government debt (bonds) that the citizens could sell to the insurance provider of their choice. Each working generation would accumulate a capital fund for its own old age, and the burden of servicing the inherited social security debt could be shared by the present and all future working generations. This is essentially how Chile managed the transition to private insurance competition while still requiring citizens to have old-age insurance.

II   Social Regulation

The following reasons have been given in favor of social regulation: (1) imperfect competition, (2) time inconsistency, (3) health and safety externalities and (4) asymmetric information (which was covered in the previous section).

If a buyer, say an employer, or a supplier, say a landlord, enjoys a *dominant position* in a local market, prices will be distorted, and the quantity will be too small. If the government or some other regulatory body were to prescribe a minimum wage equal to the competitive wage and a maximum rent equal to the competitive rent, the optimal quantity would be chosen. Unfortunately, there is no reason to believe that the government would set the competitive wage or rent. The government does not and cannot know the competitive wage or rent, and it may easily err on the opposite side. Moreover, since the median voter is a worker and tenant, the government is biased in favor of too high a minimum wage and too low a maximum rent. Depending on the elasticities of demand and supply, the welfare loss caused by the regulation may easily be larger than the welfare loss due to the initial distortion that regulation is supposed to remove.

Even if social regulation did not make things worse, it is unlikely to be the optimal instrument for dealing with the imperfections of competition. The only way of finding and bringing about the competitive price, wage, or rent is to introduce competition. The optimal instrument is competition policy, and the optimal institution is an independent competition authority that addresses specific local problem cases. It would be farther removed from electoral politics and ideally enjoy constitutional status. Competition can also be improved by raising labor mobility, e.g., in the European internal market. The problems of imperfect competition are due to a lack of choice. They will not be solved by government regulations that restrict individual choice even further.

The problem of *time inconsistency* is supposed to justify laws against dismissals and for codetermination. Otherwise, the argument runs, there would be too little investment in firm-specific human capital; in the absence of a binding commitment mechanism, social regulation ought to serve as a substitute.

Time inconsistency can be a serious problem for international contractual relations, but domestically there should be no commitment problem. Contracts are enforced by the state. If not, this is a case of government failure that can and has to be corrected. If contracts are enforced and if wages are permitted to settle at their equilibrium level, workers and employers have an incentive to agree on conditions of dismissal that are optimal with respect to firm-specific human capital and their individual risk aversion. As in Figure 1 Panel a, the period within which notice must be given will be set at t^* where the marginal benefit to the worker equals the marginal cost, if any, to the employer. The same is true for the notice to be given by a landlord or a tenant. If social regulation sets a shorter t, it will be ineffective; if the regulated t exceeds t^*, the government has caused a welfare loss equal to the shaded area. There is also a welfare loss from reduced employment, which can be shown in the standard labor market diagram (Panel b). Since the excess waiting period is worth less to the worker than it costs the employer, the demand curve shifts more (from D_1 to D_2) than the supply curve does (from S_1 to $\bar{S}$), and employment falls (from N^* to $\bar{N}$).

Similarly, if the worker wants to be protected against the consequences of dismissal and if his employer is the most efficient provider of such protection, they will agree on redundancy payments.

Finally, if arbitration is needed and if codetermination is the most efficient form of arbitration, codetermination will prevail in the market.[4]

---

[4] For the opposite view, see Levine and Tyson (1990). They argue that participation is prevented by adverse selection even though it is more efficient. Since participatory firms attract "less-motivated workers," they "will have to bear significant screening and monitoring costs" (p. 219). These external costs imposed by nonparticipatory competitors could be eliminated by prescribing codetermination everywhere (ctd.).

Nowhere, however, has codetermination emerged from institutional competition. It has been imposed by government fiat. If the degree of codetermination, c, is substituted for t in Figure 1, the potential welfare loss is apparent. Thus, everybody could be made better off if workers, either individually or at the company level, were free to sell their legal protection against dismissal and their legal right to redundancy payments and codetermination in exchange for higher wages.[5] If workers could trade their property rights, they could reveal whether, say, codetermination serves their own interest or merely the interest of trade union leaders. Thus, paradoxically, codetermination imposed by the state is incompatible with the emancipation of workers.

Health and safety risks can justify regulation if the potential externality is irreversible or if liability cannot be established. Requiring citizens to have insurance or to be vaccinated against a contagious disease is such a regulation. There may also be purely internal risks that no reasonable person would want to be exposed to. However, risk aversion differs. The demand for security increases with income. Since income levels differ considerably within Western Europe, even more than in the United States,[6] the current attempts to introduce uniform or minimum social regulations in the European Union are clearly misguided.

There are several problems with this argument. First of all, it is hard to believe that a system which, according to the authors, attracts less-motivated workers could be efficient if practiced by all. Second, it is hard to believe that the additional screening and monitoring costs that competition requires are larger than the benefits that competition for efficient forms of business organization provides. It is well known that monopolization and imposed uniformity reduce information cost. But does that mean they are more efficient overall? Finally, even if there were significant information cost externalities, they would not justify interference with the freedom of contract. A tax subsidy scheme that compensates participatory firms for their additional screening and monitoring costs (if any) would be entirely sufficient.

[5] Theologians tend to disapprove of the fact that Esau sold his right of primogeniture to Jacob for a pottage of lentils, but from an economic point of view, revelation of preference is the appropriate test, and it was proven right by the success story of Jacob and his offspring.

[6] Income per capita in Denmark and Luxembourg is three times higher than in Greece and Portugal. In the richest region, it is six times higher than in the poorest region. The Gini coefficient is much higher for the 60 EU regions than for the 49 contiguous states of the United States.

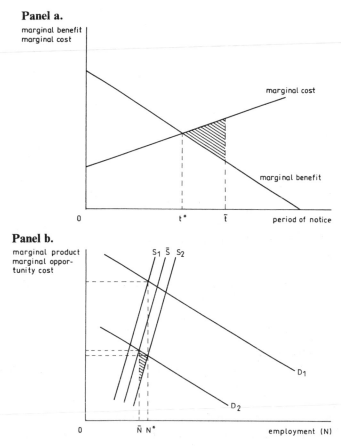

Figure 1. Contractual versus Regulated Periods of Notice.

The Social Chapter of Maastricht permits qualified majority voting on (certain) social regulations for the first time. This enables the more highly regulated member states to impose the regulations of the decisive member on the less regulated member states, and the decisive member is likely to increase his regulation because regulatory competition from the less regulated member states can now be suppressed (Vaubel, 1995a). The strategy of raising rivals' costs is well known from industrial economics and the theory of regulation. Stigler (1970, p. 2) has suggested that it explains the federal minimum wage legislation in the United States (the North suppressing the South). Even if

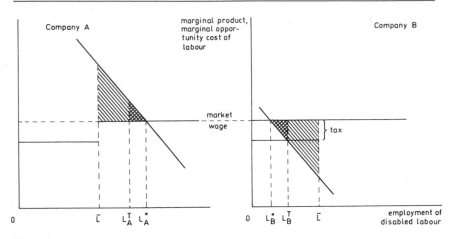

Figure 2. The Welfare Loss from Affirmative Action.

wages in Southern Europe adjust to offset the additional cost of regulation, the composition of the reward from work will be distorted: job security, hygienic standards and amenities will be excessive, and the wage component will be smaller than desired by the workers. In the absence of complete wage adjustment, unemployment in the South will rise. Moreover, to the extent that the governments of the member states adopt European regulations unanimously, unemployment may increase in the whole union. The existence of an international policy cartel will strengthen the political power of insiders over outsiders in the national labor markets, and the availability of transfers from the European structural funds will increase their incentive to use that power.

Since the 1970s, Western Europe has experimented with a new instrument of social regulation: *job quotas* for women, the disabled, etc. ("affirmative action"). This instrument is inefficient because the productivity of, say, a disabled person differs from one line of production to another. Figure 2 shows the problem. Total employment is the same in both companies but the marginal productivity of a disabled person is higher in company A than in company B. If the quota (in Germany 6 percent) is chosen in such a way that all disabled persons have to be employed, some of the disabled ($\bar{L}L_B^*$ or $\bar{L}L_A^*$ in Figure 2, both of which are equal) can be employed more productively in company A, and the welfare loss is equal to the sum of the two shaded triangles. If, as in Germany, employers have the option of paying a tax (on the shortfall of disabled persons employed by them) rather than fulfilling their quota, the welfare loss is reduced but not eliminated. The opportunity cost of disabled labor now intersects the demand curve of company B at L_B^T. Company B releases $\bar{L}L_B^T$, which is then absorbed by company A. But there remains a combined welfare loss equal to the two double-shaded areas. To avoid this misallocation, the disabled would either have to receive a lower wage that equals their lower marginal productivity or their employer would have to be given a wage subsidy that equals their productivity disadvantage. The disabled recipients would, of course, prefer an equivalent cash transfer that is not tied to employment.

III Explicit Transfers

The tax and transfer system is an efficient instrument of social policy but it is not used in an efficient way. First of all, there is broad agreement among economists that, in general, cash transfers are superior to in-kind transfers if the donors want to maximize the utility of the recipients.[7] Moreover, in practice, only a system of cash transfers can be comprehensive,[8] consistent, and well targeted. The widespread use of in-kind transfers can be explained by the interests of the social bureaucracy and private producer groups. If donors vote for in-kind transfers, this may be due to ignorance.[9]

---

[7] Notable exceptions to this rule are transfers to addicts, the mentally ill and possibly children. Tied cash transfers (e.g., housing assistance) and price subsidies (e.g., for low-quality apartment construction) that are confined to the needy are, of course, equivalent to in-kind transfers.

[8] Comprehensiveness must not be confused with spatial centralization. If the recipients of transfers are not very mobile or if the origin principle applies, the transfer system can be decentralized. In these circumstances, decentralization is efficient because transfers have to be differentiated according to local redistributive preferences and the local level of wages and living costs. Need and ability to work are also more efficiently ascertained at the local level.

[9] Bruce and Waldman (1991) argue that in-kind transfers also serve to prevent the recipients from imposing negative externalities on the donors in order to get more aid. However, if donors are exclusively interested in the utility that normal adult recipients derive from the transfer, the recipients do not have an incentive to abuse it.

Second, the current system of untied cash transfers (social assistance) weakens the recipients' work incentive much more than is strictly inevitable. As is well known, this is due to the fact that, in most countries in Western Europe, income from voluntary work is almost fully deducted from social assistance. In other words, many recipients face a marginal tax rate of 100 percent.[10]

Two remedies for the incentive problem have been tried. The first, *workfare*, obliges those who are able to work to take part in a retraining program. However, many of them may not have to be retrained or may not have a sufficient incentive to search for a job. Workfare is not sufficient, and it may even be wasteful. Alternatively, the recipients may be required to take part in public works organized by the local authorities. However, public works distort the allocation of labor between the public and the private sector. Moreover, local officials and politicians do not usually find it in their interest, and do not bother, to organize public works.

On paper, the recipients can also be required to accept job offers from the private sector. If they reject such offers, their assistance could be cut—ultimately to the subsistence level. In practice, however, this does not solve the problem because it is usually not in the interest of private employers to offer work to persons who clearly indicate that they do not want to work. Moreover, the job offered by the private employer may not be the one that the recipient would prefer and in which he would do best.

The incentive problem can only be solved if those who are able but unwilling to work are made worse off than those who are unable or willing. Either those who could but do not work could receive less assistance, or those who do could retain a larger portion of their wage.

---

[10] In Germany, recipients of social assistance retain, on average, DM 200 of income from work. The various provinces (*Laender*) have different arrangements. In the province of Schleswig-Holstein, for example, the recipients of social assistance may fully retain the first DM 130 from work plus 15 percent of additional labor income up to total retained earnings of DM 260. The Federal Government has recently suggested a similar system with a withdrawal rate of 90 percent and no cap.

Another exception is the British Family Credit introduced by Norman Fowler in 1987. With gross earnings between £70 and £150 per month, the withdrawal rate is 70 percent.

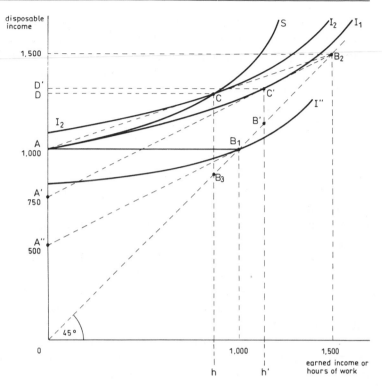

Figure 3. Variants of a Negative Income Tax.

In either case the marginal tax rate would fall. The two reforms could be combined in the framework of a *negative income tax.*

Figure 3 shows the difference between social assistance and the negative income tax. With social assistance, disposable income is equal to the social minimum, OA, until the horizontal line intersects the break-even line (the 45° line) at B_1. (If the horizontal axis is interpreted as the number of working hours, h, the 45° line is the break-even line for a wage rate equal to 1.) Now consider a negative income tax, i.e., a marginal tax rate of less than 100 percent. If the social minimum is the same as under social assistance, the recipient's labor supply curve, S, for various marginal tax rates is given by the points of tangency between a ray rotating through A and his income-work indifference curves. As can be seen, the negative income tax (the reduction of the marginal tax rate) enables the recipient to reach higher indifference curves. The donor will pick point C on the recipient's labor supply curve because it minimizes his expenditure, i.e., the vertical distance between the labor supply curve and the break-even line, CB_3. With a constant marginal tax rate, the straight line through A and C intersects the break-even line at B_2. Beyond B_2, the social minimum would be fully deducted from the income tax liability.

The break-even point of the negative income tax is higher than the break-even point for social assistance if the social minimum remains unchanged, and this is a standard objection to the negative income tax proposal. But the social minimum can now be changed. As Figure 3 shows, the transfer to those who can work can be reduced to OA' without making them worse off ($A'C'$ is tangent to I_1). For a net income of OD', they will work h' hours, and their disposable income will increase (from OD to OD').

If the disposable income rather than the utility of those who can work is to be kept constant, the transfer can be even further reduced. A welfare recipient who could earn the initial break-even income, AB_1, would receive a social minimum of A'' (provided that A'' exceeds the subsistence level). A'' is derived by drawing the tangent to the indifference curve in B_1. For those who cannot earn AB_1, the point of tangency would lie left of B_1 on the AB_1 line, so that their minimum income (the intersection of the tangent with the vertical axis) would be higher. The recipients' utility, it is true, would be lower at these minimum income levels than at A but this would merely be due to their disliking work. The transfer OA would still be available for those who can prove that they cannot work or that they are successfully attending a retraining program.[11]

The break-even point can also be lowered by setting higher marginal tax rates below the break-even point than for incomes that exceed

---

[11] This distinction is already being made in Germany. According to section 23 of the Bundessozialhilfegesetz, supplementary benefits are available for persons above 60, the disabled, the sick, pregnant women, and single parents with dependent children (one below 7 or two below 16). However, unemployed persons who have worked in the past and do not receive unemployment insurance benefits any longer receive even higher tax-financed transfers (unemployment assistance). These transfers can be renewed every year an indefinite number of times as long as the means test is satisfied. Since past work is likely to indicate ability to work in the future, this differentiation of transfers is the opposite of an incentive-compatible solution.

it.[12] Since persons with very low potential incomes are less numerous and less productive than the average, higher than average marginal tax rates and work disincentives at low levels of income can be justified. However, there seems to be agreement that marginal tax rates of 100 percent, or close to it, cannot be optimal at any income level.

If marginal tax rates and minimum incomes are reduced for those who can work without raising the break-even income, total transfer expenditure falls. Thus, if minimum incomes are reduced for those who can work, the break-even income can be raised without increasing total transfer expenditure. If marginal tax rates of more than 100 percent are to be avoided (when passing the break-even income), the basic income tax allowance must not fall short of the break-even income. As a result, any rise in the break-even income is very costly in terms of lost income tax revenue. But the loss of tax revenue can be kept small if this tax allowance is means-tested (as is the case in Germany). Those who do not pass the means test would receive a lower tax allowance because they are not likely to receive social assistance anyway.

By contrast, if the basic income tax allowance is to be the same for all, the break-even income cannot rise very much unless the negative income tax replaces other major transfer programs (for example, housing assistance, housing subsidies and unemployment assistance). Several studies show how the reform could be designed so as to leave the budgetary balance unchanged.[13]

---

[12] In Germany, social assistance (including rent and specific transfers) amounts to about DM 1,000 per month for a single-person household. If the social minimum for those who are able to work were reduced to DM 750, a break-even income of DM 1,500 would imply an average marginal tax rate of 50 percent below the break-even income. The marginal tax rate could decline linearly from 75 percent at the social minimum to 25 percent of the break-even income.

[13] A well-known study for Germany is Mitschke (1985). His simulation refers to a consumption tax rather than an income tax. In a recent paper (Vaubel, 1995b), I have proposed transforming the total west German transfer to east Germany (DM 150 billion per annum) into lump-sum payments to all east German residents. The per capita transfer could be viewed as compensation for past suffering or as an incentive to stay in east Germany. It would also avoid the regressive incidence of proportional wage subsidies. My simulation shows that the aggregate transfer plus social assistance in east Germany is sufficient to pay every east German 153 percent of current east German social assistance, or that the aggregate transfer would decrease by 35.3 percent if every east German received a lump-sum transfer equal to current social assistance.

This analysis of the negative income tax has important implications for the obligation to have insurance. Some authors argue that, if the government provides a social minimum under the negative income tax scheme, the obligation to have insurance is redundant. This is a non sequitur. There is no reason why the government should finance the social minimum for those who are sick, old or temporarily unemployed, *and* who could have insured themselves. On the contrary, mandatory insurance for the social minimum is preferable to transfers because competitive insurance providers are more likely to charge premia that reflect individual risk and reduce moral hazard. Those who, in case of need, receive (at least) the social minimum from the insurance provider of their choice have a strong incentive to overcome their dependency because, by doing so, they would regain the transfer from the tax authorities and stop the experience-rated increase of their future insurance contributions.[14]

The social and the fiscal cost of explicit transfers could also be reduced by increasing and internationalizing the tax incentives for persons who contribute to *private charities*. If individual donors do not allow sufficiently for the positive externalities that their charitable giving generates with the recipients or other potential donors, tax subsidies to private philanthropy can be Pareto-improving. If the additional private transfers replaced public transfers of less or equal quality, the social cost of aggregate transfers could be reduced because the absolute value of the tax price elasticity of private giving is significantly larger than one (as, for example, Paqué [1986] has shown for Germany). According to Paqué's estimate (an elasticity of -1.5), the sum of public and private transfers would remain unchanged if public transfers were reduced by 150 percent of tax revenue foregone. In Germany, private charitable transfers (including total revenue from the church tax) amount to only one half of the U.S. equivalent. To increase

---

[14] My proposal implies that the expected value of the social minimum for which people have to carry insurance would be lower for unemployment insurance than for health insurance and social security, since the latter two cover those who are either unable to work or are of retirement age and receive their benefits independently of whether they continue to work. The unemployment insurance provider could be required to finance the net transfer to the unemployed for a limited period of time (say, a year). By definition, the net transfer cannot exceed the social minimum.

private charity in Germany, it would be necessary to switch from the current 100 percent income tax exemption to a deduction from income tax liability of at least 41.5 percent.

Private charitable transfers to foreigners, even to charitable institutions in other member states of the European Union, are neither tax exempt nor deductible. With regard to transfers, Europe's "social dimension" is confined to public transfers that the Union grants to the governments of the poorer member states. Nevertheless, the simple correlation between total net receipts from the union budget and GDP per capita is positive ($r = 0.13$ in 1985–1989), i.e., redistribution among the states of Western Europe is regressive (Vaubel, 1994). This is mainly due to the common agricultural policy.

The European agricultural price supports and subsidies not only distort production, they are also not well targeted from a distributional point of view. If farmers are to receive special support, this aim could be reached efficiently two ways: (1) by paying direct transfers according to individual need, or (2) by compensating farmers for their environmental services. Since direct income support ought to be related to market wages in alternative local employment and since the demand for environmental services depends on the local income level, these payments should be differentiated among the member countries. Thus, agricultural policy ought to be repatriated and decentralized.

Redistribution through the European Structural and Cohesion Funds is tied to specific projects that are proposed by the member states and chosen by the Union. Since the Union is unlikely to have the knowledge required to evaluate and compare the projects, these in-kind transfers are probably inefficient and ought to be abolished.

IV   Conclusion

Few of the reforms that I have proposed are likely to be implemented in the foreseeable future. The reasons are well known from the theory of public choice. An efficient social policy that is focused on the needy is not in the interest of the median voter, incumbent politicians, welfare bureaucrats, or other influential pressure groups. However, from time to time, high unemployment and other shocks to the government budget induce politicians to search for ways of reducing the cost and obvious inefficiency of the modern welfare state. A sketch of the first-best solution[15] may be useful as a signpost that points in the right direction. Only trial and error can show how far we can advance on this path.

Appendix

The Determinants of Absenteeism: An International Cross-Section and Time-Series Analysis

Description of variables:
A: hours of absence from work per industrial worker per year,
W: number of waiting days,
R: net replacement ratio (percent),
I: index of replacement ratio and waiting days $(I = R - 8.7W)$,
$D79$: dummy that takes the value 1 in 1979 and 0 in 1990.
The data refer to the years 1979 and 1990 (Salowsky, 1980; iwd, 17/1991; Salowsky and Seffen, 1993).
The United Kingdom was omitted because a lump sum was paid. The waiting period could not be determined for Switzerland.

Data:

	A		W		R		I		û from (4) in 1990
	'79	'90	'79	'90	'79	'90	'79	'90	
Sweden	250	240	1	1	90	90	81.3	81.3	97.2
Norway	–	178	–	0	–	100	–	100.0	15.8
Netherland	222	155	2	2	80	70	62.6	52.6	42.1
Germany	151	145	0	0	100	100	100.0	100.0	−17.2
France	153	144	0	3	100	90	100.0	63.9	19.3
Italy	196	143	3	3	50	100	23.9	73.9	7.9
Austria	–	119	–	3	–	100	–	73.9	−16.1
Belgium	–	117	–	1	–	100	–	91.3	−36.2
Denmark	–	101	–	0	–	90	–	90.0	−50.8
U.S.	66	57	7	7	58	64	0	3.1	−4.5
Japan	40	36	3	3	60	60	33.9	33.9	−57.5

---

[15] A fuller account is given in my German book (Vaubel, 1990).

Regression results:

	Constant	Waiting Days (W)	Net Replacement Ratio (R)	Index (I)	Dummy (D79)	R^2 $\overline{R}^2$
(1)	162.71	−15.43	−	−	+26.55	0.30
	(7.46*)	(−2.39+)	−	−	(0.96)	0.21
(2)	−19.15	−	+1.71	−	+41.95	0.24
	(−0.25)	−	(2.04°)	−	(1.40)	0.14
(3)	90.55	−11.42	+0.73	−	+33.61	0.32
	(0.79)	(−1.26)	(0.65)	−	(1.11)	0.18
(4)	58.25	−	−	+1.04	+36.08	0.32
	(1.73)	−	−	(2.48+)	(1.30)	0.22

* significant at the 1 percent level
+ significant at the 5 percent level
° significant at the 10 percent level
Note: *t*-statistics appear in parentheses.

An increase in the number of waiting days, W, significantly reduces, and a rise in the net replacement ratio, R, significantly increases, absenteeism. One waiting day reduces absenteeism by 15.4 hours per annum. The same effect would be attained if the net replacement ratio were lowered by 8.7 percentage points. Since W and R are highly collinear ($r = -0.67$) in equation (3), they were merged into the index variable, I, by deducting 8.7 percentage points from the net replacement ratio for each waiting day. Equation (4) shows that I has a significantly positive effect on absenteeism. But absenteeism in 1990 was lower than predicted in Japan, Denmark, Belgium, Germany, Austria, and the United States (see $\hat{u}$ in the table above). The current unemployment rate or the difference between the current unemployment rate and the average unemployment rate in the previous nine years was used as an additional explanatory variable but they did not take significant coefficients. Estimation of a double-log function reduced the values of R^2 and the *t*-statistics.

Bibliography

Barro, R.J. 1978. *The Impact of Social Security on Private Savings: Evidence from the U.S. Time Series.* Washington, D.C.: American Enterprise Institute.

Bruce, N., and M. Waldman. 1991. "Transfers in Kind: Why They Can Be Efficient and Non-Paternalistic." *American Economic Review* 81:1345–1351.

Buchanan, J.M. 1968. "Social Insurance in a Growing Economy: A Proposal for Radical Reform." *National Tax Journal* 21:386–395.

Clark, C. 1954. *Welfare and Taxation*. Oxford: Catholic Social Guild.

Diamond, P.A. 1965. "National Debt in a Neoclassical Growth Model." *American Economic Review* 56:1126–1150.

Feldstein, M. 1977. "Does the United States Save Too Little?" *American Economic Review, Papers and Proceedings* 67:116–121.

Hayek, F.A. 1960. *The Constitution of Liberty*. London: Routledge.

Levine, D.I., and L. d'Andrea Tyson. 1990. "Participation, Productivity, and the Firm's Environment." In: A.S. Blinder (ed.), *Paying for Productivity: A Look at the Evidence*, pp. 183–243. Washington, D.C.: The Brookings Institution.

Mitschke, J. 1985. *Steuer- und Transferordnung aus einem Guß*. Baden-Baden: Nomos.

Paqué, K-H. 1986. "The Efficiency of Tax Incentives to Private Charitable Giving—Some Econometric Evidence for the Federal Republic of Germany." *Weltwirtschaftliches Archiv (Review of World Economics)* 122:690–712.

Salowsky, H. 1980. "Individuelle Fehlzeiten in westlichen Industrieländern." Beiträge zur Wirtschafts- und Sozialpolitik 83/84. Cologne: Institut der deutschen Wirtschaft.

Salowsky, H., and A. Seffen. 1993. "Einkommenssicherung bei Krankheit im internationalen Vergleich." Beiträge zur Wirtschafts- und Sozialpolitik 206. Cologne: Institut der deutschen Wirtschaft.

Samuelson, P.A. 1958. "An Exact Consumption Loan Model of Interest with or without the Contrivance of Money." *Journal of Political Economy* 66:467–482.

Schanz, G. 1895. *Zur Frage der Arbeitslosen-Versicherung*. Bamberg: Büchner.

Stigler, G.J. 1970. "Director's Law of Public Income Redistribution." *Journal of Law and Economics* 13:1–10.

Vaubel, R. 1990. *Sozialpolitik für mündige Bürger*. Baden-Baden: Nomos.

Vaubel, R. 1994. "The Political Economy of Centralization and the European Community." *Public Choice* 81:151–190.

Vaubel, R. 1995a. "Social Regulation and Market Integration: A Critique and Public-Choice Analysis of the Social Chapter." *Aussenwirtschaft* 50:111–131.

Vaubel, R. 1995b. "Aktuelle Möglichkeiten der Einkommenssicherung über eine negative Einkommenssteuer." Forthcoming in a conference volume to be published by the Kiel Institute of World Economics.

Lessons for Employment and Growth in Western Europe

Henri R. Sneessens

W. Europe
O47
E24

The main questions that we have to address are, to some extent, easily summarized. After *the golden sixties*, economic growth slowed down considerably and this change seems to have had quite different effects in different countries, particularly in terms of unemployment and income dispersion. Why? How can we promote growth? What can be done to cut European unemployment?

To address these questions, I first look again at the facts and recall a few key characteristics of the economic evolution of the last thirty years or so in EC Europe, the United States, and Japan (Section I). Next, I set up the theoretical framework wherein the European unemployment problem can best be discussed (Section II). In Section III, I use this framework to try to evaluate the various factors that may be held responsible for the persistence of unemployment. In Section IV, I summarize conclusions and address a few key policy issues.

I Factual Background

The slowdown in economic growth is illustrated in Figure 1, which shows the evolution of GDP growth rates[1] in the three major industrialized areas mentioned above, namely, the EC countries (EC-12), the United States, and Japan. There is a sharp contrast between the pre-

I thank B. Van der Linden, J. Drèze, and the participants at the symposium for their stimulating comments.

[1] In order to make the figure easier to read, it shows the values of a three-year moving average of annual growth rates. This manner of presentation does not alter the interpretation of the data.

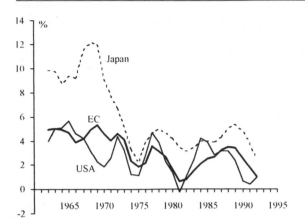

Figure 1. GDP Growth (3-year moving average of annual growth rates at constant market prices).
Source: European Economy (1993).

and post-1975 periods. After 1974, the average growth rate is cut in half in Europe and Japan (it falls from 4.56 to 2.15 percent in the EC countries, from 8.87 to 3.94 percent in Japan); the fall is slightly less pronounced in the United States (from 3.64 to 2.29 percent). One may also notice that, although European and American average growth rates have always been fairly close (and much smaller than the Japanese ones), the EC countries benefited from a significantly larger average growth rate before 1974; the situation is reversed afterwards. The figure shows no clear downward trend after 1975; the fall in the average growth rates, made the more visible by the recession of 1974–1975, probably started in each country before that date in the early 1970s, or perhaps even earlier in the United States.

The comparison of unemployment rates is made in Figure 2. The terms of this comparison are now well known. The unemployment rate in Japan has remained fairly stable, although systematically higher after 1974 than during the period before. The unemployment rate in the United States, although subject to large fluctuations, does not show any systematic upward trend from 1979 to 1990; more precisely, the upward trend of the 1970s was compensated by the impressive unemployment cuts (and job creations) achieved over the 1980s. This is in sharp contrast to the evolution observed in EC countries, where the unemployment rate rose from less than 3 percent to more than 10 percent between 1974 and 1985; it did so in two steps, as if each rise had been triggered by an oil shock, in 1973–1974 and 1979–1980, respec-

Figure 2. Unemployment Rates.
Source: European Economy (1993) and OECD (1994).

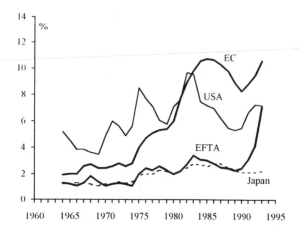

tively. Since 1985, the unemployment rate seems to have reached a plateau, transitorily lowered by the expansion of the late 1980s. All the macroeconomic forecasts made for the coming ten years suggest that the unemployment rate is likely to remain high for many years still (see, for instance, the forecasts prepared for the 1993 Economic Report of the European Commission). Figure 2 also shows the evolution of the unemployment rate in EFTA countries. In those countries, the unemployment rate remained moderate (around 2 percent) until the recession of the early 1990s; it then surged to unprecedented levels (more than 6 percent).

More information about the situation on labor markets can be obtained by looking at the relationship between unemployment and vacancies (the so-called Beveridge curve). In EC countries (left panel of Figure 3), the curve seems to have shifted continuously rightward from 1974 until 1985. This implies that inflationary wage pressures may now appear at much larger unemployment rates than during the 1960s or early 1970s. This shift of the Beveridge curve is not an artifact due to averaging the situation of different countries. Almost all European countries have suffered similar shifts, including Germany and the United Kingdom (see OECD, 1992). In the United States (right panel of Figure 3), the outward shift of the 1970s was compensated by an inward shift, so that the curve seems to have resumed its initial position. In Japan and non-EC Europe (not shown), there was a moderate

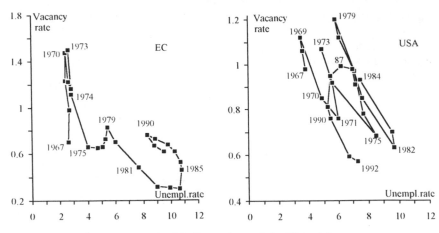

Figure 3. Beveridge Curves, in EC Countries and the United States.
Source: European Economy (1993) and Bean (1994b).

outward shift, but one which continued during the late 1980s or even the early 1990s (non-EC Europe).[2]

Figure 4 compares the evolution of real compensations per employee. During the 1960s, the average growth rate (left panel) remained much higher in Japan (around 8 percent) than in Europe (around 5 percent), and much higher in Europe than in the United States (around 2 percent). In all three cases, real wage growth began to fall in the early 1970s and eventually converged to low values (around 1 percent) in the early 1980s. They, however, started to diverge again during the recovery of the late 1980s. In sharp contrast with the other two areas, average real wage growth remained low in the United States, and even turned negative during the recession of the early 1990s. The contrast between the United States, on the one hand, and EC countries and Japan, on the other hand, is also illustrated in the right-hand panel of Figure 4, which shows that the average real wage rate barely increased in the United States after 1972, at variance with the evolution observed in the other countries.

---

[2] See Bean (1994b) or OECD (1992).

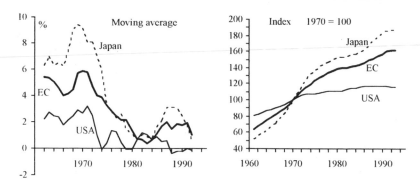

Figure 4. Growth Rate (3-year moving average) and Index of Real Compensation per Employee (total economy, private consumption price deflator).
Source: European Economy (1993).

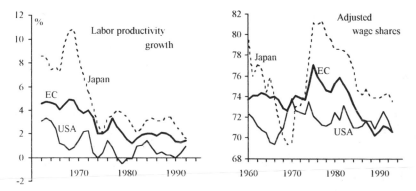

Figure 5. Labor Productivity Growth (per worker, 3-year moving average) and Wage Shares.
Source: European Economy (1993).

Figure 5 (left hand panel) shows the evolution of average labor productivity growth and of adjusted wage shares.[3] As for GDP and real wage growth, one observes a sharp decline in the growth rate of labor productivity during the early 1970s. As for GDP growth, there is no downward trend after 1974 in the case of Japan and the United States; there remains a downward trend in EC Europe until the early

---

[3] Percent of GDP at factor costs, adjusted for the share of self-employed workers in occupied population.

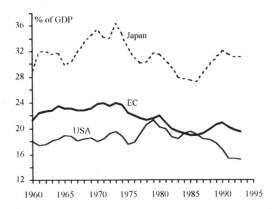

Figure 6. Gross Fixed Capital Formation (in percentage points of GDP).
Source: European Economy (1993).

1980s. The ranking of countries remains the same over the entire period; that is, labor productivity growth is consistently higher in Japan than in EC countries, and higher in EC countries than in the United States. At the same time as unemployment was sharply rising, labor productivity growth remained relatively high in EC Europe during the 1980s, at around 1.73 percent a year compared with 0.68 percent in the United States (2.68 percent in Japan). The combined effects of productivity gains and of real wage changes on labor's value-added share are illustrated in the right-hand panel of Figure 5. There is, over the entire period, no systematic trend in the case of Japan and the United States. In the former country, the huge increase of the late 1970s disappeared in the late 1980s; in the latter case, the above-normal increase of the early 1970s was eliminated before the end of the decade. In EC countries, the strong increase of the late 1970s was *more* than compensated for by the decrease of the 1980s, so that there was a negative downward trend over the entire period. In other words, real wage rises were, in the case of Europe, more than compensated for by productivity gains.[4]

Figure 6 shows how capital accumulation has changed in relation to GDP. The difference between Japan and Europe, on the one hand, and the United States, on the other hand, is worth noticing. During most of the 1980s, fixed investment (in percentage points of GDP) increased above its average value in the United States, while it slumped well

---

[4] This is not true for all EC countries. It is true for France, Germany, Italy, and Spain; it is not true for the United Kingdom. See *European Economy* (1993).

below this value in Japan and the EC countries. With the expansion of the late 1980s, investment (in percentage points of GDP) increased again in Japan and the EC countries (and fell sharply in the United States). Despite this strong recovery, the European investment share in 1993 remained substantially below the values observed before 1975 (20 percent against 23 percent).[5] This may suggest that observed aggregate productivity gains were obtained by scrapping unprofitable productive capacities rather than by replacing old machinery and equipment.

Figures 1 to 6 have stressed the similarities and differences between EC countries, the United States, and Japan. The main conclusions to be drawn from these observations can be summarized as follows:

1. There was in the early 1970s a substantial fall in the growth potential of all (EC, United States, Japan) economies. This shock does not seem to be simply the result of a lower investment effort. Because it did not occur again in 1979–1980, oil prices are unlikely to be the key explanatory variable, although they obviously contributed to accelerating the unemployment rise in EC countries.
2. In both the United States and the EC, the Beveridge curve started to shift outward in the early 1970s, suggesting increased frictions and reallocation difficulties after the productivity slowdown. Over the 1980s, the problem seems to have disappeared in the United States, but was aggravated in Europe.
3. Real wages reacted much more slowly to the slowdown of productivity growth in Europe than they did in the United States, thereby probably inducing unprofitable productive capacity scrapping and more job losses.
4. The comparison between the evolution of real wage costs, average labor productivities, and (adjusted) wage shares in Europe and in the United States suggests that wage increases have a significant negative impact on employment (an elasticity of employment to real wages larger than 1 in absolute value?).
5. The recovery of the late 1980s shows how powerful the effect of a demand increase can be. In the EC, unemployment went down and capital accumulation went up sharply, and in some countries (for

---

[5] This is true for almost all EC countries, except Portugal. See *European Economy* (1993).

example, Germany, Spain, the United Kingdom) the Beveridge
curve started to shift leftward again (OECD, 1992).

It thus appears that, although the EC, the United States, and Japan
may have been confronted, to a large extent, by similar shocks (productivity slowdown and business cycle fluctuations), their individual
response to these shocks and, as a consequence, their economic performance may look quite different. On the unemployment criterion, the
experience in the EC is obviously closer to the experience in United
States rather than in Japan, whose relatively low unemployment rates
are often explained in terms of institutional and cultural characteristics.
    It is difficult to go beyond these simple considerations and draw
more concrete conclusions and policy implications without the guid-
ance of an appropriately defined theoretical apparatus. This is precisely
the objective of the next sections.

II   Equilibrium Unemployment in Imperfectly Competitive Economies

Fluctuations in the American unemployment rate are most often
analyzed in theoretical setups with perfect competition on the labor
market, suitably modified to allow for search unemployment and
nominal price/wage rigidities. Observed cyclical fluctuations in the
unemployment rate are then mainly explained by demand shocks,
while long-lasting shifts in the Beveridge curve should be attributed to
reallocation shocks (see, for instance, Blanchard and Diamond, 1989).
The situation is somewhat different in Europe: first, because unions
have traditionally played a crucial role in the determination of wages,
and second, because the key issue is unemployment persistence rather
than fluctuations. For these reasons, the theoretical setups used to
analyze European unemployment are based on models with imperfect
competition on the labor market.

A   Wage and Price Formation

The simplest version of this type of model is the right-to-manage
monopoly-union model, where prices are set by monopolistically competitive profit-maximizing firms on the goods market, while wages are

Figure 7. Equilibrium
Unemployment and
Vacancy Rates.

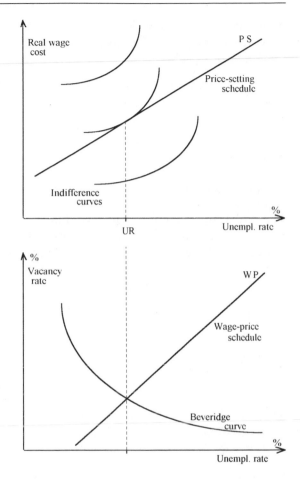

set by the (local) monopoly union on the labor market. The key elements of such an imperfect competition macroeconomic model are
illustrated in the two panels of Figure 7. Let us first consider the top
panel. The real wage cost is measured along the vertical axis, the
unemployment rate along the horizontal axis (we use unemployment
rather than employment to combine this graph with the U-V curve of
the bottom panel). In this setup, firms' pricing behavior implies, ceteris
paribus, a positive relationship between the real wage cost and the
unemployment rate, represented by the upward-sloping price-setting
schedule (PS). This schedule corresponds to the labor demand curve of

perfect competition models, amended to take into account the effects of imperfect competition. The position of the PS schedule thus depends on two types of variables:

1. *productivity variables*: technological progress, oil and raw material prices, capital accumulation, etc.
2. *markup variables*: the firm's monopoly power, itself determined by the price elasticity of the demand for goods and the many variables apt to modify the importance of tensions on the goods market (productive factor—labor or capital—shortages, mismatch and frictions, see below).

The real wage-unemployment mix that will actually be observed depends on the wage behavior of unions. Unions are assumed to maximize the welfare of their members, given the pricing and employment behavior of firms. Their preferences are represented by upward-sloping convex indifference curves. The optimal (from the unions' point of view) wage-unemployment combination is given by the tangency point between the PS schedule and one indifference curve. At given union preferences, the slope and position of these indifference curves will be affected by the variables appearing, explicitly or implicitly, in the unions' objective function. The observed wage-unemployment mix will thus depend on a third category of variables:

3. *union variables*: replacement ratio (or minimum wage), tax and price wedges,[6] union membership and representativeness (insider-outsider differences), union power (in bargaining models), etc.

In this case, the equilibrium unemployment rate may turn out to be well above Friedman's natural (or frictional) unemployment rate. Unemployment is no longer simply the result of search and matching behaviors. It also reflects the markup behaviors of agents acting in an imperfectly competitive setup. The equilibrium unemployment rate is now that particular value of the unemployment rate which, in a given economic environment, makes firms and workers income claims mutually compatible (the so-called battle-of-the-markup story); other values of the unemployment rate will generate additional inflationary or

---

[6] By price wedge I mean the ratio between consumption and value-added prices.

deflationary pressures and trigger wage-price spirals that will eventually lead back to the equilibrium unemployment rate, the only one to be compatible with a stable inflation rate (known as NAIRU: non-accelerating inflation rate of unemployment).

B   The Beveridge Curve

The same analysis can alternatively be presented in terms of the Beveridge U-V curve. This relationship between unemployment and vacancies can be introduced either via a job-matching function (see, for instance, Pissarides, 1990), or by using Lambert's (1988) result (concerning aggregation in models with quantity constraints) to obtain an aggregate employment function by means of explicit aggregation over micromarkets with different labor supply constraints (see, for instance, Sneessens and Drèze, 1986; Sneessens, 1987). In both cases, one obtains a Beveridge curve like the one reproduced in the bottom panel of Figure 7. The position of the aggregate Beveridge curve is affected by the following category of variables:

4. *matching variables*: variables affecting firms' recruitment behavior and workers' search intensity (replacement ratio, labor force composition—age, sex, etc.—disenfranchisement and share of long term unemployment, etc.), as well as structural mismatch variables (regional mismatch, skill mismatch, etc.).

The upward-sloping schedule (WP) of the bottom panel summarizes in the U-V space the wage-price behavior of firms and trade unions described in the top panel. More precisely, the WP schedule gives all the combinations of vacancy and unemployment rates that make firms' and workers' income claims mutually compatible. It slopes upward because more unfilled vacancies mean more productive factor shortages and excess demand for goods, hence larger markups; these in turn imply lower real wages, which will not be accepted by workers unless the unemployment rate goes up. The intersection of the Beveridge curve and the WP schedule determines simultaneously the equilibrium unemployment rate and the equilibrium vacancy rate. One advantage of this alternative presentation is its emphasis on the impact of Beveridge curve shifts on equilibrium unemployment.

C   Persistence Mechanisms

Actual unemployment levels may, of course, deviate from their equilibrium values, either because the effects of changes in the "fundamentals" take time to materialize (as a result of adjustment costs), or because pure nominal shocks may have transitory real effects as a result of nominal rigidities. It seems difficult, however, to explain the rise and the persistence of unemployment in Europe in such standard and simple terms. Other, less traditional and less understood persistence mechanisms may exist. Pure nominal shocks may have permanent or long-lasting effects if they induce insider-outsider effects and/or capacity shortages. One should not even exclude a priori the possibility of path dependency and multiple equilibria.

Let us first consider the *insider-outsider* story (Lindbeck and Snower, 1988; Blanchard and Summers, 1986). In the limit case where wages are set unilaterally and selfishly by those workers who are employed (the insiders), any negative unanticipated transitory shock may, at the limit, have a permanent effect on unemployment by decreasing the number of insiders, and have no effect on the wage rate. This extreme case is, of course, too simple. One should, first of all, take into account the fact that insiders are not all alike, so that the wage they would aim at need not be a simple function of the number of employed workers. If workers that are to be fired are chosen on a seniority criterion, the optimal wage is likely to depend more on wage growth aspirations than on the number of employed workers. In such circumstances, a productivity slowdown could lead to more and more unemployment by shifting indifference curves upward (top panel of Figure 7) and the WP schedule downward (bottom panel). This extreme insider-outsider story can, however, only be a partial one. It says nothing about the Beveridge curve and the bargaining power that the permanent reallocation of jobs across firms, sectors, regions, ages, etc., gives to the outsiders. The relative bargaining power of outsiders may, however, change endogenously over time, for example, when it is related to unemployment duration. Long-term unemployed workers may become "disenfranchised," either because a long unemployment spell decreases their skills and changes the attitude of firms toward them (Pissarides, 1992; Blanchard and Diamond, 1994), or because it creates a discouragement effect and reduces the unemployed workers' search effort (Layard and Nickell, 1987; Layard and Bean, 1989). In such circumstances, a transitory shock that increases the proportion of long-term unemployment will induce an outward shift of the Beveridge curve and have persistent if not permanent effects on unemployment.

When wages are not set competitively, a deep and long recession may also perpetuate itself via its effect on *capital accumulation* (capital shortage). A prolonged period of capacity underutilization will inevitably lead to bankruptcies and excess capacity scrapping, hence lower capacity employment. In other words, the recession produces a downward shift of the PS schedule in the top panel of Figure 7 (at a given employment rate, lower productive capacities mean a higher proportion of capacity-constrained firms and higher markups; see Sneessens and Drèze, 1986; Sneessens, 1987). If workers realize that there are fewer jobs available on the market, so that wage cuts can only have a little impact on employment, the new equilibrium real wage rate may remain unchanged. In the bottom panel of Figure 7, the WP schedule shifts down, while the Beveridge curve remains unaffected. In this scenario, the fall in capacity employment implies a corresponding rise in equilibrium unemployment. As in the extreme insider-outsider model considered above, one could observe unemployment changes at unchanged real wages. The reason why the number of unemployed workers has no impact on the real wage is however different. The problem comes from the fact that there are fewer jobs available, not from the fact that unemployed workers have zero market power. The larger the entry costs, the more stable the new unemployment equilibrium is likely to be.

III   What Caused Europe's Unemployment Problem?

The theoretical setup summarized in Figure 7 gives us the means to further develop the discussion about the probable causes of, and possible remedies for, European unemployment. Because it integrates the effects of many different variables into a single framework, it potentially gives us the means to discriminate between alternative stories. One should, however, not be overly optimistic. Designing a model that encompasses all the key elements alluded to above and that would at the same time remain empirically tractable is an impossible task. Disentangling the many possible influences is made even more difficult by the limited amount of information available in existing

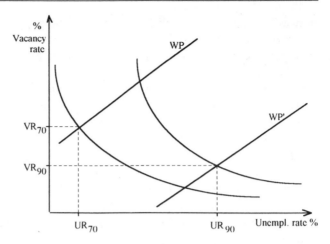

Figure 8. Changes in the Determinants of Equilibrium Unemployment in Europe over the Last 25 Years.

macro or micro data sets. Furthermore, because all the influences are so interrelated, a change in one economic variable may affect all the curves in Figure 7 simultaneously, thereby raising substantial identification problems.[7]

Given this difficulty, it is best to start from robust stylized facts and focus on the explanations that are compatible with them. Figure 8, constructed on the same logic as the bottom panel of Figure 7, illustrates the main changes observed in Europe over the last twenty-five years or so. Two things have occurred simultaneously. There has been both an outward shift of the entire Beveridge curve and a downward shift along the new Beveridge curve, the latter resulting from the downward shift of the WP schedule. The new equilibrium is thus characterized by lower vacancy rates and higher unemployment rates. This evolution is not an aggregation artifact; it characterizes most EC countries. Any explanation of European unemployment should be compatible with these stylized facts. It should also account for the fact that the rise of unemployment did not occur at once, but was spread over more than ten years and survived the short-lived recovery of the

[7] Bean (1994b) gives a fairly detailed survey of the available empirical evidence on the role played by each variable. See his paper for additional references.

late 1980s. Needless to say, this evolution may well be the result of a combination of factors rather than the result of a single shock.

To start with, let us first indicate that the rise in European unemployment cannot be viewed as a simple and direct consequence of increased market imperfections, unionization, or union power. *Increased union or firm market power* would shift the WP schedule in Figure 8 downward, but leave the Beveridge curve unchanged. It thus cannot be the whole story. Furthermore, since the mid-1970s, unionization has stabilized in EC countries as a whole (see Bean, 1994b), and has started to decline in some of them (as in France [Sneessens and Shadman-Mehta, 1995] and the United Kingdom [Layard and Nickell, 1986]). From a theoretical viewpoint, it is now well understood that the relationship between unionization and unemployment need not be a simple one-to-one relationship. The effect of unionization on the aggregate performance of the economy depends on the degree of centralization of the bargaining process. Theoretical models of behavior under imperfect competition suggest that it is better to have a strong and centralized union, rather than a lot of locally more or less powerful unions (see Calmfors and Driffill, 1988). The relatively very low unemployment rates observed (until recently) in Nordic countries have often been explained in such terms. This is not to say, of course, that market imperfections and unions' market power played no role in the economic developments of the last three decades in EC countries. It simply says that other factors (abnormally large demand or supply shocks, for example) must also be included in the story.

Among these, the *tax wedge* increase observed since the early 1970s has for some time been considered as a prime candidate. Many empirical studies have shown however that, although the tax wedge may have had its role and may have contributed to shifting the WP curve downward, it is far from being the key factor in explaining Europe's unemployment problem (see, for instance, Bean et al., 1986) and, again, cannot explain the outward shift of the Beveridge curve. There is, furthermore, a theoretical difficulty. At a given real wage cost, a wage tax increase may or may not represent a loss of income and welfare, depending on the tax's counterparts. If taxes are levied to finance social security expenditures or a public pension scheme (social security contributions), they will not necessarily lead to additional wage demands. The reaction may be different if taxes are levied to finance public consumption (direct taxes). In both cases, one should take into account distributional effects and their consequences on wage negotiations, especially when the latter are decentralized. These considerations might explain why the huge tax levels observed in Nordic countries may have had little effect on unemployment.

The rest of the discussion is organized around the factors that may have produced an outward shift in the Beveridge curve. In doing so, I shall directly focus on those factors that made EC countries' situation typical and explain the stylized facts of Figure 8. Empirical evidence on these matters comes either from direct estimation of Beveridge curves based on implicit matching functions, or from the estimation of macroeconomic models with quantity constraints wherein the aggregate employment function has been obtained by explicit aggregation over firms and micromarkets. The advantage of this latter approach is that the Beveridge curve corresponds to a mere reformulation of the aggregate employment function. The advantage is twofold. First, estimates of the Beveridge curve are part of a complete macro model; second, they can be obtained without using official vacancy data, which may not be very reliable over long periods.[8] The estimates reported in Drèze et al. (1990) for European countries and the United States over the period 1960–1986 are based on such an approach. They suggest that the Beveridge curve has effectively, over this period, shifted outward in all countries. In such studies, there is, however, little discussion and little agreement about the factors that might have caused the shift in the U-V curve.

I discuss successively the role of (1) unemployment benefits and replacement ratios, (2) hiring and firing costs, (3) insider-outsider mechanisms, and (4) structural mismatch.

1   Search Intensity and Replacement Ratios

Unemployment benefits and replacement ratios have been substantially increased in most European economies over the last thirty years (see OECD, 1994). In the standard labor market model, a better replacement ratio (level and/or duration) increases the reservation wage, thereby decreasing search intensity and lengthening unemployment

---

[8] The disadvantage, of course, is that these models are fairly complex and not easy to handle.

spells. As a consequence, the Beveridge curve shifts outward. The WP schedule may also shift outward, to the extent that increased frictions lead, ceteris paribus, to more labor shortages and higher price mark-ups.[9] Higher replacement ratios could thus produce an evolution like the one illustrated in Figure 8.

Observed increases in average replacement ratios do not seem, however, to explain much of the rise in European unemployment. In some countries (Belgium, Germany, the United Kingdom), the average replacement ratio actually reached a maximum in the 1960s or mid-1970s, well before the peak in unemployment rates. More elaborated micro- or macroeconometric investigations do not usually conclude that the increase in replacement ratios may have had, per se, a large effect on aggregate unemployment.[10] König and Entorf (1990) for Germany, Gagey et al. (1990) for France, and Andrès et al. (1990) for Spain do report significant replacement ratio effects on frictional unemployment in an aggregate model with quantity constraints. These effects do not explain much of the U-V curve shift (two percentage points of unemployment in France, between 1974 and 1986; in Germany, the variable is essentially cyclical) and do not seem very robust.

2 Hiring and Firing Costs

The effect of hiring and firing costs on firms' behavior is potentially complex. Because they render employment adjustments more costly, hiring and firing costs will affect the dynamics of employment and, by this simple fact, create persistence mechanisms (see Alogoskoufis and Manning, 1988b; Bean, 1994a). They may also affect the equilibrium employment level, albeit not necessarily in a negative way (see Bentolila and Bertola, 1990). To the extent that hiring and firing costs make the firm choosier, increasing such costs may shift the Beveridge curve[11]

---

[9] Theoretical models can be designed wherein higher replacement ratios have a negative effect on real wages and on unemployment (see Atkinson, 1990). For a critical survey of theoretical models and empirical evidence, see Atkinson and Mickelwright (1991).

[10] See also Nickell (1990) and Sneessens and Van der Linden (1994).

[11] Layard and Nickell (1986) use a U-V curve shift index as a proxy for social security and employment protection.

and generate an evolution like that in Figure 8. In the work referred to above, König and Entorf (1990) report significant and strong effects of the share of nonwage costs (in percent of total labor costs) on the position of the Beveridge curve in Germany. Because the share of nonwage costs is strongly trended, one cannot exclude however the possibility that this variable serves as a proxy for other shift factors.

The effect of employment protection and nonwage costs should probably not be overemphasized. Burda and Wyplosz (1994) show that European labor markets are characterized by large flows between employment and unemployment and that these flows have a pattern similar to that in the United States. Abraham and Houseman (1993) show that employment protection in Europe does not prevent firms' adjustment to changing conditions; the adjustment that is not made via employment is made via hours of work. They, furthermore, find little evidence that the weakening of job security regulations during the 1980s has modified the way employers adjust to output changes.

3   Disenfranchisement of Long-Term Unemployed Workers

The disenfranchisement story fits the stylized facts of Figure 8. The Beveridge curve will shift outward, because firms become choosier and/ or because search intensity weakens. The disenfranchisement of long-term unemployed workers has, furthermore, the same effect as a reduction in the effective labor force. At given vacancy rates and price markups, wage demands will be higher (outsiders' competitive pressure is reduced); i.e., the WP schedule shifts downward. This hypothesis can thus be tested via the estimation of Beveridge curves and of wage equations. Bean and Gavosto (1990) find, in a model with quantity constraints, that Beveridge curve shifts can be entirely explained by the long-term unemployment effect. They also find that a measure of labor market tightness corrected for long-term unemployment gives better results in the wage equation than the actual unemployment rate. The change in the proportion of long-term unemployment (the disenfranchisement process) is itself explained by a dynamic relationship between total and long-term unemployment. It is worth noticing that this equation also includes an industrial mismatch indicator; the replacement ratio does not appear to be significant, although, from a theoretical point of view, it should affect search intensity and the disenfranchisement process. The model explains the rise in total unemployment over the last two decades by a series of unfavorable transitory shocks between 1974 and 1983, coming mainly from union density in the mid-1970s (+2.4 percentage points increase in equilibrium unemployment),[12] demand (+3.7), mismatch (+2.3), and, again, union density (+1.6) in the late 1970s and early 1980s. Although temporary, these shocks have long-lasting effects (the model has almost a unit root) via the disenfranchisement of the long term unemployed.

The results obtained with other data sets are not so clear-cut. For Spain, Andrès et al. (1990), using a model similar to Bean and Gavosto, obtain significant shifts in the Beveridge curve, but cannot explain it by long-term unemployment. Bentolila and Dolado (1990), building on this previous work, explain the shift in the Beveridge curve by a variety of variables; the proportion of long-term unemployment appears to be significant among these variables, but its effect seems limited (the authors put the emphasis on regional mismatch). Direct estimation of a Beveridge curve on U.K. and German unemployment-vacancy data gives limited support to the disenfranchisement hypothesis. Budd et al. (1987) are able to explain 60 percent of the U.K. shift and 80 percent of the German shift by disenfranchisement effects, but their equation contains no other shift variable than the proportion of long-term unemployed, plus linear and quadratic time trends. Franz and Siebeck (1992) conclude their empirical analysis by saying that, in the case of Germany, "this variable [the share of long-term unemployment] does not appear as a suitable candidate to explain the shifts of the Beveridge curve." They insist, rather, on more specific skill mismatch variables.

4 Structural Mismatch

A last possibility is that U-V curve shifts are the result of structural shocks. Structural (reallocation) shocks shift the Beveridge curve outward. More structural problems also mean that inflationary pressures will appear at higher unemployment rates, so that the WP schedule

---

[12] The latter is *not* measured by union membership, which has been declining in the United Kingdom since 1980, but rather by the markup of union over nonunion wages, which has displayed an upward trend over time.

shifts downward. The situation is thus qualitatively similar to that of Figure 8.

Structural shocks can take different (interrelated) forms, and generate sectoral, regional, or skill mismatch. Jackman et al. (1990), following Jackman and Roper (1987), have constructed mismatch indices based either on the assumption of a segmented wage formation process or on the aggregation of group specific matching functions. In both cases, the mismatch indices are essentially equal to the variance of *relative* unemployment rates. Whatever the country or the structural breakdown considered, these mismatch indicators almost invariably suggest decreasing structural and reallocation difficulties since 1974. In other words, the shift in the aggregate Beveridge curve since 1974 would result from macro phenomena rather than from structural shocks and increasing reallocation difficulties.

This view may be surprising in view of the growing disparities between regional and professional unemployment rates. Mismatch indicators based on absolute or squared differences between *level* rather than *relative* unemployment rates may give quite different answers (see, e.g., OECD, 1992). Entorf (1993) stresses that, when unemployment rates are trended, a mismatch index based on relative unemployment rates necessarily goes to zero; such an index should thus not be used when unemployment rates are not stationary. It is thus worth looking at other approaches. More work is obviously needed on this issue.

Regional Mismatch. Regional mismatch effects are emphasized in Bentolila and Dolado's (1990) analysis of the Spanish economy. Their analysis is based on the total mismatch indicator computed by Andrès et al. (1990) of an aggregate employment function with quantity constraints. The value of this indicator rises almost continuously from 1964 till 1985. The rise remains moderate in the 1960s and early 1970s, becomes important in the ten years between 1974 and 1985, and then there is a slight decline after 1985. This evolution is well explained by a few variables, mainly regional and sectoral mismatch variables and long-term unemployment. Sectoral mismatch is measured by a turbulence index à la Layard and Nickell (1986); the effect of regional mismatch is measured by the standard deviation of regional unemployment rates (positively trended) and gross internal migration (in percent of total population). All variables are statistically significant and have the expected sign (negative for internal migration). The rest of their paper is devoted to the determinants of labor mobility. Although labor mobility seems to respond to economic incentives, it does so with very long lags. Furthermore, the authors, following Bentolila and Blanchard (1990), find that a rise in aggregate unemployment has a negative effect on workers' geographical mobility.

Skill Mismatch. Skill mismatch is another potential and poorly understood source of difficulty. In 1989, at the top of the expansion of the late 1980s, 62 percent of EC manufacturing firms reported that skilled labor supply shortages were an important factor limiting employment growth, despite the still large aggregate unemployment rate. In late 1985, only 43 percent reported such shortages. The increase was especially strong in the United Kingdom (from 37 to 62 percent) and in Italy (from 42 to 75 percent), and was not negligible in France (from 36 to 53 percent) and Germany (from 53 to 66 percent) (see OECD, 1992, Table 1.10).

Franz and Siebeck (1992)—already referred to above—cautiously conclude their study of the determinants of U-V curve shifts in Germany by saying: "Several variables such as the rate of unskilled long-term unemployed and a professional mismatch indicator are able to capture some of the movements of the Beveridge curve." Sneessens (1994) and Sneessens and Shadman-Mehta (1995) have developed a macro model with quantity constraints that builds on earlier work in this vein by explicitly distinguishing two types of labor, skilled and unskilled. As in other models with quantity constraints, the aggregate Beveridge curve is obtained from an aggregate employment function. It may shift for two reasons, either because of increased frictions on the skilled labor market, or because of increased skill mismatch. The appropriate skill mismatch indicator in this setup is approximately equal to the difference between the aggregate unemployment rate and the unemployment rate of skilled workers. The model is estimated on French aggregate data for the period 1962–1989. The skill mismatch indicator rises slightly until 1974; it then increases sharply from 1974 to 1985, and barely declines afterward. Most of the observed shift in the aggregate Beveridge curve is explained by skill mismatch rather than increased frictions on the skilled labor market. Skill mismatch is, of course, not an exogenous variable. In Sneessens and Shadman-Mehta (1995), skill mismatch results from the combination of asymmetric technological progress and relative wage rigidities. Technical progress implies, ceteris paribus, a systematically decreasing unskilled-to-skilled employment ratio (at a rate of 4.9 percent p.a. before 1974, 2.4 percent p.a. afterwards).[13] If the skill composition of the labor force does not adjust fast enough (the unskilled-to-skilled labor force ratio changed at a rate of 4.3 percent p.a. before 1974, 2.2 percent p.a. afterwards) and if the elasticity of substitution is smaller than one (it is estimated at around 0.5), the relative unskilled wage rate has to decline to maintain the difference between unemployment rates (it increased sharply). Calculated on this basis, the current *relative* unskilled wage *cost* should be decreased by about 20 percent (which would lead back to the value observed in the mid-1960s) to eliminate skill mismatch. Skill mismatch accounts for a 5.65 percentage increase in total unemployment, out of a total of 8.09. The rest is explained by exogenous technical progress (-5.57), tax wedges ($+5.10$), union power (-1.37), frictions ($+1.76$), lower capacity employment ($+2.17$), real energy prices and interest rates ($+0.76$).[14]

Finally, it is worth noticing that accounting for skill mismatch in the Sneessens and Shadman-Mehta (1995) setup amounts to introducing a difference between the actual and the effective labor force. The size of this correction is determined by the skill mismatch indicator. In the case of France, it turned out to be of a magnitude similar (slightly bigger) to that obtained by simply subtracting the number of long-term unemployed workers from the actual labor force, which suggests potential identification problems between the skill mismatch and the disenfranchisement stories.

IV Conclusions and Policy Issues

We must conclude that no simple story can explain Europe's unemployment problem. The difficulty comes from the fact that many fac-

---

[13] Exogenous technical progress is thus relatively *less* unfavorable to unskilled workers after 1974, which may look surprising. One should bear in mind, however, that, at this level of aggregation, "technical progress" actually includes various phenomena, including the effect of deindustrialization after 1974, which moved jobs from a high- to a low-productivity sector.

[14] It is worth noting that this story is compatible with the fact that most inflationary pressures at the top of the expansion of the late 1980s were, in France, due to a shortage of productive capacities rather than skilled labor (see Sneessens, 1994).

tors have played a role and are interrelated. It is difficult to account for all of them at once and to disentangle their influences. If we focus on those stories that are compatible with the stylized facts of Figure 8 (outward shift of both the Beveridge curve and the locus of vacancy and unemployment rate combinations that are compatible with stable inflation), we end up with two main stories, disenfranchisement and structural mismatch. In *the disenfranchisement story*, Europe's unemployment problem would mainly result from a succession of unfavorable macroeconomic demand or supply shocks; although temporary, these macroeconomic shocks have persistent (almost permanent) effects via the disenfranchisement of long-term unemployed workers. In *the structural mismatch story*, Europe's unemployment problem would be the outcome of both macroeconomic and reallocation shocks; persistence comes from the difficulty of solving the reallocation problem (low regional mobility, relative wage rigidities), and is exacerbated by other phenomena like capital shortages. Econometric evidence is, at this stage, not conclusive. Part of the difficulty comes from our poor understanding of the relationship between macro and micro phenomena[15] and from the lack of reliable synthetic mismatch indicators. The two stories (disenfranchisement and mismatch) are of course not mutually incompatible. It is likely that both reallocation and disenfranchisement phenomena played a role, as suggested, for example, by the fact that the proportion of long-term unemployment has increased for skilled workers as well. There is an obvious link between the two stories: persistent reallocation difficulties generate long-term unemployment and disenfranchisement.

Despite this uncertainty, I will argue that reallocation difficulties have played, and continue to play, an essential role in the EC countries. The disenfranchisement explanation alone fails to explain why unem-

---

[15] The relationship between structural shocks and macroeconomic fluctuations remains, by and large, a poorly understood phenomenon. Lilien (1982) claimed that sectoral shifts accounted for more than half the cyclical fluctuations in U.S. unemployment in the 1970s. This view was later challenged by Abraham and Katz (1986) and Blanchard and Diamond (1989), essentially on the premise that sectoral shocks should generate positive correlations between unemployment and vacancies. More recently, Hosios (1994) has shown that sectoral shocks may well increase unemployment and, at the same time, decrease vacancies, especially so when capacity employment is rigid in the short run. If so, previous empirical tests might not be valid.

ployment rates may differ so much across regions, occupations, skills, etc. That structural shocks may have had important effects is, from a certain point of view, obvious. It is fairly obvious that regions previously specialized in heavy industries are still suffering from this handicap. There is also some micro evidence that the development of new technologies is more favorable to skilled and educated workers (see, for instance, Entorf and Kramarz, 1994). The structural shock story corresponds, mutatis mutandis, to the American experience. Lasting U-V curve shifts (rightward in the 1970s, leftward in the late 1980s; see Blanchard and Diamond [1989]) and increased earnings dispersion in the 1980s in the United States are explained in terms of structural shocks and reallocation difficulties. The inability of European economies to adjust to these shocks has transformed a transitory problem into a permanent one. From this point of view, equilibrium unemployment may depend as much on relative wage costs as on average real wage levels or aspirations. Even though a productivity slowdown would, per se, have no effect on the equilibrium aggregate unemployment rate,[16] it may well make a reallocation problem much more difficult to solve. It is easier to accept relative wage changes when all wages go up than when they go down. Such a scenario is not incompatible with Alogoskoufis and Manning's (1988a) finding that European unemployment persistence is better explained by too high real wage aspirations rather than insider phenomena. If imperfect competition is apt to generate macroeconomic rigidities, it is even more likely to generate relative wage rigidities and reallocation difficulties.[17]

Turning now to policy issues, I would like to discuss a few implications of the previous analysis about the working of imperfectly competitive economies characterized by substantial real and nominal rigidities.

1. One important question is whether real wage costs are too high. It is now well known that, in an imperfect competition framework, the equilibrium unemployment rate may remain stubbornly high, not

---

[16] The neutrality of technical progress in the long run is a desirable property; it is necessary to avoid a systematic drift in the equilibrium unemployment rate (see Bean, 1994).

[17] Except for the United Kingdom, the dispersion of earnings barely increased in European countries during the 1980s, in sharp contrast to the U.S. experience (see OECD, 1993).

because the current real wage rate is too high, but simply because it would start increasing in a recovery, thereby triggering a fatal wage-price inflationary spiral. Figure 4 showed that the rate of growth in real wages in Europe started to rise again in the late 1980s, well before the return to low unemployment rates. This can be partly but not solely explained by tensions on the labor market. Wage moderation is thus needed. But the benefits of wage moderation will not be reaped unless there is, at the same time, a (coordinated) demand expansion. The presumption that equilibrium unemployment might be path-dependent is another reason why demand expansion, in combination with supply-oriented measures, may be most helpful.[18]

2. Observed evolutions in both the United States and Europe suggest that the relative wage cost of unskilled workers should be significantly reduced. Current economic trends clearly call for larger and faster adjustments on European labor markets. The challenge raised by technical progress and structural changes is twofold. We have to promote growth and at the same time avoid unacceptable income dispersions.[19] There are several options possible. The simplest approach to start with in European countries seems to be a tax (or social security contribution) exemption for minimum (or bottom) wages. Given the magnitude of current tax wedges in most European countries, it is possible to achieve in this way a sizable reduction in relative wage costs without decreasing the income of low-wage earners. The aim is to stimulate the demand for personal and "proximity services," a market that has become almost nonexistent in Europe.[20]

3. Whether unemployment persistence is due to disenfranchisement or structural mismatch, there is room for adequate passive or active labor market policies. As for passive policies, it is well known that

---

[18] Lubrano et al. (1993), analyzing Belgian postwar data by the means of multivariate cointegrating techniques, cannot reject the case with path dependency. The main channel seems to be (large) demand shocks and capital accumulation. Empirical results also show a positive relationship between the real wage rate, on the one hand, and the capital gap and equilibrium unemployment, on the other hand.

[19] Persson and Tabellini (1994) argue that inequality is harmful for growth.

[20] The interested reader may refer to Drèze and Malinvaud et al. (1994) for more detailed proposals.

existing unemployment compensation schemes do create, in some instances, poverty or unemployment trap phenomena, exacerbated by the macroeconomic situation. These defects should be remedied. This, of course, does not mean cutting benefits blindly and dismantling the welfare state, which would be unlikely to lead back to full-employment in the near future. The negative effects of unemployment schemes should not be exaggerated. The right balance has to be found between creating incentives and alleviating unemployment hardships. Full-employment is not a policy objective per se; the objective is welfare maximization, which requires taking into account the tradeoff between economic efficiency and income equality. In such a context, second-best policies may imply wage rigidities and unemployment (see Drèze and Gollier, 1993).

Bibliography

Abraham, K.G., and S.N. Houseman. 1993. "Does Employment Protection Inhibit Labour Market Flexibility? Lessons from Germany, France and Belgium." Working Paper No. 93-16. Kalamazoo, Mich.: W.E. Upjohn Institute for Employment Research.

Abraham, K.G., and L.F. Katz. 1986. "Cyclical Unemployment: Sectoral Shifts or Aggregate Disturbances?" *Journal of Political Economy* 94:507–522.

Alogoskoufis, G.S., and A. Manning. 1988a. "On the Persistence of Unemployment." *Economic Policy* 7:428–469.

Alogoskoufis, G.S., and A. Manning. 1988b. "Wage Setting and Unemployment Persistence in Europe, Japan and the USA." *European Economic Review* 32:698–706.

Andrès, J., J.J. Dolado, C. Molinas, M. Sebastian, and A. Zabalza. 1990. "The Influence of Demand and Capital Constraints on Spanish Unemployment." In: J.H. Drèze et al. (eds.), *Europe's Unemployment Problem*. Cambridge, Mass.: MIT Press.

Atkinson, A.B. 1990. "Institutional Features of Unemployment Insurance and the Working of the Labour Market." Discussion Paper No. SWP/50. London: London School of Economics.

Atkinson, A.B., and J. Mickelwright. 1991. "Unemployment Compensation and Labour Market Transitions: A Critical Review." *Journal of Economic Literature* 29:1679–1727.

Bazen, S., and J.P. Martin. 1991. "The Impact of the Minimum Wage on Earnings and Employment in France." *OECD Economic Studies* 16:199–221.

Bean, C.R. 1994a. "European Unemployment: A Retrospective." *European Economic Review* 38:523–534.

Bean, C.R. 1994b. "European Unemployment: A Survey." *Journal of Economic Literature* 32:573–619.

Bean, C.R., and A. Gavosto. 1990. "Outsiders, Capacity Shortages, and Unemployment in the United Kingdom." In: J.H. Drèze et al. (eds.), *Europe's Unemployment Problem*. Cambridge, Mass.: MIT Press.

Bean, C.R., P.R.G. Layard, and S.J. Nickell, 1986. "The Rise in Unemployment: A Multi-Country Study." *Economica* 53:S1–22.

Bentolila, S., and G. Bertola. 1990. "Firing Costs and Labour Demand: How Bad Is Eurosclerosis." *Review of Economic Studies* 57:381–402.

Bentolila, S., and O.J. Blanchard. 1990. "Spanish Unemployment." *Economic Policy* 10:234–281.

Bentolila, S., and J.J. Dolado. 1990. "Mismatch and Internal Migration in Spain." In: F. Padoa-Schioppa (ed.), *Mismatch and Labour Mobility*, pp. 182–236. Cambridge: Cambridge University Press.

Blanchard, O.J., and P. Diamond. 1989. "The Beveridge Curve." *Brookings Papers on Economic Activity* 1:1–76.

Blanchard, O.J., and P. Diamond. 1994. "Ranking, Unemployment Duration and Wages." *Review of Economic Studies* 61:417–434.

Blanchard, O.J., and L.H. Summers. 1986. "Hysteresis and the European Unemployment Problem." *NBER Macroeconomics Annual*, pp. 15–78.

Budd, A., P. Levine, and P. Smith. 1987. "Long-Term Unemployment and the Shifting U-V Curve." *European Economic Review* 31:296–305.

Burda, M., and C. Wyplosz. 1994. "Gross Worker and Job Flows in Europe." *European Economic Review* 38:1287–1315.

Calmfors, L., and J. Driffill. 1988. "Bargaining Structure, Corporatism and Macroeconomic Performance." *Economic Policy* 6:14–61.

Drèze, J.H., C.R. Bean, J.P. Lambert, F. Mehta, and H.R. Sneessens (eds.). 1990. *Europe's Unemployment Problem*. Cambridge, Mass.: MIT Press.

Drèze, J.H., and C. Gollier. 1993. "Risk Sharing on the Labour Market and Second-Best Wage Rigidities." *European Economic Review* 37:1457–1482.

Drèze, J.H., E. Malinvaud et al. 1994. "Growth and Employment: The Scope for a European Initiative." *European Economy (Reports and Studies)* 1:75–106.

Entorf, H. 1993. "Do Aggregate Measures of Mismatch Measure Mismatch? A Time-Series Analysis of Existing Concepts. " Mimeo, Département de la Recherche, INSEE, Paris.

Entorf, H., and F. Kramarz. 1994. "The Impact of New Technologies on Wages: Lessons from Matching Panels on Employees and on Their Firms." Discussion Paper No. 940. Paris: CREST, INSEE.

European Commission. 1993. *European Economy: Annual Economic Report*.

Franz, W., and K. Siebeck. 1992. "A Theoretical and Econometric Analysis of Structural Unemployment in Germany: Reflections on the Beveridge Curve." In: W. Franz (ed.), *Structural Unemployment*. Heidelberg: Physica-Verlag.

Gagey, F., J.P. Lambert, and B. Ottenwaelter. 1990. "Structural Mismatch, Demand and Capacity Constraints in the Rise of French Unemployment." In:

J.H. Drèze et al. (eds.), *Europe's Unemployment Problem*. Cambridge, Mass.: MIT Press.

Hosios, A.J. 1994. "Unemployment and Vacancies with Sectoral Shifts." *American Economic Review* 84:124–144.

Jackman, R., P.R.G. Layard, and S. Savouri. 1990. "Labour-Market Mismatch: A Framework or Thought." In: F. Padoa-Schioppa (ed.), *Mismatch and Labour Mobility*, pp. 44–94. Cambridge: Cambridge University Press.

Jackman, R., and S. Roper. 1987. "Structural Unemployment." *Oxford Bulletin of Economics and Statistics* 49:9–36.

König, H., and H. Entorf. 1990. "Strukturelle Arbeitslosigkeit und unausgelastete Kapazitäten: Ergebnisse eines makroökonomischen Rationierungsmodells". *Allgemeines Statistisches Archiv* 74:117–136.

Lambert, J.P. 1988. *Disequilibrium Macroeconomic Models*. Cambridge: Cambridge University Press.

Layard, P.R.G, and C.R. Bean. 1989. "Why Does Unemployment Persist?" *Scandinavian Journal of Economics* 91:371–396.

Layard, P.R.G., and S. Nickell. 1986. "Unemployment in Britain." *Economica* 53:S121–169.

Layard, P.R.G., and S. Nickell. 1987. "The Labour Market." In: R. Dornbusch and P.R.G. Layard (eds.), *The Performance of the British Economy*, pp. 131–179. Oxford: Oxford University Press.

Lilien, D. 1982. "Sectoral Shifts and Cyclical Unemployment." *Journal of Political Economy* 90:777–793.

Lindbeck, A., and D.J. Snower. 1988. *The Insider-Outsider Theory of Employment and Unemployment*. Cambridge, Mass.: MIT Press.

Lubrano, M., F. Shadman-Mehta, and H.R. Sneessens. 1993. "Real Wages, Quantity Constraints and Equilibrium Unemployment: Belgium, 1955–1988." IRES Discussion Paper No. 9311. Louvain-la-Neuve: Département des Sciences Economiques, Université Catholique de Louvain.

Nickell, S. 1990. "Unemployment: A Survey." *Economic Journal* 100 (401):391–439.

OECD. 1992. *Employment Outlook*. Paris: OECD.

OECD. 1993. *Employment Outlook*. Paris: OECD.

OECD. 1994. *Employment Outlook*. Paris: OECD.

Padoa-Schioppa, F. (ed.). 1990. *Mismatch and Labour Mobility*. Cambridge: Cambridge University Press.

Persson, T., and G. Tabellini. 1994. "Is Inequality Harmful for Growth?" *American Economic Review* 84:600–621.

Pissarides, C.A. 1990. *Equilibrium Unemployment Theory*. Oxford: Basil Blackwell.

Pissarides, C.A. 1992. "Loss of Skill during Unemployment and the Persistence of Employment Shocks." *Quarterly Journal of Economics* 107:1371–1392.

Sneessens, H.R. 1987. "Investment and the Inflation-Unemployment Trade-off in a Quantity Rationing Model with Monopolistic Competition." *European Economic Review* 31:781–808.

Sneessens, H.R. 1994. "Courbe de Beveridge et demande de qualifications." *Economie et Prévision* 113/114:127–138.

Sneessens, H.R., and J.H. Drèze. 1986. "A Discussion of Belgian Unemployment, Combining Traditional Concepts and Disequilibrium Econometrics." *Economica* 53:S89–119.

Sneessens, H.R., and F. Shadman-Mehta. 1995. "Real Wages, Skill Mismatch, and Unemployment Persistence, France 1962–1989." *Annales d'économie et de statistique* 37/38:255–292.

Sneessens, H.R., and B. Van der Linden. 1994. "De l'optimalité des systèmes d'assurance-chômage: Quelques réflexions." *Recherches Economiques de Louvain* 60(2): 129–162.

Unemployment in Central and Eastern Europe: East Meets West

Michael C. Burda

In his book *Economic Behavior in Adversity*, Hirshleifer (1987) describes the remarkable recovery of both Germany and Japan after severe bombing damage sustained during World War II. In particular, he makes note of the similar experiences in Hiroshima and Hamburg, which according to allied bombing reports were destroyed to considerably different degrees. His central conclusion from this experience as well as other catastrophic events over the past millennium is that the stock of human knowledge and talents is more decisive for rapid recovery from economic adversity than the lack of physical equipment and structures. In the words of Marshall, "the most valuable of capital is that invested in human beings."

The future development of Central and Eastern Europe (CEE) may provide crucial evidence for Hirshleifer's hypothesis. The transformation to a market system and the exposure to world competition after the collapse of communism has been associated with considerable adversity in these economies. As Table 1 makes clear, real GDP in these countries has declined on the order of 20–35 percent over the past four years, largely independent of reform strategies pursued by national governments. Employment has declined to a similar, if not greater, extent, mirroring the shedding of inefficient staff as well as the reduction of production levels. The result has been a rise of registered unemployment in these countries from zero before the revolution to an average of more than 10 percent today. Unemployment occupies a

This paper is an updated and revised version of a paper presented at the Annual Meetings of the American Economic Association, Boston, Massachusetts, January 3–5, 1994. I am grateful to Roland Vaubel for detailed comments and helpful discussions.

Table 1. The Evolution of Output and Employment in the CEE Economies.

	GDP at Constant Prices in 1993 (1988 = 100)	Employment in 1993 (1989 = 100)
Bulgaria		
TOTAL	72	54
Agriculture	104	53
Industry	51	48
Services	105	63
Czech Republic		
TOTAL	80	92
Agriculture	73	62
Industry	91	87
Services	64	105
Hungary		
TOTAL	82	78
Agriculture	85	42
Industry	69	73
Services	88	100
Poland		
TOTAL	83	87
Agriculture	88	85
Industry	65	79
Services	104	96
Romania		
TOTAL	63	96
Agriculture	93	109
Industry	52	80
Services	70	107
Slovakia		
TOTAL	80	82
Agriculture	70	69
Industry	85	74
Services	73	96

Source: GDP: EBRD (1994) and author's calculations. Services is a residual, includes government but excludes the informal sector. Employment: EC (1993a, 1993b), based on 1992 shares, except for Hungary (Table 4, p. 22; Statistical Tables, p. 33).

central place on the agenda of CEE politicians and policymakers alike, and there is a growing concern that unemployment in the new emerging economies will be much like that of Western Europe: high and persistent.

At the same time, the collapse of output and employment has been by no means even. Table 1 shows that the typical pattern is a sharp decline in industrial value-added and employment, while agricultural and especially service sectors have declined much less or even expanded (an exception are the Czech and Slovak republics to which we return later). This heterogeneity is also evidenced within industrial and service sector classifications, with some two- and three-digit sectors expanding and others contracting. As I hope to make clear in this paper, the transformation will be associated with a significant reallocation of labor that largely represents the unwinding of several decades of distortions and misallocation of human capital and talents. The emergence of functioning labor markets will be central to the reallocation of these resources, and to some extent, the emergence of unemployment is an indicator of this restructuring and reallocation. My objective is to survey some of the issues involved in the rise of CEE unemployment, as well as policy options available for dealing with it. Section I presents an overview of several different aspects of unemployment and "restructuring" in labor markets. Specifically, I examine reallocation of human resources across industries, occupations, space, and labor market states. In Section II, the matching function is proposed as a device for summarizing these developments. Section III briefly evaluates labor market policies in the CEE economies in this light and Section IV concludes with some speculation about what the West could learn from the East.

I   Restructuring in Transforming Labor Markets: Alternative Interpretations

It is hard to know what unemployment is in Central and Eastern Europe, since *employment* under state socialism did not correspond to conventional market economy concepts. Central planners evidently attached a social value to employment that exceeded the marginal contribution of labor to the production process. Prerevolution employment was a key means of social integration and protection. It also served as a vehicle for redistribution of national output, providing individuals with both pecuniary benefits (wages) as well as in-kind goods and services (medical benefits, additional access to goods in factory stores, vacation homes, day care), regardless of individual productivity. Enterprises were generally obliged to take on additional workers, and could finance new employment with cheap credit; it was in their interest to do so, since in a shortage economy the shadow price of any inventory is generally positive and high. Wage structures did not reflect labor scarcity. Since layoffs were not possible and unemployment was illegal, labor mobility was expressed via high interenterprise turnover.

These aspects of labor force participation and employment before the transformation raise fundamental questions about the extent and the nature of the current high CEE unemployment that must be resolved before further progress is possible. At the same time, developments in the East offer academics a fascinating opportunity to learn more about the nature of unemployment in both East and West. Does it reflect aggregate demand that will soon return or is it the result of inappropriate wage levels, restructuring, the gathering of fundamentally new information about labor and product markets, bad government policies, or some combination of all of these? In such a setting, the short-run appropriateness of the natural rate model can also be questioned. In the following sections I will pursue these ideas in more detail.

A   Reallocation of Human Capital: Restructuring across Industries

It is well known that the structure of output in the CEE was biased towards heavy industry and against labor-intensive manufacturing and especially services. Table 2 provides a picture of the fraction of GDP and employment attributable to agriculture, industry, and services (residual) in 1988 and 1992. Industrial activity represents only 27 percent of total GDP in Hungary to more than 60 percent in the Czech Republic, Slovakia, and Poland. In the planned economy, industrial structure, firm size, and location were often less driven by economic rather than political or military considerations. For example, it is well known that Slovakia's industrial base was influenced by Soviet military needs.

Table 2. The Structure of Output and Employment in the CEE Economies.

Fraction of GDP Originating in:

	Agriculture		Industry		Services	
	1988	1992	1988	1992	1988	1992
Bulgaria	11	16	61	43	28	41
Czech Rep.	7[1]	6	60[1]	68	33[1]	26
Hungary	9	9	31	26	60	65
Poland	8	8	51	40	41	52
Romania	14	20	54	44	32	36
Slovakia	7[1]	6	60[1]	64	33[1]	30

[1]CSFR.
Source: EBRD (1994). Services is a residual, includes government but excludes informal sector.

Fraction of Employment in:

	Agriculture		Industry		Services	
	1989	1992	1989	1992	1989	1992
Bulgaria	19	18	45	40	36	42
Czech Rep.	11	8	47	44	42	48
Hungary	18	10	40	37	42	53
Poland	30	29	35	32	35	39
Romania	29	33	44	37	27	30
Slovakia	14	12	46	41	40	47

Source: EC (1993a, 1993b).

As Table 1 illustrates, the transformation has witnessed sharply varying evolutions of output structures. In Romania and Bulgaria, where Stalinist-style industrialization was probably least rational, industrial production has fallen the most relative to agriculture and services. In all economies, the share of industrial employment has declined, sometimes despite a rising share in value-added. The strength of manufacturing in the Czech and Slovak republics reflects strong Western demand for their output, primarily intermediate products, as well as their considerable productivity gains. As predicted by Collins and Rodrik (1991), exports have been sharply redirected to the West, and now represent 75 percent of the total in Hungary and 63 percent in the former CSFR. The increase in agricultural activity observed in Bulgaria and Romania reflects comparative advantage (especially vis-à-vis the European Union) as well as the economic hardship that has forced a return to self-employment in farming.

A large decline in output and employment would have occurred in any event in a transition to a system in which firms do not bear principle responsibility for social security and redistribution. Furthermore, a large component of the demand shifts seen in these countries—the collapse of exports to the ex-Soviet Union and other Eastern bloc trading partners—will not return, either for reasons of comparative advantage or economic geography; the forecasts of Collins and Rodrik (1991) are illustrative in this regard and have been proven largely correct. In light of the structural change that has already occurred and that is to be expected, deficient aggregate demand is probably of secondary importance for the unemployment problem in the CEE countries.

B   Reallocation of Human Capital: Restructuring across Space

Another source of restructuring is the reallocation of labor's talent and human capital across space. In Central and Eastern Europe the pattern of regional immobility is similar to, if not more extensive than, Western Europe. Table 3 displays regional unemployment rates (registry data) for two of the smallest CEE countries, Bulgaria and Hungary, which have a surface area smaller than that of the U.S. state Arkansas. Similar results are found when unemployment relative to reported vacancies is considered instead; see Burda (1993). The differ-

Table 3. Regional Unemployment, Hungary and Bulgaria, 1993:2 (in percent).

Hungary:	13.4	Bulgaria:	15.2
Trans-Danube	14.2	Sofia town	8.8
Great plain	17.6	Burgas	15.7
Northeast	22.5	Varna	11.3
Northwest	9.8	Lovetch	14.5
of which:		Michailovgrad	20.9
Budapest	6.5	Plovdiv	19.6
		Russe	20.7
		Sofia District	15.2
		Haskovo	18.8

Source: EC (1993a, 1993b). Data refer to registered unemployment.

ence in unemployment rates between Sofia town and the surrounding administrative *oblast* (region) is particularly striking.

This regional unemployment "mismatch" is usually associated with the contraction of industry in "one-company towns" that dominated the economic landscape of regions and cities under central planning. Research is just beginning to identify the causes of immobility, which seems characteristic of Europe in general. The argument that the most mobile Europeans left long ago with the great migrations to North America can explain some, but certainly not all of current immobility. More plausible candidates are malfunctioning housing and capital markets as well as passive labor income support measures. Noteworthy is also the emergence of the distinctly West European expectation in the East that individuals should be insured against regional risks.

C Labor Force Participation: Restructuring across Labor Market States

As mentioned in the previous section, the meaning of employment in pre-revolution CEE was different than in capitalist economies, and this ambiguity carries over to *labor force participation*. As enterprises are relieved of their social protection objectives and are increasingly driven by the profit motive, they have begun to shed low-productivity staff. Registered unemployment is now a claim to social protection that resembles employment under the old system, even though reemployment prospects may be bleak or nonexistent.

This point is supported in Table 4, which shows the recent evolution of labor force participation in the total working population and by sex. Pre-revolution labor force participation in the CEE was extraordinarily high when compared with industrial countries, especially for women. Changes in labor force participation since the onset of transformation have been as dramatic as shifts in labor demand across sectors, and are more abrupt than any changes observed over the past two decades in OECD countries. There is, however, wide variation among CEE countries. Large declines in participation (especially female) have been registered in Bulgaria, the Czech Republic, and Slovakia; in contrast, females in Hungary and Poland have maintained their participation levels. In Poland, overall participation has fallen the least, and female participation may have actually risen in 1993.

Table 4. Labor Force Participation (percent of population of working age).

		Total	Male	Female
Bulgaria	1989	87.4	82.5	92.9
	1992	74.2	68.1	81.1
CSFR	1989	84.8	87.0	82.3
	1992	78.8	85.7	71.4
Hungary	1989	82.5	85.9	78.8
	1992	78.4	78.8	78.0
Poland	1989	76.1	83.6	68.6
	1992	74.5	80.7	68.2
Memo:				
France	1991	65.7	74.5	56.8
Germany	1992	69.8	80.1	59.0
Portugal	1992	74.0	85.9	62.8
Sweden	1992	80.7	82.7	78.7

Source: Boeri (1993), OECD (1993).

Evidently, part of the favorable unemployment development in the Czech and Slovak Republics can be attributed to forcing women into nonactivity; in the absence of this development unemployment in Bulgaria would have been much higher. Yet when compared with other OECD-European countries, female labor force participation remains higher in the CEE economies. If the female labor supply is more wage-elastic than that of men, the recent collapse of real wages would be expected to induce greater reduction in female than male participation. As these economies grow again, one would expect, as in the wealthier OECD economies, declining male and increasing female participation over time. Taking poorer OECD countries as a benchmark, however, further declines in participation of both sexes can be expected in the CEE economies in the future.[1]

Patterns of restructuring across labor force states will be influenced by incentives to stay in the labor force. A central element of these incentives is the administration of social safety net programs; stricter

---

[1] This has been also evident in the ex-German Democratic Republic, which saw a sharp decline in female participation after 1989.

eligibility criteria for unemployment benefits leads to a "self-selection" of low-productivity workers out of the labor force.[2] The negative social side effects of benefit policies must be weighed against maintaining unrealistic expectations of gainful employment for all individuals of working age under market conditions. Current policy, practiced to widely different extents in the CEE countries, is to shift individuals into nonparticipation, where they receive alternative forms of support (social welfare payments).

An indication of the extent to which this selection process is occurring is the degree to which declines in aggregate employment, ΔL, occur alongside increases in aggregate unemployment, ΔU (see Blanchard, Commander, and Coricelli, 1993). Although both variables are endogenous in a market economy, the primary cause of employment declines in the CEE countries in the recent past and for the foreseeable future is exogenous labor shedding in state enterprises. In a world with a fixed labor force, the ratio $\Delta U / \Delta L$ should be -1. Yet this ratio ranges in absolute value from less than 0.5 in the Czech Republic, Slovakia, and Bulgaria, to greater than 1 in Poland, and Romania. The differences across the CEE countries displayed in Table 5 seem too large to be due to chance. As might be expected, countries with stricter administration of unemployment benefit exhibit considerably greater reduction in participation. One group of countries, consisting of Bulgaria, the Czech Republic, and Slovakia, exhibits decisive reductions in labor force participation rates and thereby open unemployment rates towards OECD levels. In contrast, Hungary, Poland, and Romania exhibit a $\Delta U / \Delta L$ ratio lower than -1; in Hungary and Poland the ratio has *increased* in absolute value over the last two years.[3]

D   Obsolescence of Human Capital: Restructuring across Generations

Many studies emphasize the large gap in equipment and infrastructural capital between East and West as a barrier to rapid development.

---

[2] Recent evidence indicates that survey unemployment is highly correlated with registry unemployment, suggesting that the decline in participation is real and not merely statistical.

[3] Part of this pattern may be due to nonwage benefits (medical insurance, pension contributions) made available to registered unemploved and their family members. I thank Marek Gora for pointing this out to me.

Table 5. Changes in Employment and Unemployment, 1989–1992:4.

Country	ΔL (000s) 1989– 1992:4	ΔU (000s) 1989– 1992:4	$\Delta U/\Delta L$ 1989– 1992:4	$\Delta U/\Delta L$ 1991– 1992:4	Unemp. Rate 1993:2 (%)	Benefit Meas., 1992
Bulgaria	−1861	577	−0.31	−0.15	15.7	671
CSFR	−2656	395	−0.15	−0.05	2.6/12.5	522
Hungary	−832	620	−0.75	−1.42	13.4	3388
Poland	−2206	2509	−1.14	−1.22	14.8	1240
Romania	−741	929	−1.25	−1.02	9.3	1286

Source: EC (1993a, 1993b). The benefit measure is from Burda (1993), and depends on the replacement rate, the duration of claim, and the fraction of registered unemployed who are eligible. The larger the number, the higher the unemployment benefit.

In contrast, available data on education and literacy levels indicate high levels of human capital in the East.[4] Yet a large component of human capital consists of work experience and much experience-related human capital accumulated during socialism has been rendered obsolete in recent years. There is increasing evidence that rates of return on certain forms of new human capital have increased in the transforming economies. For example, in the three years following monetary union, data on the earnings of workers under the new regime have become increasingly available in eastern Germany, where restructuring of labor markets has been most consequent and radical. Earnings equations estimated on such data sets consistently show lower returns to experience and job tenure accumulated before the revolution than those estimated in the West.[5] This finding is less robust for education per se, especially at primary and secondary levels. These results suggest that the transformation was associated with significant human capital obsolescence for workers of all cohorts. Assuming that their tenure and experience variables are set to zero in an equation estimated on workers in the western subsample of the German Socioeconomic Panel, Bird et al. (1993) estimate income losses of up to 40 percent for eastern German workers aged 40 and older.

---

[4] See for example Begg et al. (1990), Collins and Rodrik (1991), and Hamilton and Winters (1993).

[5] See Schwarze (1993), Schwarze and Wagner (1993), Bird et al. (1993), and Geib et al. (1993).

The increase in the return to new experience signals that considerable investment in human capital will be undertaken in these countries over the next decade. Because of its time-to-build aspect, this human capital investment will be most attractive and easiest to amortize for younger workers. It follows that policies should be implemented that foster, or at least do not hinder, human capital formation for young people. One such policy would be an exemption of young people from the minimum wage; an alternative practiced in the Czech and Slovak republics is targeted wage subsidies for young labor force entrants. Another such policy that works at the other end of the age profile is early retirement. The most successful example of this program has been in the ex-German Democratic Republic, which offered the option of early retirement to males aged 55 or older who lost their job before the end of 1992.[6] By the end of 1993, more than 825,000 individuals had exited the labor force through the channel of early retirement. This policy can be viewed as a write-off of certain types of low productivity human capital, as well as an implicit insurance scheme, in which the state indemnifies individuals against catastrophic losses. Despite these problems and the cost of such programs, it is straightforward to show the conditions under which such policies make economic sense.

The following numerical example may be instructive. Suppose that a 55-year-old Hungarian with life expectancy of 75 years has a (marginal) productivity of 200,000 forints (Ft) per year, assumed constant until retirement at 65. This is roughly twice the actual 1993 gross minimum wage (Ft 108,000 year) and the minimum allowable benefit (Ft 103,200 year). (For comparison, the average take-home income in Hungary is Ft 180,000; assuming a tax wedge of 50 percent, this corresponds to a gross labor cost of Ft 360,000.) Assume that a young person aged 20 can begin work in a new enterprise at a lower initial productivity level but with a real productivity growth of 2 percent per year until his retirement at 65; if unemployed for the next ten years,

---

[6] *Vorruhestandsgeld* (implemented before unification) and *Altersübergangsgeld* (the current program offered to eastern Germans by the German Federal Employment Office). These programs provide for a prepension retirement benefit, paid by the employment office, of 65 percent of the last net wage for up to five years. These two programs account for more than half of all the participants in active labor market programs in eastern Germany. For a more detailed description, see EC (1992).

he is assumed (unrealistically) to lose no human capital (i.e., productivity remains constant despite unemployment). The current retirement benefit in Hungary is 100 percent of the last net wage up to Ft 168,000; for simplicity we assume (generously) that the retirement benefit for older, less productive workers who leave the labor force is equal to the unemployment benefit. At a real discount rate of 3 percent, the present value of GDP is raised by substituting younger for older workers as long as the younger worker's initial productivity exceeds roughly Ft 121,000 or 61 percent of that of the older colleague. At this break-even point however, a marginal early retirement causes the government intertemporal budget constraint to deteriorate by roughly Ft 180,000 in present value.

This example is meant to be illustrative, of course, and the net output gains will be sensitive to assumptions on relative productivity growth and discount rates. Even when they are productive, early retirement programs are likely to have a significant negative effect on the government budget, both in terms of current cash flow and intertemporal budget balance. Availability of external finance for such programs, as was in the case of eastern Germany, is imperative for their success. The unwillingness or inability of the state to offer attractive retirement packages to older workers (or to force them aside) explains why these programs have met with less success in Hungary and Poland.[7] On the other hand, creative solutions might be found to occupy older workers—part-time jobs as "trainers" for younger workers is an example—or, as in many CEE countries, to allow retirees to work in the informal economy. The most important aspect of the eastern German early retirement program has been its positive effect on youth unemployment (see Table 6).[8] In Hungary, where early retirement is more limited, 25 percent of all unemployment is aged 15–19, and more than 45 percent of all unemployed are younger than 30 years old (EC, 1993b). An active early retirement policy should be an important weapon against long-term unemployment of the young. Older, less productive workers have little hope of restructuring their skills, but there is also little incentive for them to withdraw from the labor force.

---

[7] If anything, the Hungarian pension system is expected to *increase* the male retirement age, for budgetary reasons, from 60 to 65 (55 to 60 for females).

[8] Of course, the German apprenticeship system must also take partial credit for this success.

Table 6. Youth Unemployment in CEE Economies, 1993:2

	Youth Unemployment Rate (%)	Overall Unemployment Rate (%)
Czech Republic	6.4	3.9
Slovakia	23.7	12.3
Hungary	22.5	12.0
Poland	29.8	13.8
ex-GDR	11.1	15.1

Source: Greenberg and Heintz (1994). Data refer to percentage of those unemployed aged 25 and younger of the labor force of the same age group.

II The Matching Process in Labor Markets in Transition

The transformation of CEE labor markets is a dynamic process that demands explicit consideration of stock-flow labor market relationships. The most important flows are from employment in the state sector into unemployment or into other jobs in the private sector, and from unemployment into new jobs, or out of the labor force. The matching approach to labor markets offers a convenient summary device for thinking about many aspects of the transformation (see Pissarides, 1990; Blanchard and Diamond, 1992). Central to the approach is the *matching function*, which relates stocks of unemployment and vacancies to the flow of new matches (which can include "matches" into household production or exits from the labor force): $x(u, v)$, where u and v are, respectively, the stocks of unemployment and vacancies. In the event that exits are time- or duration-dependent, u and v may stand for a vector of unemployment and vacancy stocks of varying durations. Normally, it is assumed that x_u, $x_v > 0$, x_{uu}, $x_{vv} < 0$, and $x_{uv} > 0$. In its intensive form under constant returns to scale, the matching function gives unconditional probability of exit from unemployment or job match $f = x(1, v/u)$ as a positive function of the relative availability of vacancies. The idea that the unemployed and vacancies require time to "find" each other is central to matching and makes it an attractive account of the facts presented in Table 3, for example.

Recently, researchers have estimated this function using regional and time-series data from transforming economies.[9] When estimated under a Cobb–Douglas specification, matching functions exhibit positive elasticities of job matches with respect to both unemployment and vacancies; values are relatively close to those in Western Europe, with elasticities of roughly 0.6–0.7 for unemployment and 0.2–0.3 for vacancies (see, for example, Layard et al., 1991; Burda and Wyplosz, 1993). Remarkably, while a positive trend is evident in the efficiency of the matching function since 1990 (Burda 1992; Boeri 1993, 1994a), the function appears stable across policy regime changes (i.e., changes in benefit provisions), so as a policy tool, it may actually survive the Lucas Critique.[10]

The matching function relates to equilibrium unemployment in the following way. Ignoring gross entry and exit from the labor force, the unemployment rate, u, is the solution to the differential equation $du/dt = s(1 - u) - fu = s - (s + f)u$, where s and f are job separation and job finding rates, respectively.[11] In the steady state, $u = s/(s + f)$, which can also be thought of as the product of an inflow rate, s, and an average duration that is the inverse of the gross turnover rate, $s + f$. This accounting exercise has little information content until we know more about the evolution of f and s. Clearly, s is rising from near-zero levels in Eastern Europe to levels typical of Western economies (1–2 percent of employment per month) and its increase reflects in part the restructuring of large enterprises, and in part the increasing role of the private sector, which has a higher turnover rate than the state sector.[12]

---

[9] Boeri (1994a) and Burda (1992, 1994) have estimated matching functions in several CEE countries and western Germany. Lehmann (1993) reports less success with a panel of Polish *vovoid*ship data. His results may reflect the high degree of measurement error in Polish job vacancy data (due to the informal economy).

[10] Burda (1992) and Boeri (1993) tested for the econometric stability of the matching function across identifiable regime changes (i.e., changes in unemployment benefit administration) and were unable to reject homogeneity. On the other hand the power of the tests may be low, since adaptation of behavior may require more time than the few months observed since the regime change.

[11] This accounting framework has been used by Hall (1979) and Barro (1988), among others.

[12] The private sector already accounts for more than 50 percent of employment in Poland.

Since f is the intensive form of the matching function, it is positively influenced by v/u, the ratio of vacancies to unemployment, which is a function of both active and passive labor market policies as well as general macroeconomic conditions. Trivially, it is negatively related to the availability of public works vacancies. It is also influenced by the efficiency of matching—information flows and job agencies, the incentive to search or wait given by unemployment benefits or the underground economy—as well as by the supply of jobs in the private sector.

Many have argued that inflows into unemployment have been too low in Eastern Europe, compared with Western economies, to be associated with a vibrant labor market (see, for example, Boeri, 1994b). This argument fails to recognize that inflows into unemployment are only one component of the restructuring process. Table 4 documents a uniform decline in CEE labor force participation since 1989, suggesting that a large proportion of the employment decline has been associated with direct exits from the labor force. Focusing on inflows into unemployment (rather than separations from state enterprises, for which there exist scanty data) will exclude these flows a priori. While such considerations will tend not to be important in mature OECD economies with relatively stable labor forces, they are important in the CEE. For example, assuming that gross exits out of the labor force from unemployment equal net flows (the most pessimistic case), the monthly outflow rate for the CSFR would have been 0.2 percent higher, in Bulgaria 0.4 percent higher, in Poland, 0.1 percent higher. These estimates go much farther in explaining the decline of state employment in the CEE countries than inflows into unemployment alone.

III Implications for Labor Market Policy in the Transition

The central implication of the matching approach is that the transformation of CEE labor markets will require time. This has implications for the pace of commercialization and privatization of state enterprises, which are associated with layoffs and plant closings. If there are social (external) costs to unemployment, there may be an optimal rate of release of labor resources from the state sector that is lower than otherwise. Heuristically, "feeding the matching function" must be balanced against the effectiveness of the matching process as well as the social costs of unemployment. The extent of geographic mismatch is extreme in CEE countries, where "monoculture" towns dominated by a single large enterprise were common. Furthermore, the supply of vacancies is endogenous and may react negatively to "shock-therapy," leading to lower outflow rates. A layoff policy that does not take the matching process and potential mismatch into account will lead to sharp increases in unemployment.

Labor market institutions will play a central role in the process, and affect the rate of job (vacancy) creation at any level of unemployment. The level and duration of unemployment benefits will play a role in the emergence of long-term unemployment, as it has in the West. It will influence the adjustment of CEE labor force participation patterns to OECD levels, as well as the rate at which individuals change occupation, industry, and location.[13] There are serious time consistency issues related to jobless pay as well; administrative extension of benefits seen in France and Spain in the 1980s seems to have occurred in Poland and Romania and may create expectations of further extensions in the future. Collective bargaining institutions can also influence the short- and longer-term macroeconomic environment. At the moment, the labor union movement is still too closely associated with communist policies and politicians to have too much impact in the ex-CSFR and Hungary but remain a force to be reckoned with in Poland and Romania.

The focus here will be directed at so-called active labor market programs. Although increasingly under fire in Sweden (see Lindbeck et al., 1993), these policies should be seriously considered as a substitute for passive income support in the CEE countries.[14] One type of active labor policies affects the efficiency of the matching process. Retraining programs and vouchers fall into this category, as do mobility grants, reinterview programs, and efforts directed at specific high-unemployment groups. The information function of labor offices is quite important in transforming economies, as workers are still learning how to search effectively for new employment opportunities. In the Czech and Slovak republics, staffing is closer to levels in the West (30:1 in the Czech republic, 123:1 in Slovakia [EC, 1993a, 1993b]) than in other CEE countries (270:1 in Bulgaria, 235:1 in Poland, 599:1 in Romania). Although there are more than three times as many

---

[13] For a theoretical exposition of this point, see Dixit and Rob (1992).

[14] It should be noted that the Lindbeck Report emphasizes short-term job creation through public works. See Snower (1994) for a concrete proposal in this spirit.

Table 7. Active Labor Market Programs, 1992.

Country (u-rate 1992:4)	Percentage of Total Spending on:					Total Spending as Percent of GDP (1992)	
	Training Programs	Job Creation	Employ. Subsidies	Business Assistance	Other	Active Measures	Memo: Passive Support
Bulgaria (18.9)	32.3	6.9	26.6	4.1	31.1	0.15	0.75
Former CSFR (5.4)	7.0	76.2	–	4.5	12.3	0.54	0.31
Hungary (13.5)	22.3	33.5	6.8	18.5	18.9	0.48	2.52
Poland (13.6)	69.2	22.5	–	8.3	–	0.27	1.73
Romania (8.4)	3.8	–	81.7	1.1	13.4	0.18	0.79

Source: EC (1993a, p. 27). Estimates for spending provided by the OECD.

unemployed in Slovakia as in the Czech Republic, Czech labor offices have more than twice as many staff and 40 percent more consultants than in Slovakia (Uldrichova and Karpisek, 1993), which suggests that high and rising unemployment with fixed staff can lead to reduced supervision, and less effective job intermediation and assistance, and possibly multiple equilibria in local labor markets. Training and reintegration programs to improve matching seem to be less successful. Table 7 shows that countries which spend the most on training as a fraction of their active labor market policies have performed the most poorly. This applies especially to Hungary, which spends almost as much as a fraction of GDP on total active labor market policies as the former CSFR. This casual evidence suggests that the skills that workers receive in such programs may not be demanded by the market.

A second type of active labor market policy is direct job creation. Decried as "make-work" or "Keynesian pyramid-building or ditch-digging," these programs have the same integrative effect as state employment under communism. These programs have many detractors: labor unions object to paying workers below contract wages, free market advocates claim that projects with low rates of return are wasteful and distortionary, and governments of CEE economies deride such programs as more of the central planning they are striving to eliminate. Nevertheless, sound economics can justify such programs, especially under the conditions currently prevailing in Central and Eastern Europe. Because information about prior productivity and effort level is usually private information to workers, hiring from the unemployment pool is risky for employers, since at least some of those workers may be unproductive or shirkers. All things being equal, employers prefer to hire those who have jobs, so being unemployed is a signal that one may, with some probability, come from the wrong distribution. This bad signal may be incorrect in individual cases *ex ante*, but to the extent that long-term unemployment deteriorates skills and work habits, may also be self-fulfilling. This labeling problem may be particularly virulent when the reasons for the initial drop in employment was systematic shedding by state enterprises of "deadwood." It is also related to the "ranking problem" (see Blanchard, 1991) in which unemployed are hired on a LIFO basis; one can imagine a bad equilibrium in which long-term unemployed are not hired because they are risky, and are risky because they have not been hired. A market failure of this type could be solved by collective action, i.e., forcing the unemployed to take a job after some prespecified spell of uninterrupted unemployment. Although the first-best solution (i.e., solving the information problem) would be superior, it may not be feasible or even possible.

There is some indirect econometric evidence in support of this claim. Recent findings by Boeri (1994b) with respect to the matching function in CEE countries indicate that long-term unemployment may indeed have less influence on the matching process than the short-term jobless.[15] This suggests a social value for make-work programs that, even though they may appear to simply "churn" the unemployed, may actually help keep workers in contact with the labor market and increase their chances of finding an appropriate match. The highly successful Czech and Slovak active labor market policies, which stress both direct and subsidized job creation and which account for 70 per-

---

[15] Specifically, he allows for the stocks of short- and long-term unemployment to enter as a CES function that in turn determines the composite u in $x(u, v)$; see above.

cent of all active labor market policy expenditures there, could be viewed in this light.[16] In addition, they target young people, the unskilled, and the long-term unemployed. Combined with rigorous administration of unemployment support, these policies have proved successful, even in Slovakia, where unemployment is considerably higher.[17] An inferior alternative to make-work is direct government subsidies to employers to maintain staffing (wage subsidies); they tend to freeze existing structures and enhance the survival probabilities of poorly performing firms. Employment subsides are more widely used in Romania and Bulgaria, and may be increasing in Hungary. Grant programs for entrepreneurial start-ups seem to play a limited role in job creation and have been scaled back considerably.

Finally, the importance of the informal, or "underground," economy, as well as its interaction with taxation and welfare systems, cannot be overlooked in designing labor market policies. High rates of income taxation and lax enforcement of existing laws have made unreported income attractive (when they can, individuals tend to hold a "regular" job that entitles them to social benefits, and then supplement this income with part-time, unreported work). For the unemployed, informal activity offers supplemental income to benefits, and job offers in the informal sector seem to be readily available.[18] While

---

[16] After the breakup of the country in January 1993, both the Czech and Slovak Republics have maintained similar labor market policies, despite the larger collapse of economic activity in the latter. See Ham et al. (1993).

[17] Although job creation is higher and unemployment is lower in Slovakia than in other CEE countries, it is unclear why Slovakia has fared so much worse than the Czech Republic. Svenjar (1993) attributes the poor Slovak labor market performance, compared with the Czech Republic, to the greater decline in industrial output, a higher proportion of Gypsies in Slovakia (who have high average unemployment rates), and the opportunity for Czechs to work legally or illegally in Germany.

[18] In the 1992 labor force survey in Hungary, 461,000 individuals reported being out of work and looking for a job (10.5 percent of the labor force), whereas 644,000 were registered with the employment offices (13.5 percent) (EC, 1993). Similarly, recent evaluation of the Polish survey data shows that in 1993 registered unemployment continued to rise, whereby survey unemployment fell. Banacek (1994) notes that from January 1991 to April 1992 some 450,000 Czechs and Slovaks quit jobs in state enterprises without reappearing elsewhere as unemployed, employed, or working abroad. The presumption is that they found employment in the informal sector.

this may reduce the financial loss to households in unemployment, the underground economy puts additional strain on public finances, and either crowds out useful active labor market programs or leads to tax increases on legally registered business. It would thus seem appropriate to design policies that neither penalize nor encourage underground activity, but rather that bring it into the light of day. Tax reform will be an important element of such a policy.

IV   Conclusions: Lessons for the West?

The East has chosen to meet the West on the latter's terms. In choosing the capitalist approach to allocating labor according to its best alternative uses, the economies of Central and Eastern Europe must accept the consequences: a period of extensive restructuring and reallocation of human capital on a scale rarely if ever seen in capitalist economies. A sizable fraction of the working age populations of these countries will at some point have to accept change of industry, occupation, geographic residence, or labor force state. Labor market institutions will play a large role in influencing the outcome, as will overall economic policy. Government intervention can create conditions that do not unduly inhibit structural change currently in progress. But CEE economies can do more: they can learn from the mistakes of Western Europe, which chose to subsidize the status quo in "rustbelt" industries in the 1970s, and to pursue passive unemployment benefit systems with little incentive for adaptation to changing conditions, effectively leaving the unemployed alone to fend for themselves. If executed properly, active employment programs can increase the chances that unemployment that is a necessary complement to the transformation will be short-lived rather than long-term. Active management of the unemployed with adequate staffing is certainly a necessary condition, as is a well-organized national job service. More market-oriented retraining and schooling programs (via vouchers, for example) would help. For older, less productive individuals who are unable or unwilling to adapt, early retirement can make room at the bottom for younger people with longer investment horizons for necessary human capital investment.

The bringing together of job searchers and open positions requires time and resources, and it is unrealistic to expect the private sector to replace the public sector overnight. Layoffs probably represent the only feasible and credible way of restructuring enterprises. Forcing unemployment is one way of restructuring the enterprises, especially as turnover is low under current depressed economic conditions. At the same time, it is recognized that unemployment is partly time-dependent, so a large state effort to prevent persistent mass unemployment is necessary. The early experience of Central and Eastern Europe teaches us that public works programs are an important element of successful unemployment policy. In the Czech Republic in 1992, 112,000 "socially purposeful" and "socially useful" public works jobs were created (in Slovakia 102,000). These measures are funded by savings on jobless benefits, explaining why active expenditures remain such a large component compared to passive unemployment support in these countries. In contrast, wage subsidies tend to freeze existing obsolete structures, remove pressure for change, and distort compensation (see Bird et al., 1993) for evidence on eastern German Treuhand firms. The Czech and Slovak experience teaches us that short-term job creation and effective targeting of marginal rather than inframarginal groups are the most appropriate responses to the current adverse labor market situation in Central and Eastern Europe.

The West can profitably learn from the adversity currently endured by the East. The situation in the CEE countries is only one point in the continuum on which Western Europe finds itself as well. Misguided passive unemployment policies in the latter have led to serious depreciation of human capital; in order to limit the damage, early retirement may be one means of easing less adaptable insiders out of the labor force in a world where retraining at an older age is considered too expensive or cost-ineffective. Finally, the European Union—especially its richer members—will be faced with increasing demands for structural adjustment as integration with the CEE economies proceeds. Labor markets in Western Europe should be restored to the key role they should hold in mediating this structural change. The ultimate irony of the next decade would be the failure of the West to meet this challenge from the East.

Bibliography

Banácek, V. 1994. "Small Businesses and Private Entrepreneurship During Transition: The Case of the Czech Republic." Mimeo, April.

Barro, R. 1988. "The Persistence of Unemployment." *American Economic Review, Papers and Proceedings* 78:32–37.

Begg, D. et al. 1990. *Monitoring Eastern Europe.* London: CEPR.

Bird, E., J. Schwarze, and G. Wagner. 1993. "Wage Effects of the Move Toward Free Markets in East Germany." Mimeo, August.

Blanchard, O. 1991. "Wage Bargaining and Unemployment Persistence." *Journal of Money, Credit, and Banking* 23:277–292.

Blanchard, O., S. Commander, and F. Coricelli. 1993. "Unemployment and Restructuring in Eastern Europe." Paper presented at the OECD-CCET Technical Workshop on the Persistence of Unemployment in Central and Eastern Europe, September.

Blanchard, O., and P. Diamond. 1992. "The Flow Approach to Labor Markets." *American Economic Review, Papers and Proceedings* 82:354–359.

Boeri, T. 1993. "Unemployment Dynamics and Labor Market Policies." Paper presented at World Bank Conference on Unemployment, Restructuring and the Labor Market in East Europe and Russia, October, Washington, D.C.

Boeri, T. 1994a. "Labor Market Flows and the Persistence of Unemployment in Central and Eastern Europe." In: OECD, *Unemployment in Transition Countries: Transient or Persistent?*, pp. 13–56. Paris: OECD.

Boeri, T. 1994b. "Transitional Unemployment." *Economics of Transition* 2:1–26.

Burda, M. 1992. "Unemployment, Labor Market Institutions and Structural Change in Eastern Europe." CEPR Discussion Paper No. 746. London: CEPR.

Burda, M. 1993a. "Unemployment, Labor Markets and Structural Change in Eastern Europe." *Economic Policy* 16:101–37.

Burda, M. 1993b. "Modelling Exits from Unemployment in Eastern Germany: A Matching Function Approach." CEPR Discussion Paper No. 800. London: CEPR.

Burda, M., and C. Wyplosz. 1994. "Gross Job and Worker Flows in Europe." *European Economic Review* 38:1287–1315.

Collins, S., and D. Rodrik. 1991. *Eastern Europe and the Soviet Union in the World Economy.* Washington D.C.: Institute for International Economics.

Dixit, A., and R. Rob. 1992. "Switching Costs and Sectoral Adjustment in General Equilibrium with Uninsured Risk." Mimeo, October.

EBRD (European Bank for Reconstruction and Development). 1994. "Statistical Tables." *Economics of Transition* 2(1): 117–127.

EC (European Community). 1992. "Early Retirement Benefit: A Bridge Between Unemployment and a Pension." *Employment Observatory: East Germany* 5 (November): 5–6.

EC (European Community). 1993a. "Statistical Tables." *Employment Observatory: Central and Eastern Europe* 4.

EC (European Community). 1993b. "Statistical Tables." *Employment Observatory: Central and Eastern Europe* 5.

Geib, T., M. Lechner, F. Pfeiffer, and S. Salomon. 1992. "Die Struktur der Einkommensunterschiede in Ost- und Westdeutschland ein Jahr nach der Vereinigung." ZEW Discussion Paper No. 92-06.

Greenberg, M., and S. Heintz. 1994. "*Removing the Barriers: Strategies to Assist the Long-Term Unemployed.*" New York: IWES.

Hall, R. 1979. "A Theory of the Natural Unemployment Rate and the Duration of Unemployment." *Journal of Monetary Economics* 5:153–170.

Ham, J., J. Svenjar, and K. Terrell. 1993. "The Czech and Slovak Labor Markets during the Transition." Paper presented at World Bank conference on Unemployment, Restructuring and the Labor Market in East Europe and Russia, October.

Hamilton, C., and A. Winters. 1992. "Opening Up Trade with Eastern Europe." *Economic Policy* 14:72–116.

Hirshleifer, J. 1987. *Economic Behaviour in Adversity*. Chicago: University of Chicago Press.

Layard, R., S. Nickell, and R. Jackman. 1991. *Unemployment*. Oxford: Oxford University Press.

Lehmann, H. 1993. "Labour Market Flows and the Evaluation of Labour Market Policies in Poland." CEPR Discussion Paper No. 161. London: CEPR.

Lindbeck, A., P. Molander, T. Persson, O. Peterson, A. Sandmo, B. Swedenbourg, and N. Tygesen. 1993. "Options for Economic and Political Reform in Sweden." IIES Seminar Paper No. 540. Stockholm: IIES.

OECD. 1993. *Employment Outlook*. Paris: OECD.

Pissarides, C. 1990. *Equilibrium Unemployment Theory*. Oxford: Basil Blackwell.

Scarpetta, S., and A. Reutersward. 1994. "Unemployment Benefit Systems and Active Labour Market Policies in Central and Eastern Europe." In: OECD, *Unemployment in Transition Countries: Transient or Persistent?*, pp. 255–307. Paris: OECD.

Schwarze, J. 1991. "Ausbildung und Einkommen von Männern. Einkommensfunktionsschätzungen für die ehemalige DDR und die Bundesrepublik Deutschland." *Mitteilungen aus der Arbeitsmarkt- und Berufsforschung* 24:63–69.

Schwarze, J. 1993. "Qualifikation, Überqualifikation und Phasen des Transformationsprozesses." *Jahrbücher für Nationalökonomie und Statistik* 211(1–2): 90–107.

Schwarze, J., and G. Wagner. 1993. "Earnings Dynamics in the East German Transition Process." Ruhr Universität Bochum Diskussionspapier No. 93-08. Bochum: Universität Bochum.

Snower, D. 1994. "Converting Unemployment Benefits into Employment Subsidies." CEPR Discussion Paper No. 930. London: CEPR.

Svenjar, J. 1993. "The Czech and Slovak Federal Republic: A Solid Foundation." In: A. Portes (ed.), *Economic Transformation in Central Europe: A Progress Report*, pp. 21–57. London: CEPR.

Uldrichova V., and Z. Karpisek. 1994. "Labour Market Policy in the Former Czech and Slovak Federal Republic." In: OECD, *Unemployment in Transition Countries: Transient or Persistent?*, pp. 113–135. Paris: OECD.

About the Authors

MICHAEL C. BURDA is Professor of Economics at the Humboldt-Universität Berlin. An American citizen, he studied at Harvard University (AB 1981, AM 1985, Ph.D. 1987) and wrote his dissertation on the rise of unemployment in Europe. From 1987 to 1993 he was Assistant Professor and then Associate Professor of Economics at INSEAD, the European Business School in Fontainebleau. He has written extensively on unemployment in Western Europe, and is currently working on labor market issues in the transforming economies of Central and Eastern Europe. He teaches macroeconomics and labor economics, and has coauthored the textbook *Macroeconomics: A European Text* with Charles Wyplosz (1993).

SAMUEL BRITTAN is an Assistant Editor of the *Financial Times*. His most recent book is *Capitalism with a Human Face* (1995). He is an Honorary Fellow of Jesus College, Cambridge, an Honorary Doctor of Letters (Heriot-Watt University, Edinburgh), an Honorary Doctor of the University of Essex, and a Chevalier de la Légion d'Honneur. He has been a Visiting Professor at the Chicago Law School, a Visiting Fellow of Nuffield College, Oxford, and an Honorary Professor of Politics at Warwick. He has been awarded the George Orwell, Senior Harold Wincott and Ludwig Erhard prizes. He was a member of the Peacock Committee on the Finance of the BBC (1985–1986). He was knighted in 1993 "for services to economic journalism" and also became that year a Chevalier de la Légion d'Honneur.

RICHARD N. COOPER is Boas Professor of International Economics at Harvard University. He studied at Oberlin College and the London School of Economics. He taught at Yale University and served in the U.S. government as Under Secretary of State for Economic Affairs.

His most recent book (with others) is *Boom, Crisis and Adjustment: Macroeconomic Management in Developing Countries* (1993).

BARRY EICHENGREEN is John L. Simpson Professor of Economics and Professor of Political Science at the University of California, Berkeley. He is a Research Associate at the National Bureau of Economic Research and a Research Fellow at the Centre for Economic Policy Research. He is coeditor, with T.J. Hatton, of *Interwar Unemployment in International Perspective* (1988).

RICHARD B. FREEMAN received his Ph.D. from Harvard University in 1969. Before returning to Harvard in 1975 he taught at the University of Chicago and Yale University. He is now Professor of Economics at Harvard University, where he teaches Labor Economics. He is currently serving as Faculty Co-Chair of the Harvard University Trade Union Program, as Program Director at the National Bureau of Economic Research, and as Executive Programme Director of the Comparative Labour Market Institutions Programme at the London School of Economics. He has served on the three panels of the United States National Academy of Science: High Risk Youth, Post Secondary Education and Training in the Workplace, and Employment and Technical Change. Professor Freeman has published over 200 articles dealing with topics on youth labor market problems, higher education, trade unionism, high-skilled labor markets, economic discrimination, social mobility, income distribution, and equity on the marketplace. In addition, he has written or edited 16 books, several of which have been translated into French, Spanish, Chinese, and Japanese.

PATRICK MINFORD is Professor of Applied Economics at the University of Liverpool (since 1976) and Visiting Professor at the Cardiff Business School (since 1953). Previously he served as economic adviser to the Ministry of Finance, Malawi (1967–1969); the Finance Director of Courtaulds Limited (1970–1971); and H.M. Treasury's External Division (1971–1974), including its Delegation in Washington, D.C. (1974). He was Hallsworth Research Fellow at Manchester University (1975) and editor of the *Quarterly Review* of the National Institute for Economic and Social Research (1976). He has been a member of the Monopolies and Mergers Commission since March 1990 and has been one of the H.M. Treasury's Panel of Forecasters ("6 Wise Men") since its inception in January 1993. He has authored articles on international, monetary, and labor economics.

KARL-HEINZ PAQUÉ is Research Director and Head of the Growth, Structural Policy and International Division of Labor Department at the Kiel Institute of World Economics, Germany. He studied at the universities of Saarbrücken, Kiel, and Vancouver, Canada, and was a research fellow at the Center for Study of Public Choice in Blacksburg, Virginia, U.S.A. His main research interests are in labor economics, theoretical and empirical research on economic growth and international trade, and selected topics in public finance. He has published extensively in these fields. He has also been coauthor (together with Herbert Giersch and Holger Schmieding) of a history of economic policy in West Germany (*The Fading Miracle. Four Decades of Market Economy in Germany*, 1992). He also teaches in the economics department of the University of Kiel, Germany.

HENRI R. SNEESSENS is Professor of Economics at the University of Louvain, Belgium (since 1985), and President of the Institute de Recherches Economiques et Sociales (IRES) at the Department of Economics (since 1994). He is also an invited professor at the Catholic University of Lille. He was a lecturer in economics at the London School of Economics (from 1980 to 1982). He is currently doing research on Beveridge curve shifts and mismatch indices, and on the relationship between skill mismatch and unemployment persistence. His most recent article (with F. Shadman-Mehta) is "Real Wages, Skill Mismatch and Unemployment Persistence; France, 1962–89," forthcoming in a special issue of the *Annales d'économie et de statistique*.

ROLAND VAUBEL is Professor of Economics at the University of Mannheim, Germany. He received a B.A. in Philosophy, Politics, and Economics from the University of Oxford, an M.A. in economics from Columbia University, New York, and a doctorate in economics from the University of Kiel, Germany. He has been a researcher at the Kiel Institute of World Economics, Professor of Monetary Economics at Erasmus University Rotterdam and Visiting Professor in International Economics at the University of Chicago (Graduate School of Business). He is a member of the Academic Advisory Council of the German Ministry of Economics, an adjunct scholar at the Cato Institute,

Washington, D.C., and a member of the advisory council of the Institute of Economic Affairs. Professor Vaubel specializes in international finance, international organizations, public choice, and social policy. His publications include *Strategies for Currency Unification: The Economics of Currency Competition and the Case for a European Parallel Currency* (1978), *Choice in European Monetary Union* (1979), and *The Political Economy of International Organizations* (1991), which he coedited with Th.D. Willet.

CHARLES WYPLOSZ is Professor at the European Institute for Business Administration (INSEAD) in Fontainbleau, France, and a Research Fellow at the Centre for Economic Policy Research (CEPR) in London. A graduate in engineering from the Ecole Centrale de Paris, he also holds a Ph.D. in economics from Harvard. His research interests include exchange rate policy, the European Monetary System and the move to a single currency in Europe, unemployment and migration, and the transition from central planned economies to market economies. He has served as an advisor to various governments and to the EU Commission. More recently, he has worked with the Russian government and conducted research at the IMF. His textbook, coauthored with Michael Burda, *Macroeconomics: A European Perspective*, has been translated into seven languages, including German and Russian. Professor Wyplosz is member of the Council of the European Economic Association, managing editor of *Economic Policy*, Associate Editor of the *European Economic Review*, and European Chairman of the International Seminar on Macroeconomics (ISOM).